PLAIN GUIDE

TO

SPIRITUALISM.

A HAND-BOOK

FOR

SKEPTICS, INQUIRERS, CLERGYMEN, BELIEVERS, LECTURERS, MEDIUMS, EDITORS, AND ALL WHO NEED A THOROUGH GUIDE TO THE PHENOMENA, SCIENCE, PHILOSOPHY, RELIGION AND REFORMS OF MODERN SPIRITUALISM.

BY URIAH CLARK.

THIRD EDITION.

BOSTON, MASS.:
WILLIAM WHITE & CO.,
158 WASHINGTON ST.

GEO. C. RAND & AVERY,
STEREOTYPERS AND PRINTERS.

AUTHOR'S PREFACE.

This volume has been in the course of preparation since 1855. After it was deemed ready for the press, I made many alterations, erasures, and additions, adapted to changes in times and conditions. Whether the work is now complete or otherwise, it embodies the labors, studies, observations, and itinerant experiences of years. If I have failed in presenting the most elaborate deductions of science, philosophy, theology, and history, or omitted any facts or elucidations deemed important to critics, it is because my aim has been to prepare a Plain Guide to Spiritualism, adapted to the masses of the people; and such a work embraces so many themes, going over so much ground, it were impossible to find room for an extensive elaboration of some topics deemed important. If I have failed to notice some of the philosophy and phenomena current in America as well as Europe, it is because such notice in some cases has been deemed undemanded, and in other cases because I lacked reliable data.

Although I have used the editorial "we" throughout this volume, it will be distinctly understood that I assume no *authority* in seeking to present either the private sentiments of individual Spiritualists, or the average sentiments of the great body of believers. I make an honest effort to sum up evidences and opinions, and leave individuals and the public to judge. I have endeavored to guard all my positions, compilations, and statements with the utmost care and consideration. I have made no attempt to dodge any of the issues of the age, or the charges, accusations, and objections arrayed against Spiritualism. The day of silence has passed, and the public platform must rock with agitation and free discussion on every theme of human weal and woe. If I have not dwelt in detail on all the civil and political questions involved in the terrible war now waging for the maintenance of the American government, it is because there are moral, spiritual, and humanitarian issues of most momentous character involved, and the spiritual stand-point enables us to entertain hopes far beyond those of conservative statesmen and politicians. I have not evaded the social problems of the age hinted in the mad and imbruting outcry about "free-love," "affinity," and similar topics, grown nauseating from the stand-point of a Billingsgate vulgarity, yet involving momentous issues; but I have endeavored to treat these topics with a delicacy causing no pure cheek to blush, and no wise souls to take alarm, yet with a fearlessness designed to arouse those who are slumbering over the volcano now threatening the disruption of all that is false and infernal in every department of modern civilization.

I have labored to present the practical as well as the theoretical of Spiritualism, yet without dealing in cant exhortations or maudlin sentimentalities. If I have recognized the affectional or religious elements of our common nature, and sometimes attempted to make strong appeals to these elements, it is owing to the need of checking a species of atheism tending to ignore all reverence, all religion, all recognition of the Infinite, the Divine, the Eternal. The harmonic Spiritualist recognizes every department of man and the universe, and occupies the medium ground between a cold rationalism and a superstitious religionism.

I ask for this book a careful and complete perusal, before any judgment is pronounced either by believers or unbelievers. It doubtless contains many sentences and paragraphs needing qualifications and elucidations which the intelligent reader can supply.

Spiritualists have long felt the need of some Text-Book, Hand-Book, or Plain Guide, embracing all the pro and con, the facts, science, philosophy, religion, and reforms of Spiritualism ; a volume for constant reference, for the centre-table, the library, the rostrum, the conference, the circle, the closet, the arena of public discussion, the pulpit, the editorial table ; a safe volume to put into the hands of friends, neighbors, skeptics, inquirers, editors, clergymen, everybody ; a volume for lecturers, mediums, reformers, conductors of Sunday schools, circles, conferences, and public meetings, to quote and read from ; a volume which shall give plain, practical hints in regard to spiritual culture, the cultivation of the "best gifts," the formation of circles, methods to advance the truth ; — in short, a Plain Guide to Spiritualism. If these objects are measurably attained, I shall be abundantly blessed, and with a deeper gratitude shall acknowledge the celestial aids I have received in the prosecution of my labors, — praying that the same benedictions whose overshadowings I have felt along the pioneer pathway of the past, may ever, through all the coming journey of life, attend each reader of this volume, like a "cloud by day" and "a pillar of fire by night," to light the spirit heavenward in triumph.

URIAH CLARK.

158 WASHINGTON STREET, BOSTON, MASS., May, 1863.

TABLE OF CONTENTS.

PLAIN GUIDE TO SPIRITUALISM.

CELESTIAL FOOTPRINTS.

WAIFS BY ANCIENT AND MODERN AUTHORS.

Millions of spiritual creatures walk the earth
Unseen, both when we wake and when we sleep;
All these with ceaseless praise his works behold,
Both day and night. How often from the steep
Of echoing hill or thicket have we heard
Celestial voices to the midnight air,
Sole, or responsive each to other's note,
Singing their great Creator. Oft in bands,
While they keep watch or nightly rounding walk,
With heavenly touch of instrumental sounds,
In full harmonic number joined, their songs
Divide the night, and lift our thoughts to heaven.

Milton.

Spirits of peace, where are ye? Are ye all gone?
A blessed troop invited me to banquet, whose bright faces
Cast thousand beams upon me like the sun.

Shakspeare.

BECAUSE I am moved by a certain divine and spiritual influence, which also Melitus, through mockery, has set out in the indictment; this, begun with me from childhood, being a kind of voice which, when present, always diverts me from what I am about to do, but never urges me on. But this duty, as I said, has been enjoined me by the deity, by oracles, by dreams, and by every mode by which any other divine decree has ever enjoined anything for man to do. — *Socrates.*

They (the poets) do not compose by art, but through a divine power; since if they knew how to speak by art upon the subject correctly, they would be able to do so upon all others. And on this account a deity has deprived them of their senses, and employs them as his ministers, and oracle singers, and divine prophets, in order that when we hear them we may know it is not they to whom sense is not present who speak what is valuable, but the god himself who speaks, and through them addresses us.

We are not to doubt about those beautiful poems being not human but divine, and the work, not of men but of gods; and that poets are nothing else but interpreters of the gods (or spirits as we now call them), possessed by whatever deity they may happen to be. And in pointing out this, the Deity has, through a poet most indifferent, sung melody the most beautiful. — *Plato.*

We should reject fables when we are possessed of undeniable truth; for, according to Pindar,

> "The body yields to death's all-powerful summons,
> While the bright image of eternity
> Survives."

This alone is from the gods; from heaven it comes, and to heaven it returns; not indeed with the body, but when it is entirely set free and separate from the body; when it becomes disengaged from everything sensual and unholy. For, in the language of Heractitus, the pure soul is of superior excellence, darting from the body like a flash of lightning from a cloud; but the soul that is carnal and immersed in sense, like a heavy and dark vapor, with difficulty is kindled and aspires. — *Plutarch.*

There is at present a sister amongst us who has obtained the gift of revelations, which she receives in the congregation or solemn sanctuary, by ecstasy in the spirit, who has converse with the angels, sometimes with the Lord, and sees and hears great truths, and discerns the hearts of men, and ministers remedies to those who want them. Also, according as the Scriptures are read, or the Psalms are sung, or exhortations are uttered, or prayers offered from the various services, materials are furnished for her visions. We had happened to be discussing something about the soul, when the sister was in the spirit. After the conclusion of the service and the dismissal of the congregation, she, after the usual manner of her visions (for they are carefully revealed that they may be examined), amongst other remarks said, the *soul was shown her in a bodily form;* the spirit-nature appeared, but was not of an empty or shapeless quality, but as something which gave hope of being embraced or held, tender and bright, of an aërial hue, and altogether of human form. — *Tertullian.*

I hold it as a truth, that a divine atmosphere surrounds our earth, — an aroma emitted from the world of spirit, in which dwell the great truths and secrets of the universe, — a great world that pours down riches upon us, as the sun pours down heat; and as, without the sun, this world would be but a formless wilderness, so without this spirit-sun would it be barren of thought or beauty. Above us and around us exists a spiritual atmosphere, more subtle than the natural one. As the latter is the supporter of physical life, so the former is of psychal. We absorb the delicate magnetic aroma from all substances, through the medium of the air, as well as the comparatively coarse oxygen; so all of our soul-life comes from this spirit atmosphere, — all thought, all feeling, all appreciation of truth and beauty. Man is the apex of earth-creation, and the basis of all heavenly life, the foundation of all spiritual existence. Standing thus in a middle plane as the highest thing of earth and the lowest of heaven, he holds magnetic relationship to both. — *T. T. Watts.*

Except freedom from sin, intense, vigorous, untiring action is the mind's highest pleasure. I would not wish to go to heaven did I believe that its inhabitants were to sit inactive by purling streams, to be fanned into indolent slumbers by balmy breezes. Heaven, to be a place of happiness, must be a place of activity. Has the far-reaching mind of Newton rested from his profound investigations? Have David and Isaiah hung up their harps, useless as the dusty arms in Westminster Abbey? Has Paul, glowing with god-like enthusiasm, ceased itinerating the universe of God? Are Peter and Cyprian, and Luther and Edwards, idling away eternity in mere psalm-singing? Heaven is a place of activity, of never-tiring thought. David and Isaiah will sweep noble and lofty strains in eternity, and the minds of saints, unclogged by cumbrous clay, forever feast on a banquet of thought, — rich, glorious thought. Young gentlemen, press on; you will never get through. An eternity of untiring thought is before you, and the universe of thought your field. — *Rev. Lyman Beecher.*

My mind has been crowded by fancies concerning these beings. Are there indeed such beings? Is this space between us and the Deity filled up by innumerable orders of spiritual beings, forming the same gradations between the human soul and divine perfection that we see prevailing from humanity down to the merest insect? It is a sublime and beautiful doctrine of the early fathers, that there are guardian angels appointed to watch over cities and nations, to take care of good men, and to guard and guide the steps of helpless infancy. Even the docrine of departed spirits returning to visit the scenes and beings which were dear to them during the body's existence, though it has been debased by the absurd superstitions of the vulgar, in itself is awfully solemn and sublime. — *Washington Irving.*

The battle's fought, the victory's won forever. The celestial city is full in view; its glories beam upon me; its breezes fan me; its odors are wafted to me; its music strikes on my ear, and its spirit breathes into my soul. Nothing separates me from it but the river of death, now dwindling to a rill, crossed at a single step. The sun of righteousness fills the whole hemisphere, pouring forth a flood of glory, in which I seem to float like an insect in the beams of the sun, exulting yet almost trembling while I gaze on its brightness, and wondering with unutterable wonder why God should deign me this glorious light. — *Dr. Payson.*

Shall we know our friends again? For my own part I cannot doubt it; least of all, when I drop a tear over their recent dust. Death does not separate them from us here. Can life in heaven do it? They live in our remembrance. Memory rakes in the ashes of the dead, and the virtues of the departed flame up anew, enlightening the dim, cold walls of our cónsciousness. Much of our joy is social here. Must it not be so there, that we are with our real friends? Man loves to think it; yet to trust is wiser than to prophesy. But the girl who went from us a little one, may be as parent to her father when he comes, and the man who left us has far outgrown our dream of an angel when we meet again. — *Theodore Parker.*

That the dead are seen no more I will not undertake to maintain against the concurrent and unvaried testimony of all ages and of all nations. There is no people, rude or learned, among whom apparitions of the dead are not related and believed. This opinion, which, perhaps, prevails as far as human nature is diffused, could become universal only by its truth; those that never heard of one another would not have agreed in a tale which nothing but experience could render credible. That it is doubted by single cavillers can very little weaken the general evidence; and some who deny it with their tongues confess it by their fears. — *Dr. Johnson.*

As to the power of holding intercourse with spirits enfranchised from our present sphere, we see no reason why it should not exist, and do some reason why it should rarely be developed, but none why it should not sometimes. These spirits are, we all believe, existent somewhere, somehow; and there seems to be no good reason why a person in spiritual nearness to them, whom such intercourse cannot agitate or engross so that he cannot walk steadily in his present path, should not enjoy it when of use to him. — *Margaret Fuller.*

It is a hard matter to deal with men who do verily believe that God Almighty and his angels encamp around about them. What do they care for earthly things or earthly power? What do they care for kings, and lords, and presidents? They fully believe they are heirs of the King of kings. In the hour of battle they seem to themselves to stand, like the great Hebrew leader, in the cleft of the rock, the glory of the most high God passes by them, and they catch a gleam of its brightness. If you come in conflict with the purposes of such men, they will regard duty as everything, life as nothing. — *Hon. Thomas Corwin.*

It is no more improbable that angels should be employed to aid man than that one man should aid another; certainly not as improbable as that the Son of God should come down, "not to be ministered unto, but to minister." . . What they do now may be learned from the Scripture accounts of what they have done, — as it seems to be a fair principle of interpretation that they are engaged in substantially the same employment in which they have ever been. . . They attend the redeemed; they wait on their steps; they sustain them in trial; they accompany them when departing to heaven. — *Rev. Dr. Albert Barnes.*

I think a person who is thus terrified with the imagination of ghosts and spectres much more reasonable than any one who, contrary to the reports of all historians, sacred and profane, ancient and modern, and to the traditions of all nations, thinks the appearance of spirits fabulous and groundless. Could not I give myself up to this general testimony of mankind, I should to the relations of particular persons now living, and whom I cannot distrust in other matters of fact. — *Addison.*

It is an exquisite and beautiful thing in our nature, that when our heart is touched and softened by some tranquil happiness or affectionate feeling, the memory of the dead comes over it most powerfully and irresistibly. It would seem almost as though our better thoughts and sympathies were charms, in virtue of which the soul is enabled to hold some vague and mysterious intercourse with the spirits of those whom we loved in life. Alas, how often and how long may these patient angels hover around us, watching for the spell which is soon forgotten. — *Charles Dickens.*

I live, as did Simeon, in the hope of seeing a brighter day. I do see gleams of dawn, and that ought to cheer me. I hope nothing from increased zeal in urging an imperfect, decaying form of Christianity. One higher, clearer view of religion rising on a single mind, encourages me more than the organization of millions to repeat what has been repeated for ages with little effect. The individual here is mightier than the world; and I have the satisfaction of seeing aspirations after this purer truth. — *Rev. Dr. Wm. E. Channing.*

The world would run into endless routine; but the perpetual supply of new genius, out of the Cause of causes, shocks us with thrills of life. The chief day of life is the day when we encounter a mind that startles us by its originality and force. Providence sends from time to time to each serious mind six or seven teachers, who are of the first importance to him in that which they have to impart. The highest of these benefit not so much by what they have to communicate, as by their spirit and modes of feeling and thought. — *Ralph Waldo Emerson.*

To be mediums on this better plan, is to be baptized with the Holy Spirit, and to be in communication with heaven. It is the consummation which all Christians have been praying for, and toward which all religious experience tends. It is the blessing of the New Covenant, promised to the last days, in saying, They shall not teach every man his neighbor, saying, Know the Lord; for all shall know me, from the least unto the greatest.—*The Circular.*

"But, ah," we say, "if there were only some manifestations; if there were only a glimpse of that blessed land; if there were indeed some message-bird, such as is supposed in some countries to come from the spirit-land, how eagerly should we question it."—*Rev. Dr. Orville Dewey.*

Immortality is not now commonly believed in as it ought to be. It wants familiarizing to our feeling. We want such corroborations of the great truth as are latent in science, history, philosophy, and the fresh experiences we are always passing through.—*Rev. Wm. Mountford.*

I long for an occasional peep at you by an "electric telegraph trip-train;" and, above all, I want the electric telegraph itself to the other world, and have a message now and then from those dear ones we have loved and lost. Oh, what a luxury would *that* be!—*Henry Rogers, Greyson Letters.*

I know of no nation, polite or barbarous, which does not hold that some persons have the gift of foretelling future events.—*Cicero.*

I am as confident of immortality, from the incontestable evidence of the spirit of God, as ever I was of any mathematical truth from all the demonstrations of Euclid.—*Phillip De Morney.*

What brightness is this I see? The day-star from on high has descended. I see things that are unutterable.—*J. Holland.*

This is heaven begun. Nothing now remains but salvation, with eternal glory, eternal glory.—*Rev. T. Scott.*

I am going from weeping friends to congratulate angels and rejoicing saints in heaven.—*Darracott.*

And I, Daniel, alone saw the vision; for the men that were with me saw not, but a great quaking fell upon them, so that they fled to hide themselves.—*Daniel.*

Now, concerning spiritual gifts, brethren, I would not have you ignorant.—*Paul.*

Believe not every spirit, but try the spirits whether they are of God.—*John.*

And behold, there appeared Moses and Elias, talking with him.—*Matthew.*

Father, into thy hands I commend my spirit.—*Jesus.*

The heavens were opened. Lord Jesus, receive my spirit.—*Stephen.*

I go away, and come again unto you.—*Jesus.*

I will pour out my spirit upon all flesh.—*Joel.*

CHAPTER I.

HISTORY OF SPIRITUALISM, ANCIENT AND MODERN—ITS RISE AND PROGRESS IN AMERICA.

Why come not spirits from the realm of glory
  To visit earth as in the days of old,—
The times of ancient writ and sacred story?
  Is heaven more distant, or has earth grown cold?
To Bethlehem's air was their last anthem given,
  When other stars before the One grew dim,
Was their last presence known in Peter's prison,
  Or where exulting martyrs raised the hymn?

JULIA WALLICE.

A PLAIN GUIDE to Spiritualism, adapted to the wants of the million, must embody many practical details, excluding a thorough history of all the phenomena extending through the ages. Though the materialist may doubt, religionists are compelled to admit the occurrence of ancient phenomena parallel with modern spiritual manifestations. Without the philosophy of Spiritualism, the mysteries of centuries are left unlocked, and the millions are enshrouded in the night of ignorance and superstition. Egyptian, Chinese, Chaldean, Grecian, Roman, Persian, as well as Jewish and Christian history, abound with evidences of ultra-mundane agencies which find no explanation without admitting the existence of a spirit-realm opened in communication with mortals, and peopled by intelligences, who under certain conditions are able to manifest themselves. Confucius, Herodotus, Plato, Pliny, Xenophon, Seneca, Socrates, Virgil, Homer, Cicero, Demosthenes, as well as the early Christian fathers, have handed down their testimony. All the ancient Hebrew authors claimed constant intercourse with the invisible world, and admitted something analogous to other nations. The birth and death of great men, the rise and fall of cities and empires, like the birth and death of Jesus, of Romulus and Cæsar; the rise and fall of Jerusalem and Rome, — all these were said to have been attended by startling supernatural occurrences. Pilate's wife had awful presentiments of the tragedy of Calvary, and the wife of Julius Cæsar was warned of his assassination. The pages of sacred history are covered with phenomena, like the cloud and the pillar of fire attending the fugitive children of Israel; the lightning and thunder of Sinai, and the delivery of the decalogue by angels; the plagues of Egypt; the fire, hurricane and earthquake of Mount Horeb; the falling of the walls of Jericho; the hurtling of chariots and warriors in the heavens over the camp of Israel; the warning hand-writing on the wall of the Babylonian court; the angelic annunciation of Jesus; the star in the East guiding the Magi to Bethlehem; the stilling of wave and tempest on the Sea of Galilee; the darkness over all the land of Judea during the tragedy of Calvary; the rending of the veil of the temple; the yawning of rocks and grave-yards, sending back their dead into the streets of Jerusalem; the rolling of the stone from the door of the sepulchre; the tongues of fire, and "the rushing mighty wind" on the day of Pentecost, and the wonders seen by John on the isle of Patmos.

The Bibles or sacred writings of all ages and nations are largely composed of phenomena, narrations, and teachings more or less in harmony with those of Modern Spiritualism. Wherever a living God or gods, demons, angels, spirits, so-called miracles, oracles, inspirations, or anything like super-mundane revelations have been recognized, there we find traces of the same spiritual philosophy now exciting the joy and wonder of the world. Sometimes it is objected that Spiritualism is of modern origin, and is only a few years old; and we are asked, If it be true, why was its advent delayed till the middle of the nineteenth century? Why have the millions inhabiting the spirit-world waited till this late day before opening communication with mortals? Why has humanity waited for ages in darkness? If it is possible for mortals now to hold intercourse, why were not the methods of intercommunication more commonly known in the past? But no sooner are these interrogations propounded than we hear it objected that Spiritualism is as old as Satan, and was proclaimed by the allegorical arch-demon in the Garden of Eden; and it is contended that all these present phenomena find parallel in ancient idolatry, heathenism, and mythology. Now, while we may admit that many of the present methods of spiritual manifestations are comparatively new, and are now for the first time becoming understood as in harmony with the laws of God and nature, we insist that history affords abundant evidence of the great law of spiritual intercourse during all the centuries. Every age and nation have had their religions and revelations, and the very idea of religion and revelations presupposes the necessity of inspiration from the invisible world, and the agency of spiritual intelligences acting as angels or ministering spirits to communicate between God and men. Let all the phenomena and the philosophy of Spiritualism become repudiated, and we can form no idea of another world, nor of the manner in which mortals can receive anything like a revelation. Let all the Bibles of the past be expurged of everything of a spiritual character, and we have little or nothing left except the skeleton of dead history and a few abstract teachings.

In the primeval age of our planet, when man first became conscious of rational existence, he began to ask questions in regard to the great CAUSE of his own existence and the existence of the boundless universe in the midst of whose temple he found himself placed, surrounded by stupendous mysteries. Whence am I, and what, and whither? How came I into conscious being, and how all this vast fabric of earth poised amid the ethereal fields of immensity? Whence all these forms of life, and yonder orbs shining in the azure dome? He questioned the oracles of earth, of his own inmost being, and the heavens, but all were dumb. He saw manifestations of power and intelligence far beyond his own finite material plane of comprehension, and he questioned the Infinite, the Unknown, the Invisible. Unable to solve the problem of his origin, his nature, and his destination, he called on the Unknown God or gods, whose might and majesty he saw displayed in every department of the universe. At last some responses came back. Faint voices were heard whispering from out the heavens. Subtle influences came stealing over him, as if from beings peopling the ethereal fields of space. Dim forms were seen, like mists fleeing before the morning light. Rays of light came stealing into the darkened chambers of his soul, opening his perceptions to the consciousness of an inner life and communion with an invisible world. The unseen elements of earth and air began to speak in prophecy of an unseen spiritual universe, peopled with myriads of living beings, and presided over by gods of supernal potency. But he could form no rational conception of God as a unity. Unseen powers and intelligences at last began to manifest and communicate themselves in such a manner as to enable mortals to indentify individual, spiritual beings. Those spiritual beings were at first seen so unlike man in the material form, so unlike the inhabitants of earth, they were regarded as gods, and as such were idolized, and set up as tutelar deities and objects of worship. Hence the origin of polytheism, or the idea of many gods, and the idolatry universally prevalent in the earlier ages of humanity. The oldest religions of which we now have any knowledge are the Chinese, the Hindoo, the Persian, and the Egyptian. All these were anterior to the Hebrew, whose history we find in the Old Testament Scriptures.

The Mosaic dispensation affords us the fullest record of ancient phenomena. Its seers claimed direct communication with God, though at the same time they recognized the agency of angelic beings coming as the messengers of the Lord, looking, acting, and talking like human beings. The controverted points here involved will be duly considered elsewhere in this volume. It is evident that these ancient seers, like John (Rev. xxii. 9), had imperfect conceptions of the communion they were permitted to enjoy, and took the messengers of God to be an impersonation of God himself, inasmuch as those messengers corresponded with their highest ideas of Deity. They often claimed to hold direct converse with God, and see him face to face, and yet it is declared, "No man hath seen God at any time." John i. 18. Yet the Jewish idea of Deity, however crude, was in advance of the polytheism prevalent in cotemporary ages. In spite of all their claims to an exclusive revelation, the Hebrew seers predicted an era when all men should hold uninterrupted intercourse with God and the invisible world. Joel ii. 23. The Christian dispensation inaugurated that era of universal inspiration and communion. Acts ii. 16, etc.; Heb. xii. 22, etc.; 1 Cor. xii. The reader will find these positions substantiated in other chapters of this Guide. The apostles and Christians of the early centuries cultivated spiritual gifts as a solemn duty, and claimed direct intercourse with the celestial world. Heb. xii. 22, etc. For several centuries a variety of phenomena akin to the modern spiritual were prevalent in the churches, and evangelists were not considered qualified to preach unless they were "endowed with power from on high," or inspired. 1 Cor. xii. 14; Luke xxiv. 49; Mark xvi.

17, etc. An able paper on the spiritualism of the early Christian church, by Rev. William Fishbough, will be found in the appendix of the Healing of the Nations, one of the most valuable volumes of the new dispensation, with an equally valuable introduction by Hon. N. P. Tallmadge. Among the most eminent of the early fathers recognizing spiritual intercourse were Origen and Tertullian. Had a faithful record of the first centuries been preserved, modern literature would have been enriched with numerous traces of celestial intercourse, now buried beneath vast tomes of theological lumber, blocking out the light of ages.

When Christianity began to be embodied in creeds and forms, and the clergy grew jealous of the rights and liberties of the people to receive and believe for themselves, then spiritual gifts began to cease, and priesthoods set themselves up as authorities to block out the light of heaven and insist on the end of all revelations and inspirations. The people must accept them as reliable expounders of what had already been revealed, rather than seek for more light. History affords abundant evidence in support of this view, notwithstanding the efforts of ecclesiastics to suppress the facts. Through all the "dark ages" we grope our way down to the so-called Reformation. Luther and his cotemporaries struck out boldly for the rights of the individual conscience against that darkening domination which for centuries had suppressed spiritual gifts, or confined them to the priesthood, and had shut out the light of heaven; but early Protestantism did not re-inaugurate the Christian era of free spiritual communion, however noble may have been its mission. Swedenborg appeared after two centuries more, and John Wesley, but no general movement indicated the inauguration of a celestial era. The strange occurrences which took place in the family of John Wesley in 17—, and which were admitted to have been spiritual by all who pursued a candid investigation, made no wide or deep impression on the public mind, and shared the fate of thousands of similar phenomena in all ages. Mrs. Crowe's Night Side of Nature gives a variety of facts extending over a wide range of history; but science and philosophy had grown too materialistic to admit any spiritual agencies outside of sacred history, and excepted the Bible only out of courtesy or policy. The seeress of Provorst appeared in Germany in 1825–28, presenting various phenomena like the later spiritual, yet one poor, feeble woman alone could accomplish but little towards battling down the walls of ecclesiastical and materialistic darkness. Jung Stilling, one of the most remarkable and amiable characters living in Germany cotemporary with Goethe, advocated the celestial philosophy in a manner to command the attention of all daring minds, but German philosophy and theology stoutly resisted the light. But while literature and theology have been so materialistic, we are not to forget the many noble minds shining out in the midst of darkness, and recognizing the gospel of spiritual communion, among which we find Luther, Melancthon, Archbishop Tillotson, Bishop Hall, Revs. Dr. Owen, Bickersteth, Townshend, Chalmers, Dick, Barnes, Oberlin, Clarke, and a score more of men equally eminent. How many have cherished the spiritual faith in one form or another, during all ages, we are unable to compute, though it is certain that belief has found a secret, undefined lodgement in the great heart of enlightened millions mourning and longing for some light from that bourn towards which all the generations have departed. "The desire of all nations" has been to solve the mystery of death and open the portals of the invisible world. With all the historical light of past revelations claiming to come from God and celestial hosts, the multitude, even in Christian lands, before the advent of Spiritualism, entertained no strong faith or radiant hope. Though Jesus rose from the dead centuries ago, the grave seemed still closed, and no beloved ones came back with messages of life and immortality. All the evangelical sects had been united for half a century in praying for a millennial era to open earth and heaven in communion, and mourners in Zion sat down sad and silent, watching for the signs predicted for ages. Second-Adventism had appointed the time for some great celestial change; cotemporary sects waited and watched in doubt, yet hopeful of something; old sciences and philosophies had grown stubborn in skepticism; the masses of the people were absorbed in material things, while new sciences like Mesmerism had startled daring minds with hopes and prophecies of celestial radiance, out-dazzling all the dreams of the past.

In the little huddle of Hydesville, Arcadia, Wayne County, N. Y., in 1844, in a humble hamlet, there resided a small family, Mrs. Ann Pulver and daughter. The mother and daughter became so disturbed by mysterious knockings around the house, they grew exceedingly alarmed, and changed their residence. In 1847, Mr. M. Weekman and family, having taken the same house, were visited by the same sounds, until they were likewise impelled to move. Mr. and Mrs. John D. Fox, with three daughters, Ann, Margaret and Catharine, moved into the same house in Dec. 1847, and in March, 1848, the knockings were resumed, and began to excite serious attention. After some time, the family began to ask questions and receive answers in the form of signals, one knock signifying *no*, two *doubtful*, three *yes;* and at last communications were rapped out in the use of the alphabet. The neighbors flocked in; the intelligence spread like prairie fires; the newspapers published startling reports; hundreds of people poured in from the neighboring towns and from every section of the land. After the most rigid investigation, nobody could solve the mystery without admitting the agency of spirits. It was certain that loud and distinct sounds were made; it was equally certain that no human beings by any possible means made those sounds; the sounds were accompanied by intelligence; it was certain that the intelligence belonged to no human being present in the form; it was equally certain that some of the intelligence could be traced back and be accounted for only by referring to beings once living in the body on earth, and those beings manifested themselves in such a manner as to enable their earth-friends to identify and recognize them beyond all doubt. This was the only possible solution of the phenomena; all else was mere conjecture or assumption. The various theories, objections, subterfuges, and slanders adduced against these palpable demonstrations of immortality and spiritual intercourse, will receive attention in subsequent chapters. But in passing it may be remarked, that one of the cruelest charges was against the character of the Fox family, the elder members of which were at that time Methodists in good standing, and the daughters too young to have any knowledge of the evils wickedly alleged against them; and since that period, amid all the temptations to which they have been exposed, they have borne unimpeachable characters.

From that humble home in Hydesville, as humble as Nazareth, the tidings spread with a joy and wonder akin to the angel tidings over Bethlehem; and the mediums were as credible as were the Mary Magdalene and the other Mary who first heralded the news of a risen Christ. A circle was soon formed in Auburn, N. Y., and new manifestations were unfolded. The Fox family moved to Rochester, N. Y., and the whole city and surrounding country were aroused. Committees were appointed, numerous private and public investigations were held, and none could account for the phenomena without adopting the spiritual hypothesis. New phases began to be unfolded, and new mediums developed. The Rev. Charles

Hammond, a humble clergyman of unquestioned character, was brought out as the first writing medium; his hand mechanically moved without any conscious volition of his own; and soon others were influenced in various ways, — some writing; some passing into trances in an unconscious state, impelled to speak, communicate messages, personify departed friends; some transported in vision into the invisible world; some rendered clairvoyant, describing disease, designating remedies, and healing by "the laying on of hands;" some used as mediums for music and the moving of ponderable bodies, etc.; in short, until from Auburn and Rochester the various phenomena since developed spread over the entire land, and at last swept their circles around the globe.

Without pausing here to define theories, specify objects and aims, state facts, or describe and classify the almost innumerable phenomena unfolded during the fifteen years since the advent of modern Spiritualism in America, we may refer to the subjoined extracts from the pulpit and the press, as appropriate to this historical chapter, and as illustrations of the magnitudinous importance of the gospel to which this volume is devoted.

If America ever becomes a Christian republic, it must be under a liberal interpretation of the religion of Jesus Christ. Already is there arising a vast movement among our people, the beginning of a new and loftier Christian doctrine and life. . . . . I see it in that worthy body of reformers, which, through evil report and good report, are applying religion to the every-day affairs of our country. *I see it in the latest and largest of liberal religious bodies* (Spiritualists), *numbering thousands of the good and wise of the land*, who are toiling to dispel the darkness that broods over the future life, who say that all worlds and places are bound into one by cords of human love, and God is over us all. . . . . The last outbreak of popular religious enthusiasm is commonly known as Spiritualism. It has two sides, the mesmeric and theological. The mesmeric certainly offers curious topics for scientific investigation, and we shall, probably, one day derive from it much light on the obscure problems of the influence of mind on matter, and the laws of mental association. But it is not as a body of people interested in mesmeric media, that this large religious denomination, now numbering four millions of disciples, chiefly concerns the observer of American theology, but as an exhibition of the popular tendencies of thought in religion. Spiritualism is a *natural awakening of the American masses to the doctrine of the immortal life taught by Jesus.* The materialism of our society has brought the popular faith in immortality to a very low ebb; while the evangelical church has so caricatured the sublime idea by its doctrines of probation, judgment, heaven and hell, that the people have begun to feel this part of their religious belief slipping from them. The natural recoil from these influences has produced that outbreak of mingled fanaticism and piety which some mistake for a new gospel; yet, all that a rational Spiritualist believes of the future life and communion of souls was taught by Jesus, an has been believed by spiritually-minded people for eighteen centuries. [Questionable.] But we, in America, were getting so far away from that sublime doctrine, in our life and theology, that human nature could endure it no longer, and by a great rebound has shown how the soul of man needs the assurance of an endless existence. I look upon the alliance of this movement with mesmerism as accidental and temporary. The tipping tables and rattling wainscots will, in good time, be left with other prodigies in the hands of curious men of scientific leisure for experiment. [Why not in the hands of the people?] But this great cry of the popular heart after a rational faith in immortality will shiver numberless churches, and burst the bonds of many a man now enfolded in materialism or petrified into theological marble. We shall learn out of it *what it means in the nineteenth century to believe in the immortality of the soul;* and it will be found that this doctrine will come to us fraught with vaster relations, suggesting larger duties, and elevating with nobler aspirations, than to the darkened masses of the early ages of heathenism or middle ages of Christianity. — *Rev. A. D. Mayo.*

The Spiritualists say, The Bible is not a finality; it is

no man's master; it is every man's servant. We, as well as the old prophets, can have communion with the departed. Christ reveals himself directly to us, as much as to Paul and Silas, Peter and James. . . . . We want a revival of religion in the American church which shall be to the church what the religion of Jesus was to heathenism and Judaism, which, though useful once, in his day had served out their time, and had no more that they could do. We do not want a religion hierarchically organized, which shall generate nothing but meeting-houses made of stone, and end at last in a priesthood. We want a religion democratically organized, generating great political, social, domestic institutions, and ending in a world full of noble men and women, all their faculties developed well, they serving God with that love which casts out fear. How can we stir that element to emotions fit for such a work? Only by a theology which shall meet the people's want, a natural and just idea of man, of God; of the relation between them; of religion, life, duty, destination on earth and in heaven; a theology which has its evidences in the world of matter — all science God's testimony thereto; and in the world of consciousness — every man bearing within him the "lively oracles," the present witness of his God, his duty, and destination. No sect has such a theology; no great sect aims at such, or the life it leads to. The Spiritualists are the only sect [not a sect, but a people] that looks forward, and has new fire on its hearth; they alone emancipate themselves from the Bible and the theology of the church, while they also seek to keep the precious truths of the Bible and all the good things of the church. — *Rev. Theodore Parker.*

Spiritualism will yet be a greater disturbing element in the religious world than it is at present. . . . The materialism of our scientific, popular and religious literature had brought about such an indifference with regard to the question of immortality; and then the popular creeds had so caricatured the Christian idea of the future life, by their doctrines of heaven and hell, that the more thoughtful of community had come to be wholly indifferent to this part of religious belief. . . . The senses may be startled by the phenomena; the higher spiritual intuitions must apprehend the pure truth. These wonderful facts will interest the curious and engage the attention of the candid; and from them much light may be shed on obscure natural laws. The intelligent masses of America want more rational ideas of God, of the soul, and of our future life. And this deep-seated want will shiver to atoms many churches, will ignore many dogmas, and reject an old, worn-out system of theology as embodied in the creeds, and will lead many millions to a rational, liberal, evangelical Christian faith. This is what the present movement is doing. Let us not oppose it, but rather temper it with a true piety, and then we shall learn what it is to have an inspiration adapted to our present spiritual needs. — *Rev. G. W. Skinner.*

In the progress the Spiritualists have made since the whole thing was but a mysterious noise in an old house at Rochester [Hydesville, N. Y.], fifteen years ago, they assume in the most confident manner to see the doom and overthrow of the entire ecclesiastical system which prevails in this country. As a theory of religion, the development of these ideas would prove, without question, the most revolutionary movement which ecclesiasticism has confronted since the Reformation. A nucleus of nearly two millions of professed and attached believers is already claimed for such a revolution. Its barricades, they say, are not, indeed, drawn up on Broadway or Pennsylvania Avenue, but in the far more vital precincts of the jury box and ballot box; in the senate and halls of legislation; on the bench, the press, and even in the pulpit itself. The movement is essentially indigenous and American, bearing the most absolute marks of its democratic and popular origin. To back up this curious and radical basis of a religion, they assert not only the Protestant principle — the right and duty of every man, woman, and child to have access to the evangelical writings — but they assume, also, the duty and the ability of every individual to become an evangelist for himself, to find access to the spiritual world, and draw thence a spiritual inspiration for his moral sustenance, as the trees absorb their own light and air. It would be useless to deny the extent to which this new superstition [?] prevails. The more noisy and preposterous manifestations of it have subsided as matters of public excitement; but the private practice of its manipulations and ecstasies are well known to have taken a deep hold of our community. Spirit manifestations make a chief and most exciting subject of attention in numberless households, especially in the stagnant social life of our country towns. Clergymen, travelling lecturers and colporteurs bear witness unanimously to its equally alarming and astonishing growth. Its real extent would be impossible to determine. Of those Christians who accord it a tacit assent, and accept its distinctive doctrine — the substantial and material being of the human soul and of God — the number is quite beyond computation. It is in this point of view that the Spiritualists have made, as yet, their only abiding impression. [Mistake.] The number of six hundred professional speakers and mediums were given in the Spiritual Register, with their names and addresses, as actively urging the movement, whilst the names of a thousand others are withheld, because it was not known how far they were willing to become subject to calls outside of their immediate circles. The same source affords an estimate of the actual number of professed Spiritualists, compiled from extensive correspondence undertaken for this object, and with the facilities of an editor and itinerant who had surveyed and gone over the ground. [Reference is here made to the *Spiritualist Register*, edited and published by the author of the present volume, five years, in connection with the *Spiritual Clarion*, Auburn, N. Y.] The sales of spiritualist books and publications would seem to corroborate this estimate. If the movement of the Protestant Reformation was the result of the printing of the Scriptures, the American revolutionary religion is still more a religion of typography. It literally substitutes the press for the pulpit, and the household for the cathedral. More than a hundred periodicals have been started for its diffusion. Over one hundred distinct publications on the subject are on the book catalogues, which are set down for as much demand as the new religious books of any other sect usually average. Certain pamphlets, in the early stages of the movement, had a more vastly extensive circulation. This enumeration is presented as one of the features of the time, and for the special consideration of that portion of our thirty thousand clergymen whose duty it should be to meet this threatening sedition in their own precincts before wasting precious time upon the barren and dangerous province of politics. It would seem that the matter is not unknown to them, for during their late visit to New York an extraordinary number of spiritualist publications were disposed of. It is well worth their attention, before it becomes too late, to see how far the religion of our sleepy churches, the Protestant loyalty to the Scriptures, are to be superseded by this religion of revolution, — the red republican project of making every man his own evangelist. — *N. Y. Herald.*

Spiritualism is the most remarkable phenomenon of this remarkable age. However we regard it, it is stranger than any other manifestation in art, science, literature or religion. If it is a mental epidemic, it proves how strong are the ties and attractions, spite of the ten thousand repellant forces of society. It teaches the solidarity of the race. If it is the devil's work, it shows that he has at least one virtue, that of industry. If it is humbug, the capacity of manufacturing and of disposing of that commodity has been wonderfully enhanced. If it is true, why cannot it be proved, what is its use, and why are not some clearer views given of the future state after death than we have had before? But, however regarded, Spiritualism is a great fact of this age. Some fire must be at the bottom of all this smoke, and thus much at least appears, that in a cold, hard, and material age, the human soul in great masses of men has shot up in ardent longings and yearnings after spiritual realities, after a stronger faith, and a more apprehensible connection with God and the spirit-world. — *New York Inquirer.*

Our readers would be astonished were we to lay before them the names of several of those who are unflinching believers in it, or are devoting themselves to the study or reproduction of its marvels. Not only does it survive, but survives with all the charm and all the stimulating attractiveness of a secret science. Until the public mind in England shall be prepared to receive it, or until the evidence can be put in a shape to enforce general conviction, the present policy is to nurse it in quiet and enlarge the circle of influence by a system of noiseless extension. Whether this policy will be successful remains to be seen; but there can be no doubt that should ever the time arrive for a revival of the movement, the persons at its head would be men and women whose intellectual qualifications are known to the public, and who possess its confidence and esteem. — *Westminster, Eng., Review.*

Notwithstanding the mighty opposition which the Spiritualists, so called, have met with since the first "rappings" in Rochester, they have increased very rapidly all over this country, and have likewise made no small progress beyond the Atlantic. They have now regularly constituted societies in almost all our towns and cities, hold regular Sabbath services, and really exert a powerful influence in almost every community. The problem of the asserted spiritual manifestations has never yet been satisfactorily solved by the opponents of Spiritualism; and the creed explaining the various phenomena involved therein, as occasioned by the direct agency of unseen and intangible beings, once the tenants of human organisms, has stood firm and immovable against all the attacks of the incredulous. — *Providence, R. I., Union.*

Spiritualism, instead of losing ground in England, is flourishing and vigorous, not only among the ignorant and insane, but among men of repute, who might fairly be looked upon as superior to any system of trickery so barefaced and wicked. At this moment there are several literary circles in London who are lending their aid to spread the delusion, and we could name more than one eminent man who is a decided victim to it. Sittings are frequent in the best circles; mediums are tolerated in the highest quarters; and even the church does not fail to add its quota to the herd of the misguided and deluded. Among the recent converts are Lord Lyndhurst, Sir E. Bulwer Lytton, Robert Chambers, Mrs. Browning, and many other literary and scientific men and women. — *Brighton, Eng., Herald.*

Though we are not believers in Spiritualism, technically so called, we regard this movement as an uprising of the human mind after something better than the existing faith of Christendom. It is the John the Baptist to a new advent. It is the morning star to a new reformation. Starved by the creeds and churches, they are neither in harmony with God's truth above, nor with man's wants below; sick of worldliness and materialism, the very words *spirits*, *spiritualism*, *spiritual medium*, come with a refreshing influence to the seared and arid heart of multitudes. — *Christian Inquirer.*

The most reliable statistics of Spiritualism will more than justify these few expressions of the pulpit and the press, selected from hundreds of a similar character published all over the civilized world. The writer has spent years in the lecturing field of all of the Northern and some of the Border States and provinces of America, visiting all the largest towns and cities, and numerous villages and rural districts; coming in direct contact with the people, with multitudes of prominent believers, lecturers, and mediums; corresponding, as editor, with every important locality; attending private circles and public conventions; watching all the signs of the popular mind, and constantly taking notes for the most accurate reports of progress. Countless phases of the spiritual phenomena have been found multiplying all over the land, and that, too, without any collusion between the numerous mediums; and all these phenomena have concurred in demonstrating the same great fact of angel intercourse. There are now in America five hundred public mediums who receive visitors constantly or occasionally, and more than fifty thousand mediums who are reliable in select circles, but are not before the public. About one hundred periodicals have been devoted wholly or in part to the propagation and exposition of Spiritualism, most of which were designed to have only a temporary mission. More than five hundred books and pamplets have been circulated, and many of them are still having an extensive sale. There are five hundred speakers who are considered especial public advocates, while more than one thousand are regarded as only occasional. Nearly two thousand places are open for public circles, conferences, or lectures, and in many places there are flourishing Sunday schools. The decisive believers number about two million, while the nominal are nearly five million. On the Eastern Continent the number may be reckoned as one million. The whole number now on the globe, supposed to recognize the fact of spiritual intercourse, cannot fall short of twenty million. The population of the United States, before the rebellion, numbered thirty-one million; of these, only about five million are church communicants, leaving twenty-six million out of the "ark of safety." The entire population of the globe is one billion, only fifty million of whom are professing Christians, and not more than five million regarded genuine; according to orthodoxy, then, leaving nine hundred and ninety-five million of immortal souls with no certain hope of eternal salvation.

These startling statistics must be met. They reveal the mighty work which some new dispensation is called on to accomplish, and the matchless mission which Spiritualism has already accomplished within the brief space of fifteen years. This gospel has become a stupendous fact with its millions of living witnesses. It is not a creed or theory based alone on the traditions and evidences of the past, like the dominant theologies of Christendom, but based on visible and accredited phenomena now manifest everywhere in our midst. From the mines of modern El Dorado, to the bleak coasts of Greenland; from the rock of old Plymouth, to the shores of Oregon; the ice-wrapped peaks of Lapland, to the jungles of the orient Indies; from the exile-realms of Siberia, to the southern promontory of the Ethiopian continent; — wherever progress has carried the intelligence of civilization, there these spiritual phenomena, which have become household realities in our midst, have broken the lethargy of materialism, and opened visions of the super-mundane universe. And these phenomena, without any collusion on the part of those who are used as mediums, are concurrent in demonstrating the agency of some power and intelligence other than that belonging to the sphere of material causation, and referable only to spiritual beings capable of manifesting themselves to man on the normal plane of earth. It is behind the time to contend that these manifestations are not a reality. Neither magic nor art, magnetism nor electricity, psychology nor theology, can account for them. Thousands of intelligent witnesses have closely investigated them, and their testimony is before the world, with an array of strength never equalled in behalf of any other system of science, philosophy, or religion. Neither astronomy, geology, nor phrenology, for more than a quarter of a century, had as many advocates as Spiritualism now has, after only fifteen years since its lowly advent; and it may be doubted whether Christianity, in a century from the birth of Christ, numbered as many as the Spiritualists of to-day. Allowing the Spiritual ranks to number two millions, composed of every grade of intellect and moral estimate, to suppose all these either deceived or deceiving, were more marvellous than to admit the spiritual hypothesis itself, since the multitude could have no motive, on the one hand, to deceive themselves, and, on the other, it were morally impossible that the mediums, acting without concert or collusion, should have been able to cheat all the caution, science, philosophy, and intelligence combined in the investigation of the phenomena. To suppose this, were to throw doubt into all evidence, and undermine the foundations of all history. The rise of Christianity, of the Roman Empire, and the Reformation of the sixteenth century, are events transmitted to us on the evidence of departed witnesses; and it were just as reasonable to deny all those witnesses, and discredit the events concerning which they testify, as to dismiss with silence or contempt all the living witnesses who stand up to-day, with a bold front, in testimony of the existence and manifestation of spiritual intelligences.

The churches have found Spiritualism sweeping the world with its broad, angel wings, and have risen in alarm. It has been found embracing all that is good and true in the past and present; all science, philosophy, religion, and revelation. Conservatism, sectarianism, and skepticism, have been blindly desperate, and ransacked all the spheres of life in search of weapons with which to beat back the descending hosts of heaven. But still they come in spite of all misrepresentations and contumelies. The opposition has been so violent and unfair, it has reacted; and the result is, converts have been added by hundreds of thousands. The tone of the pulpit, the press, and the people, though still anon violent, is fast becoming modified; and Spiritualism is recognized as the gospel of millions of living men and women, ranking among all classes, and reaching over both continents. It has grown into a power so popular, it has attracted certain classes of impostors, whose time, however, is short, for the intelligence of the million is on the alert. Many of its public advocates, though acknowledged to possess excellent gifts, have received no education for public life except that which has come from nature, self-culture, and spiritual influence. They stand up "endowed with power from on high," and speak as they are moved by the "Holy Ghost," or the holy hosts of heaven. They do not ignore the graces of the schools, but rely more on the influxes of the spirit. Many of them are not up to the highest standard, but they are aiming to accomplish a noble work, and are cheered on by angel inspirations. In addition to these public advocates, are the thousands of mediums and the manifold phenomena. The influence of all these public speakers and private mediums is incalculable; and when we endeavor to realize that millions on millions of spirits are endeavoring to reach millions of their earthly friends, and all these are coöperating with millions of believers and inquirers, we have a culmination of agencies unparalleled in human history. Add to these the periodicals, tracts, pamphlets and books, constantly issued and scattered over the continent, and Spiritualism becomes seen and felt as a power no ally on earth can stay back.

Humanity, long buried in the night of materialism, sat mourning at the sepulchre, waiting for some divine agency to roll away the stone that blocked out the light of God and the invisible world. Sages, philosophers, and priesthoods built their temples over and around the sepulchre, and erecting their systems, forms, and creeds as authority, said the stone should not be rolled away; the dead should not come back; humanity should not see its Christ until he returned in vengeance, but should weep and mourn with no light, save that which came down through centuries, shining dimly in the pages of history, or through the stained windows of temples over whose altars priests sat mumbling their creeds and swinging their dark-lantern lights out into the air of a worse than Egyptian night. But, lo! the earth began to vibrate as if beneath the march of angel armies, and sound after sound came thundering on the old rocks blocking out the light of heaven. "We must stop these manifestations," hoarsely whispered the opposing conclaves. Judaism said this of Christianity, and it martyred Jesus, blocked up his sepulchre, and set a Roman guard on watch. But what whipsters of impotence are mortals when leagued against heaven! Had that Roman guard been millions of the sons of Hercules, all would have fallen as dead men before the power descending and shocking the tomb with angel presence. And what can avail all the powers arrayed against the celestial world to-day? Why, let the churches propose to martyr every pioneer of Spiritualism, excommunicate its legions of believers; let them preach their funeral sermons, and consign us again and again to the deepest, darkest grave of diabolism; let them marshal their clerical guards in pulpits, printing-offices, and theologic halls, to keep watch, armed with wealth, pride, pomp, and old creeds, backed by the authority of ages, and artillery loaded with the mock-thunder of present and eternal damnation, — yet, in spite of all these, the stone shall be rolled away; the grave shall give up its dead; the dear departed shall yet linger near with messages of that better land, and the armies of the Lord of hosts shall yet come with a power and glory to silence opposing priests and people into grateful awe and admiration.

> "Oh, hear their shouts,
> And list their heavy tramplings! On they come,
> Shaking the firm-set earth, which rocks beneath
> Their mighty footsteps. Hear their song! — it throbs
> With its great burden, and the trembling air
> Is filled with anthems of triumphal music."

At the commencement it was predicted that Spiritualism, in less than a quarter of a century, would inaugurate revolutions without parallel in the history of humanity. It was announced that the inhabitants of the spirit-world would open a new dispensation of the kingdom of heaven, to modify or supersede the old; thousands of mediums be unfolded as the agents to demonstrate immortality anew; old authorities in church, state, and society become weakened, and the individual souls of men and women, infused with inspirations from the eternal world, should arise in their divinity and stand forth born anew in the light and liberty of heaven; that alarming signs should appear in the social, civil and religious worlds, threatening the overthrow of all conservative institutions, customs, and opinions; and that amid unprecedented revolutions, an era of celestial glory should dawn on the waiting and wanting millions. How far these predictions have been fulfilled, let the signs of the times designate. Without any sectarian, social or civil organizations; without any leaderships, creeds, pledges, oaths, compacts, platforms, hireling influences, or authoritative organs; in the face of all the old, organized sects, exhibiting an animosity unparalleled since the advent of Christianity, Spiritualism has gone on with its silent work of triumph.

From the beginning, many predicted that Spiritualism would prove short-lived, and there are many who to-day talk as though this gospel had entirely died out, and, instead of advancing, was fast disappearing from the face of the earth. But the facts show a steady, gradual, irresistible increase, and afford no signs of retrogression. Though physical manifestations have not increased, more profound thought, inquiry, and reading have been elicited. There has been less superficial agitation or curiosity, but more deep sentiment and research. Many laborers and believers have gone through terrible ordeals, exposed to the severest criticisms of opponents, but all these experiences have only tended to develop individual souls and prepare the world for more startling trials and revolutions. The darkest suspicions and calumnies have culminated on the heads of Spiritualists, but they are taught to heed nothing save the dictates of God, and their own better natures unfolded beneath celestial influences, and go on calm and uncompromising in accordance with their highest and holiest ideals of a true life. Amid the revolutions in civil, sectarian, and social life, it is inevitable that some disruptions will ensue, calculated to excite sympathy, misconception, alarm, and denunciation; but all these are essential. They are the travails of the soul in preparation for the new birth of the spiritual dispensation.

All the disruptions, agitations and revolutions of to-day, seen from the spiritual stand-point, are tending towards the individualism essential for every man and woman to recognize. If civil, sectarian and social unions are threatened with dissolution, it is because they are not based on the harmonic principles of God and humanity, and we are called to seek and sustain relations established in accordance with the eternal laws of our being; seek the kingdom, the church, the social relations in harmony with God and angels. Times of unparalleled tribulation are already at hand, and Spiritualists must be prepared, not to mingle in scenes of strife and alarm, but to stand up calm and firm in the wisdom, truth and love now beaming from supernal spheres. While we pledge ourselves to no entramelling creed or clique, yet we are bound by bonds of fraternal sympathy, first to cherish and defend the household of our own faith amid impending calumnies, and breathe nothing but the angelic song of peace on earth and good-will towards the opposing world. The value of Spiritualism is to be tested by its influence on the lives and hearts of genuine believers. Let skeptics and inquirers seek for manifestations, with the desire to become wiser and better, and to lead spiritual lives, and abundant evidences will be afforded. We are to judge of the progress of this cause, not merely by outer signs, by the number of its open professors, mediums and public advocates, but by the principles involved, the hopes, joys and affections moving the inmost souls of the people, the silent workings of its influence on thousands and millions who secretly rejoice at the thought of communion with the spirit world, and by the deep under-current of inspirations and aspirations which speak in prophecy of that glorious era in which earth and heaven shall become one.

As already intimated, the science and philosophy of the age, as well as theology, demanded some new light from other spheres. Take, as an illustration, the science of astronomy. On a clear night, gazing heavenward, who has not questioned the starry world whose dim glory comes streaming down the celestial pathway? Are those orbs inhabited, and the homes of intelligent beings bearing the image of God and eternity? Who can answer? Alluding to the science of astronomy, Gilfillan says: —

It seems to us that in this science we are fast approaching a point where we need the guidance rather of a new Plato than of a new Bacon or Newton. The telescope of Lord Ross has sounded our present astronomy to its real depth. Few more great prizes are reserved, we suspect, in that starry sea. We have attained the knowledge that the stars are old, that they are of one stuff, and that there is no visible end to their numbers. What more of any moment, in this direction, by our present methods, is ever likely to be reached by us? It is like walking through a pine forest of great extent and uniform aspect; a few miles tire and satisfy us. So now, the news of "stars, stars, stars," pouring on us in everlasting succession, all like each other, all distant, all inscrutable and silent, the moral history of all unknown, produces very little effect, and the midnight heavens of modern astronomy become again, as to the eye of childhood, a mighty and terrible pageant or procession, the meaning and the purpose, the whither and the whence of which, we do not understand. And we are tempted to say to astronomers, as they prate of their new firmaments, and planets, and comets, "We knew something like this long ago; can ye not give us some light on the meaning of these distant orbs? or read us off some worthy lessons of moral interest from that ever-widening but never-clearing page?" And to cry out to the stars, "Speak, as well as shine, ye glorious mutes in the halls of heaven! Shed down on some selected and favorite ear the true meaning of your mystic harmonies! Hieroglyphics, traced by the finger of God on the walls of night, when shall the Daniel arrive to interpret you, and to tell us whether ye contain tidings of hope or despair? Star-gazers have looked at you long enough, and mathematicians weighed and measured you; when shall the eye — the Rossian eye of a true seer — lift itself up to your contemplation, and extract the heart of your mystery? If not, men may soon turn away from you in disappointment, and look with as much hope on the bright foam-bells of an autumn ocean as on you, the froth of immensity."

Material science here makes a wonderful concession in

regard to its impotence. And what, we ask, can supply the need of light from these celestial worlds? Placed here, on this little earth-planet, in the midst of an immeasurable universe studded with countless orbs of immense magnitude and supernal glory, can we know nothing more than astronomy reveals? Is there no Great Father Spirit whose intelligence rules in and over all? no beings of like mould, who can commune with each other, and telegraph from world to world the tidings of like hopes, loves and aspirations? If man is immortal, whither have gone the millions of departed generations? Are their homes in those shining planets, fixed stars, and suns that gleam on the brow of night? Answer us, O ye mute oracles of heavens! The blue firmament bends in solemn silence and grandeur; meteors flash; comets wheel their courses; clouds, tempests, storms and thunders anon pass with their awful pageantries; but no response comes, save through the messengers recognized by the celestial science and philosophy of modern Spiritualism! And who shall limit the revelations yet destined to be unfolded? It is well known that several of the most important late astronomical discoveries were first heralded by spirits; and when the laws of spiritual intercourse become more throughly understood, we may anticipate celestial unfoldings far beyond the conceptions of the loftiest imagination. Man shall yet tread the mount of beatitude in communion with angel worlds, and star telegraph to star the glory of God and the stellar universe.

The holy aspirations of all great and good souls, for ages, have been breathing heavenward; and streaming eyes have watched the stars for signs of the long-foretold era, when man should behold descending hosts bringing again tidings of the everlasting gospel, bearing the olive of peace and good-will, and singing the song of glory in the highest. The worn sentinels on the ramparts of Zion, amid their weary vigils, have anon lifted the cry, What of the night? and anon priest and people, rousing from their slumbers, have sent back the response, The morning dawneth! For more than a quarter of a century the Christian press and church were filled with prayers and predictions that God would open the heavens anew, that the Holy Ghost would come down with power, that Jesus Christ would descend in glory and majesty, that angel armies would marshal themselves for fresh battles with earth and hell, that some mighty manifestations would be made from the skies to flood earth with overwhelming showers and flame-like tongues of fire, and thunder with vibrations to quake the dead souls of the apathetic masses, and jar from their centre the very walls and foundations where multitudes congregated. But the very first, faint sound coming in response to these prayers and predictions sent terror into the heart of modern Christendom. While in the very act of praying and predicting that some celestial manifestations of power and majesty might be made, lo, a feeble sound was heard on the altar floor or pulpit case, and priest and people were seized with alarm; they turn pale with affright; their prayers shake them, and they take them back; they pray God to forgive them for asking for more than they were prepared to receive; Catholics cross themselves and Protestants beg to be absolved; through the blue goggles of their dogmas they see "hydras, gorgons and chimeras dire," pale phantoms of alarm, shrieking ghosts, wandering wild in the midnight air, and weird hags, like those mumbling in Macbeth; and they cry out, Delusion, Beelzebub! Back, demons damned, ye legioned throngs clothed in the alluring light of the spheres!

In spite of all opposing obstacles, history affords nothing parallel with the progress of Modern Spiritualism. Only fifteen years, and its journals are numbered by scores, its volumes and public evangels by hundreds, its mediums by thousands, its believers by millions. Conservative to all good, and radically revolutionary to all evil, beneath its angel influences the church, state and society of to-day are rocking like stranded barks amid ocean-waves. Adapting its manifestations to every phase of life, to the lowliest hamlets and loftiest palaces, the home and the wilderness, the field and the workshop, the highway and the fanes of holiest worship; teaching man all his duties and relations, and expanding his being with great thoughts, mounting beyond the mouldering vault of death; breaking down all barriers dividing the children of God; lighting the material universe, as the temple of Deity vocal with anthems of harmony; opening communion between man and the myriads peopling the spiritual empires; flooding our hemisphere with glory-gleams of the Divine and eternal; flashing the fires of celestial influx through the massive walls of materialism standing for ages between earth and heaven, — why need we wonder that multitudes are startled into new-born gladness, shouting, "Glory to God in the highest!" Before the advent of Spiritualism, the masses of the people lay in spiritual night. Zion was mournful and desolate, watching in vain for the millennial morn to break. The multitudes plodded on with no certain light of the future. Children huddled in silent awe over the dead. Death was a blinding, frightful mystery. Homes sounded hollow with the wail and woe of bereaved hearts. Marys watched lonely at the sepulchre, but no resurrection morn dawned on their tear-dimmed eyes. Young men and maidens, aged and middle-aged, mourners all, hung desolate over grave-yards and blasted hearth-stones, calling for the dear departed; and the dying lifted their wan hands and faces towards that drear unknown from whose bourn no traveller had been supposed to return.

Amid the silence which for ages had hung like a pall almost unbroken over the grave, sounds were heard; gentle sounds like "footfalls on the boundary of another world." They came again and again. From home to home they vibrated, till oceans and continents were crossed, till every ear was startled, till the whole globe trembled as beneath shocks from off some celestial battery touched by the fingers of Omnipotence, flashing the electric flames and rolling the thunders of Sinai over the angel-trod mountain-tops of the century. Messages came startling the world with overwhelming evidences of immortality. The weary, working masses lifted up their eyes with joy and wonder, and new hopes gleamed on their toiling way. The young crouched in terror no more, but talked of brothers and sisters only gone on before; and the orphan saw a dead mother transformed into a guardian angel, watching over the lone one by night and day, and singing songs of the everlasting home. Young men and maidens tripped on their gladsome way, with new hopes and loves. The lost son of the lone widow came back, and wiped away her tears with hands reached out from the spirit-land where the prodigal shall wander no more. Fathers and mothers, and the long train of mourners who wept and wailed over the dead, lifted their faces heavenward, and, lo! the veil was parted by beloved ones, and the home of "many mansions" hymned to earth the song of angel-loves forever sheltered beneath that Father's dome where no clouds lower or storms beat on the bared soul. Old men and women, tottering over the grave in despair, started up on their staves, bent low their eager ears, and, lo! the dear departed of other years came back to guide their trembling steps up the mount of God, where age blooms in eternal youth, and the sainted dead are gathered to their fathers.

A gospel like this cannot be resisted! We welcome it as the richest legacy of life. When its evidences take hold of our minds and its inspirations warm our souls, we are prepared for whatever scorn, derision, wrath, persecution and suffering the world may pour on us. Throngs may follow us with curses, calling us dupes or knaves; poverty and proscription may haunt the pioneer who goes forth breasting the public storm; yet we can afford to go on enduring, laboring, waiting, assured of angel smiles, and glories fast unfolding for humanity. The time is coming when opposing priest and people shall file in with the gathering ranks of progress. Another Pentecost shall see thousands born in a day. This generation shall yet realize the light foretold by ancient seers and sages. "Blow ye the trumpet in Zion; sound the alarm!" "They shall come from the east and the west, the north and south!" Many shall come in the midst of private griefs and disasters, sorrows and deaths, or in the midst of revolutions, rocking thrones and empires, or dread calamities sweeping continents with consternation and alarm; yet the time hastens when God's celestial hosts shall gather in majesty to awake the slumbering millions to a solemn consciousness of the reality of things spiritual and eternal.

CHAPTER II.

THE VARIOUS PHASES OF SPIRITUAL MANIFESTATIONS — HINTS AS TO DIVERS GIFTS OF MEDIUMSHIP — A MULTITUDE OF POINTED FACTS.*

THE backbone of the whole theory of spiritual existence in every school is, that there is immanent with man a spiritual essence, which, while the body exists, forms a part thereof, and when it decays, still remains and continues to exist, under such change of conditions as the death of the body has induced. Under this theory it is fair to infer, that the spirit which has been set free from the body of one person by death, and continues its existence in the distinctive spiritual state, is but an emanation from the structure of the body which it once inhabited, and possesses the same general character, as an entity, with that which resides in the body of another person now remaining on the earth. That the spirits in their disembodied condition can communicate with those in the flesh, is, therefore, as easy to conceive as that they can do so with their ethereal companions, since, in both states or spheres, they partake of the same generic constitution; and whatever differences there are between them, are

* E. W. Capron's Modern Spiritualism; Owen's Footfalls on the Boundary of Another World; Spiritual Telegraph Papers; Spiritual Clarion; London Spiritual Magazine; Banner of Light; Gridley's Astounding Facts; Herald of Progress; Judge Edmond's Spiritualism, 2 vols.; Brittan and Hanson's Discussion; Seeress of Provost; Mrs. Crowe's Night Side of Nature, etc.; Newton's Ministry of Angels; Caganet's Celestial Telegraph; Healing of the Nations; Woodman's Review of Dwight; Hare's Spirit Manifestations; Fowler's New Testament and Modern Miracles; Lewis's Spiritual Reasoner; Stilling's Pneumatology; Ballou's Spirit Manifestations; Davis's Philosophy of Spiritual Intercourse, Present Age and Inner Life, etc.; T. W. Higginson's Results of Spiritualism; Tuttle's Life in the Spheres; Whiting and Jones's Discussion; Snow's Spiritual Intercourse; Tiffany's Spiritualism Explained; Miller and Grimes's Discussion; Redman's Mystic Hours; Home's Incidents of My Life. Reference is made to these, among numerous other works, not because the authors claim any uniform endorsement. They are named as aids to investigation and not authorities. Spiritualism canonizes no books as wholly sacred, final, or infallible.

due, not to the different elements of their nature, but to the different states and degrees in which their common nature is developed. — *Beckwith.*

While the narration of spiritual phenomena may excite curiosity, they must be witnessed or experienced in order to satisfy certain minds; yet the testimony of reliable witnesses, now numbering millions, can no more be ignored than we can ignore testimony on other subjects. Another has said: "It is more reasonable to admit unaccountable facts, than to deny good evidences." Many of the sciences are accepted, by the majority of minds, more on the investigation of others than on their own researches. All Christendom to-day bases its faith on miracles, revelations and inspirations coming ages ago. Christians have undoubted faith in the resurrection of Christ, yet they never claim to have seen him. He arose eighteen hundred years ago, and was seen only by about five hundred persons then living; not a thousandth of the number of witnesses who to-day testify as to the spiritual manifestations. We ask for a careful comparison between the ancient and the modern records. If the modern fail, the ancient must share a fate still worse. The candid reader will judge of this, in perusing subsequent chapters of this volume, and will find all the popular theories, subterfuges, evasions, queries and objections anticipated as far as our limits will permit.

This chapter deals mainly with facts. Facts are what the people need, and they can then form their own opinions and theories. Are the phenomena called spiritual adequate to substantiate the spiritual theory? Let the skeptic reject nine-tenths of what passes for spirit-manifestations, yet if one-tenth remain unanswerable on any other hypothesis, it is sufficient. Suppose we are unable to explain all the laws, forces and conditions involved? We are unable to explain some of the simplest phenomena of life and nature. Suppose some of the manifestations are seemingly insignificant and trifling? Little things sometimes have a sublime significance. The falling of the apple on Newton's head; the chips and seaweed seen by Columbus, and the kite of Dr. Franklin, were trifles, yet they suggested mighty truths. The electric telegraph seems a little machine, and its clicking sounds are nothing in themselves, yet they have a significance which anon rocks the continent with thrilling intelligence. Just so with those spiritual manifestations which thrill millions of souls with news from friends peopling that realm whither the generations of ages have gone. If religionists regard these phenomena insignificant and undignified, let them be compared with those recorded in the Bible. (See Chapter III., the last twenty propositions, and the ninety-five questions in Chapter V.)

To enumerate and classify the various manifestations, phases of mediumship, and methods adopted by spirits in communicating with mortals, would be as difficult and impossible as to attempt the same thing with reference to the various phenomena, phases of character, and methods of communication found on earth; for the spirit-world is only a higher type of our world, and spirits are human beings; only, in proportion to their progress passed on to a higher sphere and unfolded on a higher plane in communion with worlds and intelligences far beyond our material vision. It were unwise, therefore, for us, at the present stage of development, to insist on any rigid theories or systems, or to map out the spheres of eternal being; though we may obtain all the light indispensable for our guidance, and stop not in our investigations either here or hereafter. (See Chapter VI.) Persons are continually inquiring who are mediums. Our philosophy teaches that, as all human beings are spirits, created in the image of the great Father Spirit, all have within themselves the elements of some kind of spiritual mediumship waiting to be quickened and unfolded. Those who are mediums for the production of physical manifestations, like the sounds, the moving of ponderable bodies, etc., are so by virtue of the peculiar organizations they inherit; and when they are in the right condition of body and mind, and are surrounded by harmonic influences, the phenomena will be induced. The spirits use certain elements found in the mediums, in connection with other imponderable elements, and can act only while all the conditions are right. The same law holds true with reference to all mediumship. Those who would develop their gifts must study and heed all the laws of life and health,—physiological, moral, social, fraternal, and religious; and must seek to make their hearts and lives accord with the laws of spirit-life, in order that they may attract spiritual beings in sympathy and coöperation. All the higher and more practical phases of mediumship depend in a measure on our own culture. 1 Cor. xii.

"Spiritual gifts" are not miraculous, but belong to our common nature, and only wait for us to unfold them in communion with that spiritual world whose atmosphere is around us, on whose influences we are constantly dependent, and whose inhabitants are ever seeking to exercise over us a celestial guardianship. We do not claim the right to specify what gifts individuals should seek to unfold; they must judge for themselves, test themselves. All phases have their uses, but ultimately all will become merged into the natural, the normal, the harmonic. Thus far in the history of Spiritualism we have an indescribable variety. At first "rapping mediums" were most numerous, and afforded the most satisfactory evidences. Good mediums of this class are exceedingly rare, and their gifts usually change into phases deemed further in advance. There are mediums for writing, some by impression, and some are mechanically influenced; mediums who are wholly entranced, and some who are partly or in whole conscious; mediums who see spirits, and describe them to be identified by their friends; mediums who are influenced to personify departed friends, and go through scenes of past experience; mediums who describe disease, clairvoyantly or sympathetically, prescribe remedies, or directly impart healing influences; mediums who are impelled to execute music, paint, sing, speak, and manifest other gifts not apparent in the normal state; mediums who prophesy, speak and write in tongues, give warnings, presentiments, describe past life, incidents, accidents, events, traits of character, offer counsels and cautions, etc. These and manifold other phases of mediumship have all been thoroughly tested, and have rendered unmistakable evidence of the manifestation of powers and intelligences belonging to ultra-mundane spheres of existence. The more common and practical phases of mediumship, however, are those in which individuals seem to be in a state perfectly natural, in full possession of all their external senses, yet with their spiritual senses quickened in such a manner as to enable them to realize not only their own spiritual existence, but the existence of the spirit-world engirting them with celestial influences, and spirit-friends as the angels of God evermore watching, guarding, guiding, warning, gladdening, impressing, encouraging, inspiring, and anon giving them glimpses and glory-gleams of the land of beatitude and the endless pathway of progress trod by the myriads passed on triumphant over death. Towards this lofty plane of development all mediums and all seeking souls are tending, and on this plane there are now numerous apostles going forth, speaking as they are moved by their own quickened intuitions, and by the powers of the eternal world.

In order that those who are not familiar with spiritualism may have a more distinct idea of the data on which we stand, a brief summary of a few facts may here be submitted. Our reference to a few Bible phenomena will be found on page 93, etc., and the sacred histories of all nations record some analogous manifestations. In Tedworth, England, 1661, '62, the Rev. Mr. Glanville testified that in the house of John Mompesson, loud noises were heard all around the house and on top; noises hurtled in the air; furniture was moved, lifted and thrown around, yet so softly nothing was injured; intelligent responses were drummed out; witnesses, to their dying hour, declared the phenomena to be more than earthly. In the Wesley family at Epworth, 1716, '17, loud knockings, the sound of footsteps, rustling of dresses, responses during prayer time, etc., were repeatedly heard. Dr. Adam Clarke, and many other good and learned men, credited these occurrences as facts against materialism. The seeress of Provost, in Germany, 1828, was a medium for sounds, and other indications of spiritual gifts. In South East, N. Y., 1790, rappings were heard, and intelligence was manifest. In Paris, France, 1859, Hon. Robert Dale Owen testifies to having seen a Mrs. Kyd lifted four or five feet from the floor, in her chair, no person being near. Mr. Owen likewise asserts that he saw in the same city, 1858, in the house of a French nobleman, a heavy table moved and raised without any human contact. Dr. Bell, of the Massachusetts Insane Hospital, testifies to similar phenomena in his own house. Judge McDonald and lady, Glens Falls, N. Y., 1855, had similar manifestations; L. Parker and family, Manchester, Ct., 1859; Mr. and Mrs. Shepherd, Albany, N. Y., 1855; John Reynolds, Puttneyville, N. Y., 1860; the writer of this volume, Providence, R. I., 1851, and hundreds of others, testify to similar occurrences in their own households. Charles Partridge, Drs. R. T. Hallock, Gray, and other responsible men of New York, declare to the playing of musical instruments, and the raising of persons and ponderable bodies, under circumstances precluding the possibility of human agency. Among the early phenomena reported in Capron's History of Spiritualism are the following:—

A murder was exposed by the invisibles through the Fox girls in Hydesville, 1848; audible voices heard, ponderable bodies moved, persons touched, mechanical writings produced, billets of wood thrown about, etc., alarming sounds and rumblings heard on the roof and around the house; the spirits in Rochester, N. Y., telegraph in regard to a death sixty miles distant; hundreds flock to the house of the Foxes to witness the manifestations; remarkable predictions are given; public committees in Rochester are baffled; the spirits in Auburn, N. Y., make music and produce other physical phenomena; they give warning against a fire; the house of Rev. Dr. Phelps, Stratford, Ct., is besieged by invisibles, and numerous visitors of the most celebrated and sagacious character are unable to account for the occurrences without admitting spiritual agents; Gordon, the medium, is lifted up bodily; Judge Edmonds becomes developed as a spirit-seer, and receives positive demonstrations of spirit-presence. The Spiritual Telegraph paper reported the discovery of medicinal springs by spirits; the cure of a cancer; the production of spirit lights; the rescue of an orphan girl by her angel mother, and various other indications of celestial power and intelligence. The Clarion paper published a desperate case of cholera suddenly cured through Dr. A. G. Fellows; a person supposed to be dying, restored; a prodigal saved by the interposition of a spirit friend; a mechanical instrument vibrated without contact; a case of death forewarned; a dwelling illuminated, and converse held with celestial visitors; life saved by spirit forewarning; violent disease stayed, and the patient restored; a spirit-brother identified; death predicted thirty years in advance; a child saved by spirit-interposition; the likeness of a spirit-boy painted; a piano played by no visible hands; angel music heard in Indiana; spirit seen and described; spirits telegraph to California; the life of a lady saved by spirits; a clergyman silenced in his pulpit by invisibles; a child saved from cruel treatment; insanity cured; the lame made to walk; poison neutralized; melodeon played on without human contact; palsy cured; a railroad conductor saved; a boy and table lifted; a lost boy found; portraits of departed friends painted; a man lifted by spirits; a bed, with an invalid, raised; a public cure wrought, and numerous tests descriptive of life, character, incidents, accidents, diseases, and spirit-friends, given before public audiences.

S. B. Brittan and others testify to having seen a piano in Charlestown, Mass., weighing over one thousand pounds, lifted without contact; Stephen Albro, and scores of others, testify to similar phenomena in Buffalo, also to the production of voluntary music in perfect harmony, through a medium wholly unacquainted with the musical art. Prof. M—— testifies to having received through a young woman-medium more valuable scientific and philosophical information than through all the books of the past. Col. Ellsworth, Gen. Baker, and other eminent heroes falling in the war against the rebellion, had distinct spiritual premonitions of their death. Mrs. D. S., Melrose, Mass., had positive warning of an accident to befall her husband, and he was killed accordingly. J. F. Coles, three months before, predicted the death of the Emperor Nicholas, and the prediction was literally fulfilled to a day. The Crimean war, the war in India, and the American war against the Southern rebellion, were distinctly predicted by various mediums. A New York medium described the loss of the Arctic several days before any news was heard. Judge Edmonds had premonitions of the accidents befalling the steamers Henry Clay and Reindeer. The family of Thomas Ely, Deansville, N. Y., for weeks had their house visited by various startling sounds and other physical phenomena, and an audible voice spoke for hours in open daylight in the parlor. Numerous persons have written letters to spirit-friends, sealed them securely, and received remaıkable answers without the letters having been opened. Numerous persons afflicted with disease, abandoned as hopeless, have been cured by invisible agents. One healing medium can now exhibit a dray-load of crutches once used by persons whom he cured by the "laying on of hands." Writings have been produced by spirits, while pencil and paper were locked up in drawers, or placed under tables beyond the reach of human hands, and fac-similes of their hand-writing have been produced. John C. Calhoun is reported as having written thus, through the Fox girls. Hon. J. F. Simmons, Providence, R. I., testifies that writing was done in the use of a lead pencil placed in a scissors-bow, in open light. Before hundreds of public audiences appointing skeptical committees, through the agency of a well-known lady medium, the spirits have produced sounds audible to the whole house, and given tests of intelligence impossible of solution without the spiritual theory.

Now, in alluding to these few illustrations, let it be understood that we do not include any of the thousands of questionable phenomena occurring under circumstances of a suspicious character; we cite only those which came under circumstances baffling the most rigid skepticism and abiding the severest tests. Nor have we cited the hundredth part of that which has been and is still occurring. The largest volume ever issued could embrace only a small proportion of the phenomena current during the last fifteen years. If a book filling the "world" would have been required to "contain" everything relating to Messiah, modern Spiritualism would require a volume as vast as the spheres. With a few more phenomenal selections this chapter may close: —

A father relates that he was suddenly aroused, as seemed to him, from a sound sleep, and saw in his room what appeared like a small bright cloud. He looked again and the cloud assumed a human form, and his first wife, long since deceased, stood before him. He saw her as plainly as he saw us while relating the story. He spoke to her, and said, "Have you come for me?" To which she promptly and distinctly answered, "No, not for you, but for Charley." She said no more, but withdrew as she came, gradually vanishing from his sight. Charley was the name of the youngest son, at home with his mother five hundred miles away. At the time of the vision, the father had no knowledge of his child's sickness, but the telegraph soon told that his little Charley had been taken suddenly ill and removed from the world, about the very time when the spirit of his wife appeared and told him that she had come to take him away.

Mrs. Ely, of Bristol, Indiana, after a year's illness, left the form. About two hours before her death there came a number of voices singing in at the front door. No persons were visible to the natural eye. The voices seemed to come in over the top of the open front door, and passed along through the parlor into the room of the dying woman, over her head, and continued in the most beautiful strains for several minutes. A number of persons were in to witness the dying scene, and the music was heard by all. After the singing had continued a short time, the dying woman aroused and said, "My friends, you need not be alarmed; these are my children singing."

Uriah Roundy, of Spafford, New York, relates a fact connected with the death of his grandmother. She was nearly ninety years old, and had been blind twelve years. Just before her exit she lay a long time in a state of torpor or trance. At last she suddenly raised her head, and, addressing a friend present, said, "You tell Laurens (her son) I can't wait any longer; there comes a band of angels, with my mother at the head, and I must go!" She fell back, and her spirit instantly departed in peace.

W. Smith, a citizen of Red Creek, New York, states that his eldest daughter was engaged to a professor of music, and the day and hour of the marriage was fixed. A few days before the appointed nuptial-time, the professor was killed by an accident on the railroad. The wedding-day arrived, but mourning was in the place of feasting. The parlor, with the piano at which the intended had often sat discoursing the richest melody, was deserted, and the bereaved bride was wrapped in silent grief. Just as the clock struck announcing the hour the wedding was to have taken place, the young lady was startled by the sound of a familiar tune on the piano in the parlor, and the playing was in such imitation of her intended, she arose and ran towards the room with mingled emotions of awe and wonder. But no one was found in the parlor or near it. The whole family heard the music, and testify to the fact that it must have been by the invisible bridegroom, who came to fulfil his promised engagement.

A gang of fast, gambling young men, in Springfield, Massachusetts, one night were startled in the midst of their games by loud raps in several parts of the room. The spirits entranced one of their number, and poured out such burning appeals, the whole company trembled and wept, and then broke up, with no more gambling, at least for that night.

A little girl seven years old, in West Newton, Mass., one morning suddenly stopped playing, and said, "I am going to die; I am going to heaven; I shall be an angel." On that very evening she was seized with the croup, and made her exit, with these last words: "Do you see the angels over there?"

M. H. Barton, Jerusalem, New York, while sitting in Hester-street Church, New York, Quaker meeting, in 1823, was moved by the spirit to rise and pronounce the Quakers a backsliding and persecuting people, and to predict their ultimate dismemberment. For more than two hundred years the Quakers had been peaceful and united. They took Barton to be crazy, and forced him out of their house. Since that time the Friends have become divided into six or eight parties.

Mrs. J. R. Pierce, of Oswego, New York, one day, while she and her sister, a medium, were sewing, near her work-stand, on questioning the spirits the stand was suddenly moved entirely away from her to the opposite side of the room, and then by request was brought back, no person touching it or near it.

Mr. McFarland, of Brooklyn, New York, on relating in a public conference meeting how all the things in his parlor were one night mysteriously turned upside down, two lady mediums were simultaneously moved to go up to him afterwards and say that the meaning of the manifestation was, that his house was about to be broken up. Within three months Mrs. McFarland cast off the form, and Mr. McFarland broke up housekeeping.

Mrs. Benning, of Buffalo, New York, alleged that a Mr. Booth and herself were conversing on Spiritualism, one evening, when at last they agreed between themselves that whichever died first should, if possible, come back and give the other some manifestation of supermundane existence. Mr. Booth left Buffalo for Toronto, C.W. Three evenings after he left, Mrs. Benning was seated at her writing-desk, when she was suddenly influenced to write, "I have come in fulfilment of my promise. I left the form in Toronto, two hours ago." Mrs. Benning was startled at the intelligence; she ran and communicated it to her daughters. The next morning brought news by telegraph that Booth had died at the time specified.

Marcenus Wright and lady, of Victor, New York, relate that they were on business in Springfield, Illinois, and called at the New England House for rooms. They were shown into large apartments which seemed to have been seldom occupied. After a few days they began to hear strange sounds on the floor. Questions were asked, but no definite answers could be obtained. The noises, however, continued and constantly increased, until Mr. and Mrs. Wright felt not a little annoyed, if not alarmed. During the night, at intervals, the rappings became frightful, jarring the whole room, and they were impelled to change quarters. They asked one of the Irish girls of the house why the room was not usually occupied, and she intimated that the devil seemed to have taken possession of it. On making further inquiry, Mr. Wright learned that a young man had died from injuries received on being violently thrown out of the haunted apartment.

Dr. J. W. Russell, of Winchester, N. H., affirms that an invalid brother of his promised that if he died first, and it was possible for him to return in spirit, he would indicate his presence by some unmistakable tests of identity. The brother died. Dr. Russell soon after met a medium who was influenced to delineate a scene and conversation concerning which none had any knowledge save himself and brother. He afterwards visited Mrs. Hayden, in New York, and received the most satisfactory evidences, not only from his brother, but his father. The spirits gave their names through Mrs. Hayden, though Dr. Russell was an entire stranger, and not the least thing had been communicated. Loud rappings were heard, and a large table was lifted entirely free from the carpet, and made to vibrate to and fro in a manner to demonstrate the utter impossibility of any human contact or the agency of any material machinery.

The late Hugh Miller thus alludes to an early experience: — Day had not wholly disappeared, but it was fast posting on to night, and a gray haze spread a neutral tint of dimness over every more distant object, but left the nearer ones comparatively distinct, when I saw the door open, within less than a yard of my breast, as plainly as ever I saw anything, a dissevered hand and arm stretched toward me. Hand and arm were apparently those of a female; they bore a livid and sodden appearance; and directly fronting me, where the body ought to have been, there was only blank, transparent space, through which I could see the dim forms of the objects beyond. I was fearfully startled, and ran shrieking to my mother, telling what I had seen. I communicate the story (he adds) as it lies fixed in my memory, without attempting to explain. Its coincidence, in this case, with the probable time of my father's death, seems at least curious.

In the house of the writer, in open light, in the presence of nine witnesses, all of whom were sane, all away from the table, with nothing touching it save two fingers of the little girl-medium, the table, with a weight of about one hundred and fifty pounds thereon, moved in every direction requested, loud raps being heard at intervals. An aged clerical friend from Boston, overwhelmingly convinced of the presence of super-mundane beings, solemnly exclaimed, "My God! is it possible we are in the presence of immortal spirits!"

The writer in the Telegraph says:—While at the house of a friend in Troy, New York, when retiring late one night, a few moments after, a spirit-form, in the garb of a genteel mariner, came near the bedside, and giving a graceful salutation, in a moment disappeared. After several inquiries the next day, the spirit was identified as a friend of Mrs. Coan, the medium, who was on a visit with us at Troy.

Another night I became disturbed by various singular sounds around my head. They seemed like efforts to tune stringed instruments of music. Two or three times something like a tuning-fork appeared to shoot through the brain, leaving a sound behind more novel than agreeable. Doubting my senses, I arose in bed and sat upright. But the sounds grew more distinct and harmonious, and snatches of beautiful tunes smote my ear. It was along toward morning, the night was dark, stormy, and tempestuous. The wind smote with clattering strokes on the tiles of house-tops; window-blinds and shutters swung with discord, and the rain pattered down dismal drops, anon changing to torrents, threatening the desolation of a deluge. I sprang to the floor, to be reassured of my senses, and looked out up to the darkened heavens. At that moment I distinctly heard the closing bar of a magnificent tune, which seemed to be played by an innumerable band, sweeping through the aerial realms at the distance of about one mile, and up at an angle of about forty-five degrees. I threw up the window, and listened to hear if any voices or footsteps were audible. But all was silent, save the elements of a dark and stormy night. Nobody in Troy could aid me in finding material cause to account for that midnight melody, notwithstanding the most persevering inquiries.

Falling into a drowse on a lounge one afternoon, while residing in New York, Mrs. —— was reading an article on Keats and Shelley, and she made some remark, unheard by me, in regard to Shelley's being present. Soon after, I awoke with a thrilling consciousness of the poet's presence, and with him I seemed to have just gone to his distant tomb, and wandered through the oriental scenes among which he revelled on the eve of his mournful departure from a world which knew little of his bright and burning soul before it took its celestial flight.

At the close of one of the writer's public lectures and test-meetings in Boston, on Tuesday evening, November 1, 1859, as a subject for examination the audience selected Benjamin Danforth. After passing through the usual preliminaries, we began to refer back to the past life of the subject. We spoke of a peculiar difficulty with the right arm and shoulder, and described certain movements indicating the cause of the injury. We were shown a scene in the boyhood of Mr. Danforth, and described, somewhat in detail, an old gentleman who, in the said scene, was earnestly talking and gesticulating with a cane; and we likewise represented the same old gentleman as the present guardian spirit of Mr. Danforth. In addition to these, we closed with minute delineations of the character and tendencies of our subject, all of which were admitted correct by well informed acquaintances in the audience. Mr. Danforth confirmed what we said about the arm, and made due explanations. He admitted that the boyhood scene was perfect to the life; said our description of the old gentleman was accurate, and that he had frequently communicated to him through other mediums. These public tests are illustrations of hundreds given by the writer in all the Eastern, Middle, Western, and Northern States, including numerous small towns and villages, as well as the cities of Bangor, Boston, Providence, New Haven, New York, Philadelphia, Baltimore, Syracuse, Auburn, Rochester, Buffalo, Cleveland, Detroit, Columbus, Louisville, etc.

A beautiful incident, demonstrative of the re-visits of departed spirits, took place at the meeting of Rev. T. L. Harris, New York. After Mr. Harris's prayer, he stated to his congregation that although, while engaged in his public ministrations, it was seldom granted him to perceive the presence of individual spirits, he had just then enjoyed that privilege. Clothed in paradisiacal garments there had appeared a radiant form which he distinctly recognized as that of a little girl whose funeral he had attended at the far South a little over a year ago. Mr. Harris added that the child had not before appeared to him since her entrance into the spirit world, and that in no other way could he account for her presentation *now* than by the supposition that some of her earthly friends, with whose sphere she was *en rapport*, must then be in the audience. After the conclusion of the services, *the father* of the spirit child came forward and spoke to Mr. Harris, which was the first external intimation he had that the latter was present, or indeed that he was in the city. How welcome to that fond parent must have been the intelligence, coming in this unmistakable manner, that his loved one, though unseen by external eye, was still following and watching him in his journeys and dangers, and clinging to him with a filial tenderness which an angel child alone can know.

Strange sounds, like rappings, began to be heard in the house of Thomas A. Ely, Deansville, New York, in Aug., 1855, and various manifestations continued for some time. Mrs. Crandall first heard the sounds towards midnight. They grew louder and louder. The family, all sleeping up stairs, were aroused. Lights were struck, and diligent search made, but the mystery was unsolved. They retired again and put out the lights, but the noises came again so loud the whole family grew alarmed. Lights were struck again, and all the beds moved down stairs for the night, but the sounds came. On asking questions, the spirit of Mr. Crandall and Mr. Ely's first wife announced themselves, and the household became less alarmed. Night after night the manifestations increased for months, and numerous messages, of a highly comforting and religious nature, were given through the alphabet. Mr. Ely at first believed the whole thing a work of the devil. But tests and communications came at last allaying all fears and convincing the whole family. For more than a year no person out of the house had any knowledge of what was going on. Sounds like torpedoes; like pounding with boots, hammers, and mallets, jarring the whole house; like hurried footsteps, rustling of dresses, etc., were distinctly heard by every person in the family. For several nights the family kept lights burning, slept in rooms adjoining each other, left the doors all open into each other's rooms, and the sounds and tramplings were heard, and their bedsteads were lifted, rolled and tumbled, as though the entire house was haunted with hosts of Samson-like invisibles. Iron candlesticks were lifted up in sight of all; and in open daylight heavy articles, like flatirons, wedges, etc., were carried or thrown about like shuttlecocks, yet no person or thing ever injured in the least. But the most marvellous of all, the family heard audible voices in the air, in open daylight, distinct to all. Hour after hour these voices were heard, sometimes when every member of the family was present, and sometimes otherwise. The voice changed its location, and was heard under circumstances precluding the possibility of its coming from any other than a spiritual source. Hundreds of visitors heard it and went away overwhelmed with awe and conviction. Mrs. Crandall sat and listened hour after hour, taking down messages, and she wrote one from her husband requiring an uninterrupted sitting of five hours. Mr. Ely and family knew these things were genuine productions of the invisible world, and all the teachings accompanying the phenomena were of the most sound, moral, religious, and Christian character.

Dr. J. R. Newton, of Newport, Rhode Island, affords numerous illustrations of the remarkable healing powers unfolded beneath celestial influence. J. H. Hibbard, of New York, confined three years with spinal disease, able to walk but little even on crutches, was relieved in about five minutes, and, after three operations by "the laying on of hands," testifies that he was entirely cured. John Corkery, of Philadelphia, partly blind and deaf for twenty years, was relieved after a few manipulations. C. F. Muench, of Harrisburg, Pa., nearly helpless for years with rheumatism and internal bleeding, was cured from his first interview with Dr. Newton. D. G. Taylor, of New York, suffering from cough and other symptoms of consumption for fifteen years, was made entirely free from all signs of disease after an operation of about ten minutes. Eliza A. Tolles, of Vincennes, Ind., suffering and nearly helpless for more than twenty years from spinal disease and ailings peculiar to woman, testifies to an entire cure after a brief interview. These cases are illustrations of thousands of others coming under the treatment of healing mediums, though it is not claimed that conditions will warrant cures in every instance of disease.

While the writer was in Montague, Mass., in May, 1860, he was visited by a father and mother coming from Northfield for the purpose of having an examination of their little daughter, who was about two years old. They took particular pains to avoid communicating the least thing in regard to the child, and declared if the examination proved true it would afford them adequate evidence in demonstration of the presence of superior intelligences. The mother took the child in her arms, and sat off four or five feet distant from where we sat. We closed our eyes, and in about five minutes the spirits discovered to us a piece of metallic substance in the child's stomach. The parents were so startled, they immediately revealed to us the fact that the little girl had swallowed one of the small, new, one-cent coins. On our sitting down to the examination we had no clue to the fact; we were perfectly blank; the child gave no external indication of anything, and the parents had been profoundly silent.

Miss Ada Hoyt, the test-rapping and writing medium, held a public investigation in Stuyvesant Institute, New York, February, 1856. The skeptics of the audience appointed a committee of seven skeptics to take the platform, and proceed in the investigation. As soon as the committee were seated with the exception of two members, the sounds began loud and distinct to the whole house. Some of the committee, however, were at first suspicious of the others, and were quite sure the rappings were made by them. It was settled at last that the sounds were not made by anybody in collusion with the medium, and the investigation proceeded. Twenty-five or thirty test-questions were propounded, beyond the possibility of the medium to answer, and yet they were answered in such a manner that every one of the committee arose at the close and declared themselves unable to solve the phenomena. At a subsequent meeting in the same place, Dr. Achilli was chairman of the committee, and put his questions in the Italian language, with which Miss Hoyt was wholly unacquainted. His inquiries were in relation to the birth, disease, death, etc., of his mother, who died in Italy, and concerning whom, Dr. Achilli stated, no one in this country could have had any knowledge besides himself. So accurate and startling were the answers to his questions, at the close he emphatically declared to the audience that *he knew his mother's spirit must have communicated!*

The New York Philosophical Society of the Mechanics Institute employed Miss Hoyt to give sittings for a scientific investigation. Mr. Rosevelt, the president, was on the platform, which had been prepared for the occasion, and Alderman Purdy proposed the first questions. The initials of his spirit friend's name were given, disease, and age. Mr. John Reid next took the stand. The name of his spirit friend was given, age, disease, and the number and sex of children left behind. A strict investigation was then instituted as to how the raps were made, and it was decided that the medium could not produce them. Dr. Vandewine asked a series of questions in the German language, of which Miss Hoyt had no knowledge, never having studied or spoken any language except the English.

In Norwich, N. Y., the writer was invited to a confidential interview with a music-teacher and a young lady pupil of hers, who had come under some mysterious invisible intelligence. The young lady pupil began to take lessons on the piano, and it was perfectly certain she had not been in practice long enough to acquire even the first rudiments of the art. About two weeks previous to our interview, one day her teacher sat down to the piano and commenced practising on a long and a very difficult operatic composition of which she nor her pupil had any knowledge. On a sudden, the hand of her pupil was controlled by an invisible power; she was made to seize a baton, and commenced beating out the time and tune of the composition the lady was practising. Whenever the teacher made the slightest deviation from the notes, the hand of her pupil was suddenly controlled, and the baton made to point to the defective note, meanwhile the pupil having no agency in the movement, and often looking in a direction opposite the piano and music. Though they were wholly unacquainted with the spiritual phenomena, they made inquiry for the spirit, and the pupil's hand was controlled to write out that Mozart was interested in the matter, and that he could control the young lady every day for so long a time, until the teacher should become perfected in the execution of the piece in question.

A little girl ten years old was developed as a medium in the family of Mr. and Mrs. R. H. Willard, Louisville Landing, New York. Numerous witnesses testified to the fact that large tables were rapidly lifted and moved across the room, while nothing was in contact except the fingers of the medium. So powerful was the influence sometimes attending her, she seemed almost transfigured, and wore the appearance of a spirit. Her health failing, she was confined to the bed for some time. The bed was placed in the centre of the sitting-room. At intervals it was lifted entirely from the floor, with none near except the little girl, who lay on top almost helpless. An old uncle, belonging to the family, had repeatedly witnessed the tables move, but persisted, in his ignorance, in attributing the phenomena to electricity. One day while the bedstead was being lifted up and let down with the most startling sounds, the old man was called in to pronounce his opinion. He stood gazing for a moment with awe and wonder, and then exclaimed, "That's not electricity."

Col. R. B. Harwood, of Whately, Mass., states that Mrs. R. Craft was thrown into a state of entrancement, and seemed borne away in spirit among the distant islands of the Pacific Ocean. The scene of a terrible storm and shipwreck was presented to her vision, and while convulsed with agony in intense sympathy with the endangered mariners, she gave a graphic description of all the details. She gave the name of the vessel, Clinton, No. 3, Captain Andrew Jackson Wing; told what port it left, and its place of destination; said the vessel had struck a sand-bar, not laid down on any marine chart, near one of the small Sandwich Islands, and at last described the crew as all landing safe from the disaster. Col. Harwood had sufficient confidence in the communication to relate the details to some of his neighbors in order that the matter might be tested. He was willing to risk his faith and reputation. After a sufficient length of time had elapsed, he wrote to Howland Company, extensive shippers in New York, and received information confirming all the particulars as described by Mrs. Craft.

Mr. C. K. Bennett, conductor on the Southern Michigan and Northern Indiana Railroad, a resident of Toledo, Ohio, relates that while he was standing on the platform of one of his cars, going west at moderate speed, he was suddenly seized on the shoulder by some invisible power, and forced from his position on the platform. Immediately after, an express train came dashing along and ran into Mr. Bennett's train, smashing the platform from which he had just been ejected, and doing a work of destruction which would have inevitably cost him his life had he not been rescued as he was. The spirit thus interposing in his behalf claimed to be the father of Mr. Bennett.

Mr. A. F. Newman, of Circleville, Ohio, had a son who died when about four years old. G. C. Walcutt, the painting medium, of Columbus, was called on for a portrait of the boy. As soon as the conditions were favorable, the spirits, through Mr. Walcutt, in one hour produced a superior oil-painting, with a portrait of the boy so strikingly accurate, the father and friends, on first seeing it, stood speechless with wonder and joy.

In September, 1847, with Rev. E. A. Holbrook and A. M. Convis, a medium, the writer visited Auburn State Prison. After passing through the various departments, Mrs. Lewis, the matron, invited us to spend a season in her private parlors. Mr. Convis was requested to allow his guardian spirit to manifest himself. The influence immediately came on; and, after the spirit had made a few introductory remarks, he began to recognize some of the spirit friends of Mrs. Lewis. He described one of them as a young man. Then drawing back, he brought his hand with a sudden blow against the right side of his forehead, fell back, and represented the act of dying. Mrs. Lewis at once identified her son, Charles Lewis, who was killed out West a few months before, and brought home a corpse. It is certain Mr. Convis had no knowledge or recollection of the tragedy.

Mr. A. Hogeboom, of Shed's Corners, New York, states that the wing part of Mr. T. Harris's house, for two evenings in succession, was shaken with violent shocks, for which nobody was then able to give any cause. Immediately after these shocks, the family observed written on one of the upper panes of glass, in one of the wing windows, the name of James Cary. The name had been there for years, and hundreds of curious neighbors had examined without being able to account for it. Mr. Hogeboom received permission to take out this pane of glass and submit it to some spirit-test. He learned that one James Cary formerly resided in that vicinity, and the spirit of this Cary claims to have caused the electrical shocks experienced at the house of Mr. Harris many years ago, asserting that they were produced by a current of electro-galvanism which he used in writing his name on the glass.

Mr. Amos Rodgers, of Willowvale, New York, relates that one of his boys, six or seven years old, had wandered away from home and become lost. Long and diligent search was made, but no boy found, and fears were entertained that he might have been drowned in the stream or pond near by. Mr. Rodgers, however, did not abandon hope. He walked out calmly, and wound his way up one of the winding paths of his rural, romantic domain, till at last he seated himself on a rough, rural lounge erected on the lofty summit of his lands. Remaining quiet a moment up there in the pure air of nature, he heard an audible voice in the direction of Clinton, saying, "*Father, I am coming!*" Mr. Rodgers immediately hurried down the hill, ordered his carriage, started towards Clinton, and had not gone far before he met the boy walking on the way home to Willowvale!

CHAPTER III.

HOW TO INVESTIGATE — GENERAL PRINCIPLES OF SPIRITUALISM — SPECIFIC STATEMENT OF THE SPIRITUALIST BELIEF — THE BIBLE EVIDENCES.

To investigate Spiritualism, it becomes necessary to divest the mind of all prejudices and influences calculated to bias the judgment or intercept the light of impartial truth. Those who fancy their opinions and preconceptions are already infallible; those who take ground on the authority of pre-existing creeds, sects, systems, and associations; those who assume themselves in possession of all truth; those who are fortified with self-conceit; those who are evermore looking back with idolatry for the past, and bowing down with adoration for its traditions, fearful of looking forward for new unfoldings, and those who are governed by a popular policy, rather than by a sterling principle of independence, — are but poorly prepared to begin an examination of the claims of modern Spiritualism. We are to commence, remembering that God has endowed every human being with individual rights and capacities to read, reason, reflect, investigate all facts, truths, and phenomena; and, having decided, to speak and act according to the divine standard erected by conscience; and that, too, without fear of molestation on the part of any authority outside of heaven, so long as is observed the golden rule respecting the rights of others, and doing unto them as we would have them do unto us, under similar circumstances. Nor are we to be intimidated by conservatives who are continually croaking in regard to the fancied results of such fearless investigation. No new unfolding has ever been made on earth without creating alarm on the part of bigoted, unenlightened, and prejudiced opponents. Primitive Christianity was regarded as the archest heresy and infidelity, threatening the overthrow of all deemed sacred by Jew and Gentile. Every newly-unfolded system of science and philosophy, every art, invention, and discovery, have been met and opposed by conservative alarmists, predicting dreadful disasters as the result of the radical revolutions threatened.

So with reference to Spiritualism. Religionists have established their creeds, formulas, churches, sects, ideas of revelation, and their mediums, in the form of self-ordained priesthoods; and all these are sustained by sacred traditions, customs, and associations. They seem dependent on these for salvation "in the life that now is, and that which is to come." And when Spiritualism is announced as a new unfolding in continuation of the past; as a gospel of present inspirations, seeking to inaugurate the kingdom of heaven in every human soul; to make a church, a priesthood, a medium of every mortal; to unfold all in the light and liberty of God and the angel-world,—these religionists grow alarmed, and predict nothing but danger and destruction. But who is to judge? Our religious opponents, or ourselves? Our authority is as good as theirs, if not far better; for many who have now passed into the experiences of Spiritualism, who have witnessed and received its manifestations and communications, who have realized its beneficent influences, have likewise passed through the experiences of the church, and are prepared to pronounce its doctrines, teachings and tendencies as not only inefficient to the salvation of the soul, but harrowing to the best feelings and affections of humanity, inadequate to meet the wants of the skeptical and the wandering, and dangerous to the weal of the world; while, on the other hand, our religious oppo nents have never experienced Spiritualism. Many, however, are already prepared to admit that the idea of angel intercourse is beautiful and attractive. Yet they affect to regard it dangerous, because it is so beautiful and well adapted to the affections of the human heart. On this ground, then, we must reject everything that is lovely and attractive, and receive that only which appears ugly and repulsive. Not so. We claim that the attractiveness of Spiritualism is proof of its divinity, and of its divine adaptation to human needs. Let it be tested. Let every mind and heart claim its own God-inherited right and duty to "prove all things, and hold fast that which is good."

In the social and political world, there are those who take alarm at this new dispensation, and are seeking to intimidate the masses of the people. And why? It has been the course of the demagogue, the despot, the aristocrat, and the conservative, in all ages. False institutions, false governments, and false conventionalisms have ever sought to shelter themselves in compact with false systems of religion and mythology. Spiritualism seeks no alliance with any political party, fanatical faction, or social clique of conservatism, nor does it aim at the direct destruction of any of these. While it maintains a due regard for the temporary expediency of these, and seeks to preserve all that is good and true in the past and present church, state, and society, nevertheless, as the highest object of its mission, it aims to unfold the individual man and woman in accordance with those higher laws of the eternal world which rise supreme over all that is temporal, transitional, and incidental to the rudimental state of society. Our prayer is, "Thy kingdom come, and thy will be done on earth as it is done in heaven." In communion with God's ministering angels, we seek to know the DIVINE WILL as revealed within the sanctuary of the soul; and to feel, think, speak, and act accordingly, regardless of all that is false, external, institutional, political, conventional, or sectarian. Whoever takes alarm at this position, must likewise take alarm at Christ and the apostles, and every hero, martyr, or reformer who has dared to rise up in the authority and right of heaven and humanity, regardless of time-honored and tampering conservatisms.

But let none take false alarm from the misrepresentations of the opponents of Spiritualism. As Spiritualists, claiming to know the legitimate teachings and tendencies of our own faith and philosophy, as citizens of a republic granting us equal rights and privileges in common with all other religionists and reformers, as intelligent beings belonging to the great family of mankind, we claim the right to define our own position, and decide what Spiritualism is and what it is not. But we assume no right to decide for any except our individual selves. We claim no authority over each other as a body of believers and investigators, nor over those who stand outside of our ranks. We present our evidences and opinions, and leave inquiring minds to come to their own conclusions. We ask all skeptics and inquirers to take the same liberty which we take, in reasoning and investigating, in receiving or rejecting. Let us begin on equal grounds, and treat each other as brothers and sisters. If Spiritualism is false, let us find it out and reject it. If it is true, let us know it, cherish it, proclaim it, practise it, though all earth should rise in wrath, and the gates of Hades jar with thunders of denunciation.

Spiritualists, as a body, claim no authority to bind any "grievous burdens" on the human soul, or to erect standards of faith, formula, philosophy, or theology like the schools and sects hitherto holding domination over the public mind. We have no councils, conventions, tracts, books, periodicals, colleges, theological institutions, priesthoods, censorships, mediums, lecturers, or leaders to be regarded in the light of bishops, cardinals, or popes, endowed with infallible authority to dictate in matters of faith and practice. According to the Jeffersonian Declaration of Independence and Equality, we hold that "all men are endowed by their Creator with certain inalienable rights," not only in a civil, but in a social and spiritual sense, — at least, all intelligent, normally organized beings. "Why even of yourselves judge ye not what is right?" was the significant question of Christ. Luke xii. 57. To know who Spiritualists are, and what Spiritualism is, then, we are to consult no arbitrary standards, whether claimed by individual believers or associated bodies of believers, or by those who set up an authority outside of our ranks. Individual investigation and experience alone can determine for each individual what Spiritualism is in its deepest, divinest essence, when applied to the mind, the heart, and life. It can no more become embodied in a creed, form, or church, than can the air or the sunlight of heaven. And yet there are certain facts and principles with which to begin our investigation, though we are not to take these as absolute authority, any farther than they commend themselves to reason and intuition. In order that we may ascertain what these are, it becomes necessary to give heed to the published or oral statements of the most representative minds, sum up the testimony of the whole, take an impartial position, and form an opinion according to our better judgment. Spiritualists erect no authoritative standards of faith or practice outside of the divine authority the Great Father enthrones in the enlightened consciousness of every soul. While we take this ground, there is no authority for any human being to sit in judgment or condemnation of another, or to interfere with another any farther than it becomes absolutely necessary for the protection of the individual rights of all. Hence, it becomes our first duty to look to ourselves, to judge ourselves alone, to analyze our own natures and needs, to commence the work of self-culture in communion with those spiritual intelligences who have already passed the discipline of this rudimental life, and learn to see ourselves and all other human beings in the light of that celestial world where even the highest angels of God veil their faces and fear to pronounce an unjust judgment. On this ground there is no room for intolerance on account of diversity in opinion, belief, character, condition, or practice. Science recognizes differences in our organizations; philosophy unfolds various mental and moral tendencies in human nature; the spiritual as well as the true primitive Christian religion teaches us we are all children of one family and Father, each endowed with an individuality of our own, though all are linked and allied by a common tie of fraternal sympathy. Hence the need of exercising the broadest toleration and charity, without which none can be regarded genuine Spiritualists, however well convinced they may be of the fact of spirit intercourse, or however loud and zealous their professions. The religious sects have failed for the lack of exercising these principles, and have been rent by endless janglings about creeds, and denunciations of individual differences in life, character, and custom.

Though spiritual believers may agree as to general principles, they allow no right to dictate the individual conscience. It is possible that some of our statements as to what Spiritualism is, may not meet the entire approbation of all believers. The writer alone is responsible, and invites the freest criticisms. Each must judge from his own individual standpoint. The aim of this volume is to present every phase of spiritual phenomena, philosophy and opinion. In seeking to present a plain guide, so many principles and responsibilities are involved, the utmost care and discrimination are needed. It must be remembered that modern Spiritualism is yet in its infancy, compared with the old schools of religion. Its believers have come out of all the other sects, and represent every phase of society, character, culture, and opinion; and, as a matter of necessity, there are crude, complex materials among them. When Christianity arose in Judea, eighteen hundred years ago, its believers represented every class of the people, from the lowest to the highest; the multitudes at first following Christ and his apostles with no matured convictions, but governed only by motives of curiosity and wild hopes of some new-found gospel. So with the masses to-day coming out under the new-found gospel of heaven opened in communion with the inhabitants of earth, long darkened and mournful beneath the palls of theology and materialism. At first, it was enough for them to know the silence of death was broken; the dead still lived and loved; the departed came back with startling manifestations of power and intelligence, to awake slumbering souls into a consciousness of the reality of man's spiritual nature, and the glories of an eternal world; that angel hands parted the portals of the tomb, held the beacon light of immortal life, reached down to lead the weary and worn pilgrim along the dusty highway of duty and trial, wipe the tears from mourners' eyes, and point to the land of re-union with the beloved. No marvel that multitudes arose with streaming and wondering eyes, without waiting to inquire for all the principles involved in this new-found gospel. Thousands of men and women grew almost wild with joy to find themselves delivered from the thraldom of old errors, ignorance, and superstition, and born anew in the light and liberty of heaven-descended truth. Under these circumstances, it could hardly be expected that much harmony of sentiment would exist at first, or that any general unitary movement would arise among the body of believers. Besides, the fear of sectarian tendencies has operated to deter many from making any efforts in regard to organization. The idea of individual freedom has been uppermost from the beginning, and the spirits have invariably cautioned against all action tending in the least towards compromising personal liberty or personal responsibility. Hence, while Spiritualism is understood to embrace certain principles, each individual must assume the responsibility of applying those principles, and take the consequences of their use or abuse. With this fact in view, Spiritualists, as a body, claim no right to prescribe specific phases of reform, or to judge censoriously in regard to moral distinctions, except in cases which involve absolute evil or infringement on the rights of others. The doctrine of individuality requires each person to place himself in the position occupied by others. But "we most emphatically declare that no theory or practice which tends to abrogate moral distinctions, to weaken the sense of personal responsibility, or to give a loose rein to animal indulgences, by whomsoever taught or received, can with any propriety be considered a part of Spiritualism. Since man's spiritual welfare in this and the after life is intimately connected with his conduct, habits, occupations, surroundings, beliefs, and motives, we recognize the importance of all questions relating to human improvement and practical reform."

Those whose souls come in clear and serene communion with celestial intelligences, take no alarm at whatever agitation is moving either the church, state, or society. During every political campaign, the whole Union becomes intensified with startling issues, and certain conservative croakers put on woful countenances in prediction of the anarchy and ruin of the government. But the country usually comes safe out of the contest, and rather improved by the excitement. At every new unfolding of spiritual truth the churches grow alarmed for the cause of religion, and predict a coming reign of ruin and terror. But God still reigns, the earth rejoices, and humanity is safe. Similar alarms and predictions prevail with reference to the social agitations of the age, and some timid conservatives entertain serious apprehensions of danger. In the light of Spiritualism, the laws of conjugal love, of true marriage, of sexual purity, of home harmony, and of the relations between parents and children, are being unfolded and demonstrated in such a manner as to reveal the falsities and infernal discords of the past, and inspire hopes of a new era, in which men and women shall overcome all that is evil and at war with genuine conjugal, monogamic relationships. And why should we fear the result? Doubtless there is some danger of temporary evils, some hasty disruptions, some abuses and perversions; but these are incidental to every age of agitation. We may have no fears in behalf of aught that stands on solid foundations. Houses, homes, relationships, compacts, parties, churches built on the rock of eternal truth, shall withstand all the waves, the storms, the shocks of the age. An eminent reformer says, "everything is now breaking up." In one sense it is alarmingly true. Yet this "breaking up" process augurs the drifting away of the ice and floodwood floating on the sea of society.

Spiritualists as individuals will hold themselves responsible only so far as they participate in these questions of to-day, but if they are true to their teachings they will feel no undue sensitiveness or alarm, nor pronounce any hasty judgment. The signs of the times are ominous of radical revolutions. It is now as it was when Jesus walked Judea centuries ago; the elements are coming in fearful conflict; agitations are stirring the deep waters covering the face of humanity, and divisions, dissensions, are rending state, church and society in preparation for "the kingdom of heaven which is at hand."

A true spiritual philosophy is absolute in demanding the practice of principle instead of exercising any time-serving policy. Yet few, it is feared, are prepared to practise according to the demands of sterling principles, while the many are governed by policies or expediencies. Take as an illustration: many individuals are convinced of the error of old opinions and habits, and have evidences of the truths and duties inculcated by Spiritualism. Yet policy withholds a confession of their errors, and keeps them from a practical acknowledgment of the truths newly unfolded to their minds. They fear the prejudice, the opinion, the frown, the disapprobation of an opposing world, and ask, What will certain persons think? how will they feel? what will they say? Their first question should be, What is true? what is right? what is just and divine in the sight of conscience, of God, and the host of heaven? Thousands are thus kept in menial service to a blind, unprincipled, short-sighted policy! They cannot realize that the demands of conscience are first and supreme, and that all these policies will soon pass into insignificance before the stern ordeals in which all souls must be tried. They are living false lives, whose masks must at last be torn off and reveal the lurking hypocrisies long worn from the gaze of the outer world. It is pitiable to contemplate the condition of all those who to-day are inwardly convicted of the truths of Spiritualism, yet whose policy prevents them from coming out openly, and living in acknowledgment of the principles involved.

And it were well for all those who are called Spiritualists to ask themselves whether they are living in strict conformity with the principles of their philosophy and religion. But few of us can answer in a manner to make an entire acquittal of our consciences. In many things we are governed more by policy and prejudice than by principle and ideas of absolute right. Many are more sensitive about their reputations than about their principles. They are still prone to ask, What will the world think? say? what impressions will opposers form?

It were not wise for us to fly into the face of the world, or seek to outrage its prejudices; yet there are times when stern duties compel us to speak and act regardless of all popular prejudices and conventionalities. Sometimes there are men and women brought under the influence of Spiritualism who are regarded by opposers as unpopular; and shall we condemn and cast them off merely because such a course would seem politic in the eyes of the world? Sometimes we are prone to judge each other from the standpoint of the vulgar multitude. We may know nothing that is absolutely wrong in itself, but, on the contrary, may feel assured all is right and just and pure when considered in a true light; yet we grow sensitive in regard to the prejudices and suspicions of others, and recommend a corresponding policy. But there is a divine judgment and action, on which we are sometimes compelled to stand, though we fall martyrs before the false sentiment of the superficial world. God grant us the inspiration of eternal PRINCIPLE, with wisdom to guide and charity to enlarge our hearts.

Spiritualists are no sticklers for mere names, titles or terms of designation, nor are we pledged to any specific forms or ceremonies. Yet, while we are all confessedly more or less on the plane of the external, and dependent for an understanding of each other on the use of external language, it becomes necessary for us to adopt some forms of expression in attempting to designate our sentiments, sympathies and aims. Some difference of opinion may exist among us in regard to the adoption of any fixed name by which we shall be known to the world. Some persons are exceedingly sensitive about the adoption of any name, and they have fears that the use of a common name will eventually tend to sectarianism. But the adoption of some name is inevitable; and unless we select for ourselves, the outside world will select for us. Most of the names by which the sects are now known were first applied by their opponents, and afterwards became adopted as titles of convenience. Who first used the term Spiritualist or Spiritualism we are unable to state, though none will deny its appropriateness. In adopting names to designate classes of individuals, it is impossible to avoid a tendency in some minds to extremes. Whatever title is adopted is found susceptible of being tortured into something opposite to that which is intended by its originators. Every name under heaven may be charged as having some tendency to partyism or sectarianism. The terms Freethinker, Infidel, Friend of Progress, Harmonial Philosopher or Reformer, are just as open to the charge of sectarianism as the term Spiritualist or Spiritualism. And yet some persons have objected to the latter, while they have insisted on thrusting forward one or more of the former names, as though they were thereby going to accomplish some extraordinary results.

We can find no term more free from objections, more natural or appropriate, than the one in general use to designate spiritual intercourse, viz., SPIRITUALISM. The mightiest laws and forces in the universe are SPIRITUAL. God is a SPIRIT; man is the SPIRITUAL image and offspring of the Infinite Father; his highest attributes and noblest triumphs are SPIRITUAL; as a SPIRIT he is immortal, and through SPIRIT-BIRTH he passes into the SPIRIT-WORLD; our loftiest joys and grandest achievements are in communion with the SPIRIT-WORLD, and the highest hopes of humanity are centred in the inauguration of a SPIRITUAL or celestial kingdom on earth in fellowship with SPIRITUAL hosts of heaven. Spiritualism, therefore, becomes significant of all that is great, good, glorious, grand and divinely ideal. No term in the English language can be found so appropriate and full of meaning. The name may sound unpopular and opprobrious to certain itching ears, but to the believing soul it is significant of the sublimest inspirations, and becomes the password of eternal progress in all that is godlike and angelic. Let scoffers, skeptics and bigots sneer at us and ironically exclaim, "Spiritualists!" but what care we, save to glory in that glorious epithet and repeat it as significant of our loftiest ideals and aspirations? The invisible world is peopled with myriads of spirits gazing down on the highway in which we are called to walk with heroic footsteps, and may no coward souls prove unworthy of the guardianship of God's celestial monitors.

The largest Convention of Spiritualist lecturers, mediums and believers ever assembled, was held in Providence, R. I., in 1860. The following "definitions of Spiritualism and its aims" was unanimously adopted by that body, though the author does not confine himself to the letter of the original statement:—

1. *Who are Spiritualists?* Those who believe man is an immortal spirit; that human spirits exist after the death of the body, and can and do come back, so to speak, manifesting themselves and communicating to mortals, in the use of various methods demonstrating immortality, the reality of a spirit world, and tangible intercourse with the inhabitants of earth.

2. All who recognize the fact of spiritual intercourse may be regarded as Spiritualists in theory, without reference to life, character or profession; while practical Spiritualists, the true, the genuine, the reliable, are those who seek to make their lives, characters and professions in harmony with the teachings and inspirations of the purest spiritual intelligences communicating with mortals and the divinest standard of the unfolded soul.

3. Spiritualists as a body claim no authority to dictate systems of philosophy, morality, reform, civil policy, theology or religion, for the arbitrary government of individuals, nor do they claim any uniformity of sentiment on any other ground than the fact of spiritual

8

intercourse, nor hold themselves responsible for each other's acts or opinions any farther than they choose to enter into fraternal compacts with an understanding as to the responsibilities to be borne.

4. We believe that differences of opinion and practice are inevitable to the differences in states of development and planes occupied by different individuals, and that entire harmony can exist only where there is an entire equality in organization, culture and condition. But,

5. We recognize a fraternal plane on which all may come in harmony, on moral and religious ground, where all are identified as brothers and sisters of one common Father-and-Mother-God, and one family in communion with celestial spheres, each with guardian angel influences breathing the divine love which mortals should ever seek to exercise towards each other, regardless of all transient differences and conditions. The Spiritualist creed is summed up in the Golden Rule and the Christian commandment of love to God made manifest in love to man, and is enforced by all the solemn obligations which belong to intelligent beings made conscious of the dignity, the divinity, the eternal and undivided destiny of the human family.

6. *What is Spiritualism?* Spiritualism, in its modern, restricted sense, may mean nothing more than the mere fact of spirit existence and spirit intercourse. But the term is often also applied to a system of philosophy or religion based on this cardinal fact; a system embracing all truth relating to man's spiritual nature, capacities, relations, duties, welfare and destiny; all that is now known or can be known relative to other spiritual beings, and the occult forces and laws of the universe. It is thus catholic and comprehensive; and Spiritualism, in short, may be regarded as the culmination, the essence of all truths, inspirations and revelations brought down to the

present age, and demonstrated, confirmed by unmistakable manifestations of spiritual power and intelligence.

7. While modern Spiritualism began with the phenomena in Hydesville, Wayne Co., N. Y., in 1847–8, it likewise recognizes similar phenomena traceable through all past history, and especially in what has been regarded sacred history, though it is no indispensable part of Spiritualism either to affirm or deny the truth or authority of the Bible as interpreted by any of the religious sects, each Spiritualist being at liberty to place his own estimate on the value of that and of all other ancient records, whether called sacred or profane. The masses of believers, however, find abundant evidences in the sacred Scriptures, so called, harmonizing with modern Spiritualism, and are inclined to recognize the pure, primitive teachings and authenticated phenomena recorded in the New Testament as in essential unity with the unfoldings of the present spiritual dispensation. But there is a diversity of opinion in regard to interpretations of the Bible and the extent of its authority and authenticity, the nature of Deity, the character and mission of Christ, and as to what modifications and rejections should be made in regard to the evangelical doctrines, denominated the "fall of man," "human depravity," "vicarious atonement," "the Trinity," "future judgment," and "endless punishment;" the majority of Spiritualists repudiating these doctrines as they are stated by the sects, and, in accordance with their own intuitions and the teachings they receive from spirits, advocating the law of human progress; the natural tendency to good in humanity; the need of retributive justice mingling with mercy, instead of a scheme of vicarious salvation; the certainty of present judgment, rewards and punishments, administered according to the natural law of cause and effect, and continued no longer than is necessary to subserve the aims of benevolence in the reformation and consequent holi-

ness and happiness of the transgressor; the divinity of Christ as a type of the divinity God has stamped on all his children, and the mission of Christ as representative of the mission of the truly unfolded spiritual man, without any intervention of the so-called miraculous; the unity of the Godhead in contradistinction to the Trinity; and finally a method of interpreting the Bibles of all past ages precisely like the method adopted in the investigation of modern Spiritualism. The spiritual gospel, therefore, cannot be confounded with any one species of philosophy, science, deism, atheism, pantheism or dogmatic theology, however noted may be the advocates, party or sect, whether they are men still in the form or so called disembodied spirits; none are recognized as infallible authority, though each may afford some truth belonging to Spiritualism.

8. All Spiritualists agree in affirming that the grand aim of Spiritualism is "the quickening and unfolding of the spiritual or divine nature in man, to the end that the animal or selfish nature shall be overcome, and all evil and disorderly affections be rooted out; in other words, that the 'works of the flesh' may be supplanted in each individual by the 'fruits of the spirit,' and thus mankind become a brotherhood, and God's will be done on earth as it is done in heaven."

9. *Its Relation to Specific Reforms.* — Since man's spiritual growth and welfare, in this life and the future, is believed to depend in some measure on his physical health, his habits and surroundings, as well as on his beliefs and motives of action, all departments of human improvement and practical reform come legitimately within the scope of a broad Spiritualism. Hence earnest and philanthropic Spiritualists cannot fail to take a deep interest in the promotion of objects like the following, though they may differ in regard to methods of action:

10. Physiological reform in general, whether as relates

to injurious habits of food, drink, dress, labor, indulgence, or stimulation, or to erroneous systems of medication — to the end that every human body may be made a fit temple for the indwelling spirit, and a healthful instrument for its use.

11. Educational reform — that body, mind, and spirit may be unfolded and cultivated symmetrically, and by the use of the most enlightened methods.

12. Parentage reform — that every child may be secured its right to a healthful organism, and an introduction to life under favorable circumstances.

13. The emancipation of woman from all civil and social oppressions — that she may freely choose her own occupations, and become best fitted to be the mother of noble offspring.

14. The equal enlightenment and consequent ultimate liberty of all human beings, and the abrogation of all oppression, civil inequality, domestic tyranny, or mental and spiritual despotism — because freedom is the birthright of all, and the instinctive demand of every growing spirit.

15. Theological and ecclesiastical reform — since deliverance from error and from external authority is requisite to the best spiritual advancement.

16. Social reform and ultimate re-organization — because the present selfish and antagonistic relations and institutions of society are unsuited to a higher spiritual condition.

Lastly, in any and every effort calculated in their individual judgments to improve the condition of mankind.

17. *Its Bearing on Organizations.*—While Spiritualists have no general organization or authoritative creed, and cannot consistently combine for the purpose of controlling each other's opinions or setting bounds to inquiry, yet they may properly associate for such objects as the following: — The promulgation of what they deem important truth; the promotion of fraternal intercourse;

and the affording of mutual encouragement and aid in a true life.

While believers have no blind faith in the authority of conventions, or any other large bodies, yet, when such bodies truly represent the masses, they ask their opponents to treat them with due regard. If Spiritualism is assailed, we insist it ought to be assailed on fair ground, free from all caricatures, slanders, and misrepresentations. Opposers are prone to attack us on ground which we do not occupy; they quote books, papers, persons, and opinions which we have never acknowledged as authority. As yet we have adopted no books or individuals as our standard. The foregoing statement is the only one most widely adopted and endorsed. As the leading opinions of all parties and peoples are determined by the principles or platforms adopted by public representative bodies, we ask that Spiritualism be judged in the same manner, and not by unreliable reports.

We have a variety of individual statements of the spiritual philosophy, among which is the subjoined, by Prof. G. Beckwith: —

1. That this life is a sphere of existence in which are developed the rudiments of a being which is to exist without end.

2. That after the occurrence of the chemical change called death, mankind continue to exist as conscious spirits.

3. That all spirit-faculties possessed in the body are retained and exercised in the spirit-life.

4. The type of character which an individual has cultivated or sustained in this life determines the state or condition of the spirit in the beginning of the next. In other words, the spirit-life may be compared to a graded school, in which the spirit is assigned to a class for which his discipline in the earth-life has qualified him.

5. That the capacity for improvement and progression, possessed by the spirit while in the form, is retained in the spirit-life. Hence, —

6. That the state (sometimes called sphere) into which

a spirit at first enters on leaving the form is not of necessity fixed; but the spirit, at its own volition, can attract more refined and elevated spirits, by whose coöperating influence it can pursue an endless course of progression in purity and excellence, forever assimilating itself more and more to the ultimate of DIVINE PERFECTION.

7. That under certain favorable conditions spirits can and do manifest themselves to, and communicate with, persons in the flesh; and for this purpose they sometimes make sounds upon material substances, or move such substances, and sometimes employ the organism of mortals who are susceptible to their influence, inspiring them to write, speak, personate those who have died, of whom they had no knowledge, tell the events of the past, present, and future, perform acts of healing, and do many other things commonly classed as miracles.

8. That observation has shown, that by our mental, moral, and physical state we can aid or hinder the approach of the spirits to the earth. But the laws by which we are able to do this are as yet but imperfectly understood.

9. That persons who are susceptible to the influence of departed spirits are likely to attract those which are of a like character with themselves.

10. That the spirits which can influence one organism may not be able to affect another; and in case where the same spirit influences different persons, it will be likely to do it in different ways, and for different uses, according to the varying organism.

The following is another valuable statement, modified from A. E. Newton's Tract No. 2: —

1. Spiritualism demonstrates that the spirits of departed human beings now hold tangible, intelligible intercourse with man on earth.

2. Man has a spiritual nature surviving the material body, and is born into spirit-life at the dissolution of the material.

3. The spirit-world is a "house of many mansions," or spheres, in which all take their place or plane, according to their character, though none are debarred from progress.

4. The spirit-world is not essentially a fixed locality,

but rather condition, though it may be difficult to divest mortals of all ideas of location.

5. Spirits are endowed with power to act on the human mind and body without destroying human responsibility, and under certain conditions can act on material objects, affording physical manifestations.

6. All human beings have spiritual senses, which, when cultivated and unfolded, render them mediumistic; hence, spiritual gifts and inspirations corresponding with those of ancient times, confirming the past, and demonstrating past and present phenomena as in harmony with the laws of nature.

7. No inspirations, manifestations, or communications, either ancient or modern, can be regarded perfect or infallible, since all come through finite, fallible mediums, and must be tested by individuals receiving them. "Prove all things."

8. Heaven and hell are states or conditions, rather than fixed places, and so are what are called spheres.

9. All human spirits are destined to endless progress towards an ultimate state of universal harmony, in accordance with the laws of Him who "doeth his will in the armies of heaven and among the inhabitants of earth."

10. All the mightiest forces in the universe are spiritual. "The things which are seen are temporal, but the things which are not seen are eternal."

11. There is one Supreme Intelligence, "the Father of all spirits."

12. Spiritualism enables man not merely to believe but to realize immortality, and to receive constant aids and inspirations in spiritual life.

13. All inordinate fear and mourning are banished, and the future life is revealed with hope and joy.

14. The idea of constant angel guardianship elevates all human aims and aspirations, restrains evil, quickens the noblest faculties, aids in purifying the heart and life, and uplifts the affections in communion with the beloved and beatified ones gone on before.

15. Constant communion with the spirit-world, peopled by the myriads of all past ages, aids man in becoming more conscious of the individuality, dignity and divinity of his own nature, enables him to throw off all false, external authority, and to stand up heeding the voice of God within the temple of his own being.

16. This communion keeps alive the holiest affections for the living and the dead, or departed, and enables us to realize the whole family of man as one on earth and in the heavens; it awakens the deepest religious emotions in oneness with the Father, the Holy Host, the Christ, and all Christ-like spirits, coming on errands of mercy to mankind; and finally enkindles the fires of philanthropy as man realizes angel throngs in sympathy with the race, and singing songs of joy over "one sinner that reformeth."

As already stated, those who would know what Spiritualism is must consult its acknowledged believers and representatives, fall back on their own intuitions, and then judge for themselves. Yet every believer has some phase peculiarly his own; hence, an individual opinion, or a number of opinions by different individuals on a given point, may not fairly or fully represent Spiritualism as a whole, as accepted by the body of believers. In order that the subject may be presented in its broadest sense, as adapted to conscientious religionists, we submit the subjoined summary, comparing the modern with the ancient Bible Spiritualism: —

1. Spiritualism, as generally understood, teaches the existence of a supreme Spiritual Intelligence, unfolding, pervading, and animating the universe; a God of infinite attributes and perfections, and the Father of all spirits, whether in or out of the mortal form.

The heavens declare the glory of God, and the firmament showeth forth his handy work. God is a spirit. Whither shall I go from thy spirit? Have we not all one Father? Psalms xix. 1; cxxxix. 7; John iv. 24; Mal. ii. 10.

2. It teaches that man is the spiritual offspring of God, — "made in his image and likeness," — with God-like attributes, individualized and immortal.

Men are made after the similitude of God. James iii. 9; Gen. i. 27.

3. Man having a spiritual nature, God-derived and

God-sustained, a compound of all the essences of subordinate objects in creation, in that nature is eternal and progressive.

There is a natural body and a spiritual. This mortal must put on immortality. Now we see through a glass darkly, but then face to face; now I know in part, but then shall I know even as also I am known. 1 Cor. xv. 44, 53; xiii. 12.

4. As a *personal*, essential, intelligent being, man is a spirit; in this earth-life, as an *individual*, clothed with a material form or body, and made to pass through a state of discipline initiatory to other spheres of existence.

Our light affliction, which is but for a moment, worketh for us a far more exceeding, eternal weight of glory. 2 Cor. iv. 17; Romans viii. 18.

5. When the spirit has fulfilled its mission in this earth-life, and the body has done its office work, the material form is thrown off in the process of death, and man enters the spheres of spiritual being.

That which thou sowest is not quickened except it die. It is sown a natural body, it is raised a spiritual. In my Father's house are many mansions. 1 Cor. xv. 37, 44; John xiv. 2.

6. In proportion to his unfoldment in truth, wisdom, and love, man on entering the spirit-world may so control certain imponderable elements and influences, under certain conditions, as to come back to earth, — in various ways communicate with those who are still in the body, and produce manifestations to demonstrate to mortals the agency of spirits, minister faith to the unbelieving, joy to the sorrowing, strength to the weak and weary, comfort to the mournful, love to the lonely and neglected, hope to the despairing, and eternal life to the dying.

If I go to prepare a place for you, I will come again. I will come to you — will manifest myself. Lord, how is it thou wilt manifest thyself unto us, and not unto the world? Moses and Elias talking with Jesus. And he shall go before him in the spirit and power of Elias. In heaven their angels do always behold the face of my Father. Angels came and ministered unto Him. We, also, are compassed about with so great a cloud of witnesses, etc. (See whole of Heb. xi.) There was a great earthquake; for the angel of the Lord descended from heaven, and came and rolled back the stone from the door, and sat upon it. The spirits of the prophets are subject to the prophets. When I had heard and seen, I fell down to worship before the feet of the angel which showed me those things. Then saith he unto me, See thou do it not; for I am thy fellow-servant, and of thy brethren the prophets. The gods are come down to us in the likeness of men. Behold, I stand at the door and knock, etc. He that hath an ear to hear, let him hear what the Spirit saith unto the churches. The Comforter, which is the Holy Ghost, whom the Father will send in my name; he shall teach you all things. John xiv.; Matt. xvii.; Luke i. 17; xviii. 10; iv. 11; xxvi. 53; xxviii. 2; 1 Cor. xiv. 32; Rev. xxii. 8, 9; Acts xiv. 11; Rev. iii. 30; John xiv. 23.

7. While still in the body, man, according to his spiritual culture and unfolding, may hold direct communication with the spirit-world; may realize the influences of the holy host of heaven; may commune with the ever-revealing, ever-inspiring Father-spirit of the universe; may read the souls of his fellow-men, with an interior eye; may sometimes penetrate time and space with a prophetic glance; may have such command over the invisible elements, in coöperation with unseen intelligences, as to control disease, heal the sick, bless the unfortunate, and dismantle death of its dreads.

The heavens were opened, and I saw visions of God. The Spirit took me up, and I heard behind me a voice of a great rushing. A spirit passed before my face. Behold,

I see the heavens opened. I will come to visions and revelations of the Lord. I knew a man in Christ, about fourteen years ago, whether in or out of the body I cannot tell, — such a one caught up to the third heaven, caught up into paradise, and heard unspeakable words, not lawful for man to utter. If a man love me he will keep my words; and my Father will love him, and we will come unto him, and make our abode with him. Come, see a man who hath told me all things that I ever did. These signs shall follow them that believe. A vision appeared to Paul in the night. There stood a man of Macedonia, and prayed him, saying, Come over unto Macedonia and help us. Ezek. i. 1; iii. 12; Job iv. 15; Acts vii. 56; 2 Cor. xii.; John xiv. 23; iv. 29; Mark xvi. 17; Acts xvi. 9.

8. On entering the spirit-world, man takes the plane or state corresponding the nearest to the plane, the interior condition, the predominant character of his earth-life; though opposed by nothing in the divine economy to prevent the overcoming of all evil, the eternal progress of the spirit, and the ultimate reign of harmony throughout the empire of Him who shall become all in all.

Every man in his own order. Star differeth from star in glory. Of him, and through him, and to him, are all things. 1 Cor. xv. 23, 41; Rom. xi. 36.

9. The bond of all true unity is love, the essence of God, the element of the angel-world, the life-current of all spiritual communion, the test of Jesus, the touchstone of all noble souls whose deeds have blessed humanity, the criterion of all faith, all fraternity, all forms, all mediums, and all fellowship with earth and heaven.

Keep the unity of the spirit in the bond of peace. God is love. He that loveth is born of God, and knoweth him. All the law is fulfilled in one word, in this: Thou shalt love thy neighbor as thyself. By this shall all men know that ye are my disciples, if ye have love one to another. Eph. iv. 3; 2 John iv.; Gal. v. 14; John xiii. 35.

10. Spiritualism is in harmony with all sound revelation, reason, philosophy, and religion; and without seeking any direct antagonism with seemingly opposite systems, seeks rather to recognize the good and the true in everything, and to harmonize all things according to the laws of eternal progress as under the guidance of Him who governs supreme, through men and angels, over all worlds and intelligences.

Ye shall know them by their fruits. I come not to destroy, but to fulfil. God doeth according to his will in the army of heaven and the inhabitants of earth. Matt. vii. 16; v. 17; Dan. iv. 35.

11. It recognizes the sacred histories and Scriptures of all ages and nations; accepts Christianity in spirit, not as embodied in creeds, but as taught and exemplified by Christ and his apostles; each believer claiming the Protestant right of private judgment to read and interpret for himself, accountable for his opinions to none except God at the bar of his own conscience.

All Scripture given by inspiration of God is profitable for doctrine, etc. I have found no fault with this man (Jesus). Who went about doing good. Go to the lost sheep of the house of Israel; heal the sick, etc. Let every man be fully persuaded in his own mind. 2 Tim. iii. 16; Luke xxiii. 14; Acts x. 38; Matt. x.; Rom. xiv.

12. It claims that modern spiritual manifestations, in their multiplied forms and phases, are in entire harmony with so-called miracles, revelations, inspirations, angel visitations, and demonstrations of invisible power and intelligence recorded in the Bible; that both are accounted for by the same laws; that the same laws are eternal and unchangeable in their operations; that in each grand epoch in the history of the world manifestations have been and will continue to be adapted to the needs of man as a being

of unending progress; that the past, present, and future are indissolubly linked as one; and that no contempt is thrown upon the past, with all its noble heroes, martyrs, seers, sages, saints, mediums, and Messiah, in accepting the manifestations of the present, and in contending that the same heavens whose light shone on the brow of Olivet are still open to-day for man to commune with God and angels, and receive foretastes of the divine life.

There are diversities of gifts, administrations, and operations, but the same spirit, same Lord, worketh all in all. I have yet many things to say unto you, but ye cannot bear them now. I am the Lord, I change not. I will pour out my Spirit upon all flesh. Many shall come from the east and the west, and sit down with Abraham, Isaac, and Jacob, in the kingdom. 1 Cor. xii.; John xvi. 12; Mal. iii. 6; Joel ii.; Matt. viii. 11.

13. To thousands who have no faith in the past, and who are without hope, Spiritualism gives *demonstrations* of immortality, and they go on their way rejoicing.

Thomas, because thou hast seen me, thou hast believed. John xx. 29.

14. To thousands who have only a faint and feeble faith it gives like demonstrations.

Him that is weak in faith receive ye, but not to doubtful disputations. Rom. xiv. 1.

15. To those who mourn in Zion over the coldness of religion it gives new life, and inspires them with a glowing consciousness that God and the holy host have not withdrawn from the world.

Ye are come to Mount Zion, and unto the city of the living God, the heavenly Jerusalem, and to the innumerable company of angels, etc. Heb. xii. 22, 24.

16. It demonstrates anew, and reäffirms with life-quickening power, all the divine precepts of Christ, and those who have gone before, making them the living truths of to-day, and enforcing them home on the heart and life

with all the pathos, the unction, inevitable in realizing the presence of loving spirit-friends and of angel beings pleading in the name of the Father and the holy dead.

The Holy Ghost shall bring all things to your remembrance, whatsoever I have said unto you. The letter killeth, but the spirit giveth life. There is joy in the presence of the angels of God over one sinner that repenteth. John xiv. 27; 2 Cor. v. 6; Luke xv. 10; Matt. xviii. 10.

17. Spiritualism recognizes the foreshadowing of some truth in all the false mythologies, superstitions, forms, creeds, and religions of the past and present, and, instead of first making aggressive war on these, proposes to lift man up and out of them, and build up in him the true church, and a temple fit for the indwelling of the divine Spirit and of angel-guests.

Let both grow together till the harvest. First the blade, then the ear, after that the full corn in the ear. Know ye not that ye are the temple of God, and the Spirit of God dwelleth in you? Matt. xv. 10; Mark iv. 28; 1 Cor. iii. 16.

18. It maintains that spirits produce audible concussions or raps, accompanied by tests convincive of spiritual agency; move material objects not in contact with any human organism; present spirit-forms and spirit-scenes; hold intercourse with mortals; communicate messages manifesting superhuman intelligence; make impressions on the minds of mediums; read, write, speak, think, act and personify through persons who are suitably susceptible; identify themselves to their earth-friends; read and transmit to a distance thoughts and messages; describe distant objects, scenes and persons; sometimes make accurate predictions and give reliable counsel; speak in tongues and interpret language unknown to the mediums; examine, describe and cure diseases; raise persons and ponderable bodies without regard to the law of gravita-

tion; exhibit spirit-lights; touch persons and cause them to feel their influence; execute music audible to the sense of hearing; and in the hour of closing nature reveal themselves to mortals and welcome them home to the spheres.

In the Mosiac allegory it is said the Lord walked and was seen in the garden of Eden. Gen. iii. 8. An angel tells the abandoned Hagar where to find water to save herself and boy. Gen. xxi. 17. An angel guides in the choice of Isaac's wife. Gen. xxiv. 7. Jacob has a vision of a ladder on which angels descend and ascend, and he is afraid. Jacob wrestles with an angel; is touched, smote on the thigh, thrown to the ground, lamed; asks the spirit's name, gets no definite answer. Gen. xxxii. Terrible manifestations — the plagues of Egypt, ending with the slaughter of all the first-born infants. Ex. vii. to xii. Miriam sings and plays by inspiration. Ex. xiv. Physical demonstration on Mt. Sinai. Ex. xix. The mediums, Aaron and Miriam, grow jealous of Moses. Num. xii. 2. Balaam's ass speaks and sees an angel. Num. xxii. Balaam becomes a trance medium, with his eyes open. Num. xxiv. Jericho falls by invisible power. Josh. vi. An angel cooks cakes and a kid for Gideon. Ju. vi. 21. Samson is trained under angel direction. Ju. xiii. The child Samuel is inspired. 1 Sam. iii. The ark of Israel becomes dangerous to the Philistines. 1 Sam. v. 6. Samuel becomes clairvoyant and tells Saul of his lost asses. 1 Sam. ix. David's harp allays the evil spirit of Saul. 1 Sam. xvi. Saul goes to the medium of Endor and meets the spirit of Samuel. 1 Sam. xxviii. Elijah touched and fed by an angel. 1 Ki. xvi. Elisha makes an axe swim. 2 Ki. vi. The heavens open, and spirit-hosts are beheld by Elisha. 2 Ki. vi. The shadow on the dial of Ahaz turned back ten degrees by Isaiah. 2 Ki. xx. Eliphaz sees a spirit. Job iv. Jeremiah accuses the Lord of deceiving him. Jer. xx. Ezekiel eats a spirit-book; he hears great noises. Ez. ii. Is made to shave his head. Ez. v. Angel saves Shadrach, etc., from the fiery furnace. Dan. iii. A voice warns Nebuchadnezzar. Dan. iv. 31. Spirit-writing and spirit-hand on the wall. Dan. v. Daniel entranced, thrown on the ground, is touched; the men quake. Dan. ix. An angel comes to Mary. Matt. i. Angels sing over Bethlehem. Lu. iii. Jesus can call legions of angels. Matt. xxvi. Mighty miracles of humanity are done by Jesus. Matt. xi. 5. Awful manifestations take place at the crucifixion. Matt. xxvii. An angel rolls away the stone. Matt. xxviii. The spirit-Christ reappears first to Mary Magdalene, the medium out of whom he had cast seven demons. Matt. xxviii. The mediums of Pentecost speak in tongues, and startling manifestations shake the whole place. Acts ii. Zacharias made dumb, and writes. Luke i. Saul hears the spirit-voice of Jesus; is smote from his horse, blind for three days. Acts ix. Peter and Cornelius telegraph to each other. Acts x. The apostles are attended with signs and wonders. Mark xvi. 10. An angel preaches the everlasting gospel. Rev. xiv. 6. Paul exhorts the Corinthian circles to preserve harmony. 1 Cor. xiv.

19. It teaches that all mortals have within themselves the elements of mediumship to commune with the spirit-world; are more or less in communication with the spirits in and out of the form, and measurably influenced by them, either for good or ill, whether they are conscious of it or not; and the influences, manifestations, impressions, and communications they receive will in a measure, if not entirely, correspond with the moral plane mortals occupy, the affections that predominate, and the life they lead; and hence the need of a true life in order to attain a true, harmonic *Spiritualism.*

The true light which lighteth every man. The manifestation of the spirit is given to every man to profit withal. Try the spirits whether they are of God. Covet earnestly the best gifts. John i. 9; 1 Cor. xii. 7; 1 John iv. 1; 1 Cor. xii. 31; John xiv. 23.

20. While it prescribes no ceremonies or creeds to coerce or cramp the conscience, it recognizes the doctrine of individual liberty and responsibility; the duty of individual regeneration, in conformity to physical and spiritual laws; the self-retributive elements of wrong; the self-recompense of the right; the necessity of practising love, purity, justice, and humanity in the attainment of harmony, happiness or heaven, either in the present or future life; and the right and duty of every man to seek all the light he needs as his guide and settle for himself all matters between his own conscience and God.

Judge ye what I say. Ye shall know the truth, and the truth shall make you free. Ye must be born again. He that sinneth wrongeth his own soul. My peace I give unto you — not as the world giveth. Cease to do evil, learn to do well. Do justly, love mercy, and walk humbly with thy God. Follow peace with all, and holiness, without which no man shall see the Lord. 1 Cor. x. 15; John viii. 32; iii. 7; Prov. viii. 36; John xiv. 27; Isaiah i. 17; Mic. vi. 8; Heb. xii. 14.

CHAPTER IV.

THE POPULAR OBJECTIONS AND THEORIES ANSWERED.

Most of the objections and theories now adduced against Modern Spiritualism have appeared in some form with equal force and pertinence against almost every new unfolding in the past. Yet modern objectors invariably talk and write as though their positions were original, and seldom give credit to those who took the same positions long ago. And they assume that Spiritualists are ignorant of these objections. The fact is, almost every believer in spiritual intercourse began his investigations with these objections in mind, and was called on to grapple with them and dispose of them before yielding his doubts. We have gone over the entire ground now occupied by those who stand out indifferent or opposed, and can sympathize with them and anticipate all they have to offer. We are not unmindful of the fact that there are many honest and conscientious unbelievers. It is our earnest desire to meet them fairly, listen patiently, and answer all their questions candidly. We would state their objections in the strongest, clearest manner, and omit nothing calculated to have an influence in retarding the progress of truth.

Objection 1. It is objected that Spiritualism is of modern origin. If it be true, why did not God or angels or the spirits of departed human beings unfold similar manifestations and communications in the earlier ages of the world? Have not the needs of humanity been the same in all ages and among all nations? If departed human beings are able to come back now, why have they not come before, and left the most tangible evidences in sacred and profane history? Since Spiritualism is of modern origin, it must be an innovation of human invention and not of God.

Answer. This objection is based on an assumption, and these questions suggest their own answers. As already intimated, we have abundant evidence that something like modern spiritual intercourse has been known to man during all ages. Every nation and tribe have claimed some intercourse with invisible intelligences. The Bible abounds in accounts of interviews with angelic beings, who are described as looking, acting and communicating like human beings, like men, and they are called men. (See *Bible Statement of Spiritualism*, p. 93.) Some of the methods of modern communication may not be exactly like the methods adopted by spirits in other ages, nor may all the modern teachings prove in exact accordance with the ancient, though in import or in spirit they are essentially the same. But allowing they are not the same, may we not suppose it probable that spirits have made some advancement during ages; and may it not be legitimate for them to adopt some new methods of holding intercourse with mortals? If mortals are permitted to progress here in this world, and to adopt new methods of communicating with each other, why may not spirits likewise progress; and as higher knowledge of the laws of the eternal world is unfolded, why may they not discover and adopt some new methods of celestial communion? In one sense "there is nothing new under the sun," and yet we know there are new unfoldings of old eternal laws and principles. In every other department of life and nature we rejoice in recognizing things seemingly new. Why not adopt the same with reference to things spiritual? The angel of the Apocalypse exclaimed, "Behold, I make all things new." Rev. xxi. John saw "a new heaven and new earth," and all the ancient prophets predicted a period in which man should enjoy new privileges for celestial communion. So, while we deny that Spiritualism is of modern origin, even admitting some of its methods and unfoldings are peculiar to a progressive age, we find in this fact nothing to militate against its truth.

Objection 2. Spiritualism is a reproduction of ancient mythology, necromancy, witchcraft, the work of the devil, Satan, demons, and is therefore prohibited as profane and dangerous.

Answer. In offering this general objection, our opposing brethren refer to the Bible, and cite passages said to prohibit all intercourse with the invisible world. (See again our *Bible Statement*, p. 93.) It will be observed that the objection under consideration is not in entire harmony with the objection first offered. If Spiritualism is identical with ancient mythology, etc., it must be conceded as of very ancient origin. We are willing to admit that many modern spiritual phenomena are in accordance with the same laws by which we are enabled to understand phenomena anciently attributed to demons and evil or undeveloped spirits, though we question the actual existence of any semi-omnipotent, semi-omnipresent deity in the form of a personal devil or Satan, or the existence of any infernal world peopled with myriads of irredeemable devils beyond the control of God. A rational interpretation of the Bible will dispense with such a fabled existence. (See Jahn's Archæology, etc.) To admit the existence of such an arch enemy and such an infernal world, sending forth millions of fiends to seduce and destroy man, would be to impeach God and throw contempt on the divine government; for if God is good and almighty, we can admit the existence of no infernal powers or intelligences permitted to rule over his children or thwart his purposes. But suppose we admit the existence of such an infernal world, and that such infernal beings have been permitted to visit our earth on errands of evil, and are now permitted. Is there no angel world inhabited by better spirits, and can they not likewise visit our earth on errands of mercy? Does God permit the gates of an infernal world to be opened for our ruin, and yet shut the gates of heaven, and allow no angels to come as his messengers in behalf of humanity? If evil spirits can come, why not the good? These questions suggest their own answers, and may lead us to understand all the phenomena in ancient times. In earlier times men were unprepared to understand the laws of spiritual intercommunication, and but few were developed far enough to receive high and harmonious influences. They attributed all the evil influences around them to the agency of infernal spirits, and attracted spirits of an unprogressed order. They were unable to discriminate. Miscellaneous spiritual intercourse often grew dangerous; hence the evils of witchcraft and similar phenomena, hence the prohibitions of the Old Testament. But in the light of modern spiritual science and philosophy we are now enabled the better to understand and control these things, according to the law of conditions, and to discriminate between the good and the evil, the mundane and supermundane, and see all these reconciled under the guidance of high and holy intelligences.

Objection 3. Do not the teachings of Spiritualism come in conflict with divine truth, sound morality, and the teachings of the Bible? If so, may it not be the work of the devil and of evil spirits in his service?

Answer. In the first place, we regard no spirit teachings as perfect or infallible, since all must come through the mediumship of imperfect or fallible mortals, and must be judged by individuals according to their intrinsic value as tested by external and internal evidences. Consequently we cannot concede anything like infallible standards of truth or authority. We must each decide for ourselves according to our own enlightened consciousness. Who, then, shall claim to have discovered the perfect standard of divine truth by which Spiritualism is to be judged? There are various sects which claim authority to decide, but who endowed them with authority? The founders of these sects were fallible men, and their successors are alike imperfect and incapable of becoming our authority. And what do they mean when they accuse Spiritualists of coming in conflict with divine truth, sound morality, and the teachings of the Bible? They mean nothing more than that we do not see as they do; do not sanction their ideas of divine truth; do not entertain their peculiar notions of morality; do not interpret the Bible as they do; do not regard it an orthodox book; do not subscribe to their creed; do not support their churches, forms or ministers. The fact is, there is simply a difference of opinion between us; and we have as good a right to our opinions and our interpretations of the Bible as they have to theirs. In the light of nature, reason and the unfolding spheres, we maintain our honest convictions; and we have just as good a right to call others errorists, fools, fanatics, heretics, knaves, lunatics, infidels, atheists and devil-deluded, as they have to apply these epithets to Spiritualists. "By their fruits shall ye know them." Why, then, is Spiritualism said to be of the devil and his angels? We believe it is mainly because its teachings do not entirely accord with the teachings and interpretations of orthodoxy. Every newly unfolded truth in science and religion has been at first attributed to the devil. Christ and the apostles were charged as in league with Beelzebub. The art of printing was first assigned to Satan. Every new sect has met with a similar charge. Universalists are told their doctrine was first preached by the serpent in Eden. There is no originality, therefore, in attributing Spiritualism to the devil, nor is there any reason for it, notwithstanding men like the Reverends Messrs. Beecher, Butler and Tyng, and our brethren of the Advent school, have fallen back on this diabolical hypothesis, as the easiest subterfuge to blind and intimidate the superstitious masses of the people. Is there anything immoral, dangerous, devilish or infernal in the teachings of this angel gospel? No. It recognizes all that is good and true in Christianity; all the well-authenticated facts, inspirations and moral inculcations recorded in sacred or profane history; all the important truths underlying systems of mythology and theology; all the better elements embodied in every system of science, philosophy and religion; and in addition to these, Spiritualism gives manifestations and communications not only in confirmation of all that is good and true in the past, but in positive proof of a living God, living Christ, and holy hosts opening the heavens in communion with man, imparting the most elevated influxes of celestial wisdom, truth and love, and demonstrating the reality of immortal life and eternal progress.

It seems almost impossible to conceive how any enlightened minds can attribute a gospel like this to the agency of infernal beings; and we believe but very few are really apprehensive of what are called devils or demons. Who really fears anything infernal will result from forming circles and calling on the spirits of dear departed friends? We may have more fear of the devils within our own perverted natures and the diabolical influences incidental to this rudimental sphere of existence, than from any demons liable to come from the invisible world. Through all our mediums, these spirits inculcate principles and practices indicating no infernal purpose, but rather missions of mercy, purity, justice, benevolence, humanity. And under their influence, thousands have been redeemed from unbelief, sorrow and despair; from passions, appetites and propensities over which nothing else could triumph; thousands have been healed in body and soul, and tens of thousands "brought from darkness to light," and sent "on their way rejoicing" in the guardianship of angels and the glorious hope of demonstrated immortality.

Objection 4. It is objected that the spiritual manifestations, so far as they are genuine, are referable to some unknown laws of nature, or to the agency of Mesmerism, animal magnetism, psychology, biology, pathetism, electricity, etc.

Answer. To say these phenomena are in accordance with some unknown laws of nature, is to leave us in utter darkness. What do men know about unknown laws of nature? And what can they ever know about these laws, so long as they ignore all investigation of these phenomena? As rational and intelligent beings we are unable to rest satisfied in ignorance and mystery. We are bound to find some adequate cause or laws to enable us to account for all the phenomena of life and nature. It is sheer assumption to assert that these manifestations belong to the realm of unknown causes, or are referable to Mesmerism and its kindred isms and ologies. Most of those who now contend that Spiritualism is nothing but Mesmerism or some similar phenomena, professed to have no faith in Mesmerism until Spiritualism arose. Then they became suddenly converted to what they had hitherto denominated a humbug, and fell back on Mesmerism as their only subterfuge against Spiritualism; and should something else now arise still more startling, they would doubtless fall back on Spiritualism, and refer it to the agency of spirits. Such is the strange inconsistency of those who oppose the cause of human progress. Now those who are most familiar with the genuine phenomena of Mesmerism know perfectly well that all those phenomena are referable to spiritual laws, and cannot be understood otherwise. Those who deny the agency of spirits, and fall back on Mesmerism, are unable to tell us what Mesmerism is. When mediums describe distant persons, scenes and events unknown in their normal condition, it is said the phenomena are clairvoyance. But what is clairvoyance? We answer, it is clear-seeing, seeing spiritually, seeing as spirits see, measurably independent of external senses. The natural way for a man to see while in the body is in the use of the natural, material organ of sight, the eye. If one sees with the eye closed, he demonstrates the existence of a spiritual sense of sight, and that this spiritual sense can act measurably independent of the external organ; and if it can act independent of the external organ, may it not likewise exist independent of the material? So with all other of man's senses. There are spiritual senses in perfect correspondence with the material. The phenomena of Mesmerism demonstrate that all these senses have manifestations at times independent of the material body, and if they manifest themselves independent of the body, they may likewise exist independent of the same, and become organized in a spirit form after the body is thrown aside in the transition of death. The manifestations of these spiritual senses demonstrate the existence of spiritual laws and elements higher than the material plane; and all clairvoyants, at times, admit the agency of those laws and elements, and the aid of spirits out of the body. Moreover, every clairvoyant subject throughout the world, even before the advent of Spiritualism at Hydesville, in 1847–48, predicted the coming of this spiritual era, and recognized the agency of departed human spirits in opening intercourse between earth and heaven, and in the inauguration of all the late phenomena of the age. We claim all the mesmeric phenomena, then, as only initiatory to more tangible spiritual phenomena. Many of the spiritual phenomena, however, transcend any of the mesmeric occurring before the advent of modern Spiritualism. Under the auspices of Mesmerism most of the subjects were affected only as they came under the influence of operators or in sympathy with persons of positive minds. Spiritual mediums, however, pass under influence without coming in communication or contact with persons in the form. Under the auspices of Mesmerism, no physical manifestations occurred like the rappings or the moving of ponderable bodies without machinery or human contact. No phase of Mesmerism ever demonstrated that persons had the will-power to produce the slightest sound like the rappings, or to move the smallest ponderable body; nor that the human system is charged with any magnetic or electric force capable of being projected by the will to the production of these physical phenomena, unless under the direction of spirits. Nor has it ever been demonstrated that there is any force or element in nature adequate to account for the intelligence accompanying the phenomena in question. The intelligence accompanying these phenomena, when seriously questioned, is invariably attributed to the agency of spirits; and we are bound to accept this solution until we are able to receive some explanation more solid and satisfactory.

Our aim in this Plain Guide is to present all the pro and con, in a style adapted to the appreciation of the humblest minds. We make no effort to appear very profound, scientific or philosophical in any technical sense. Many of the attempts to explain and defend Spiritualism have been altogether too elaborate, speculative and metaphysical to prove adapted to the hearts and understandings of the masses of the people. Something more than fine-spun theories, or lofty flights into the unknown, or long, elaborate speculations, are needed. Plain facts, direct appeals, positive evidences, common sense, unvarnished arguments, are demanded. The people need weapons capable of being used on every occasion of attack, that they may always be prepared to "give a reason for the hope that is in them, with meekness and fear," or rather with wisdom. To this end we adapt this Plain Guide, and those who read to the close will find themselves furnished with hints covering over the entire ground. And let it be remembered that we do not write merely to cater to the critical student of spiritual lore, but rather for those who need the arguments and evidences with which initiated Spiritualists are already familiar.

It has been intimated that Mesmerism and all kindred phenomena belong to the introductory phases of Spiritualism. Most of those who were at first mesmeric subjects are now acknowledged as spirit mediums; and most of those once regarded as powerful mesmeric operators are now either mediums or open advocates of Spiritualism. Dr. J. B. Dods, once considered among the most successful magnetizers, now declares the powers he then claimed as his own were only delegated by spirits. The writer's experiments in Mesmerism, nearly twenty years ago, satisfied us that there were persons and intelligences in a measure beyond mortal agency. It is commonly said that the magnetizer has control over his subjects. But the most experienced operators must admit, after all, that they have little or no absolute control over their subjects; that all they have to do is to find certain persons and conditions, establish confidence between themselves and their subjects, open as it were a sympathetic communication, give their subjects the cue with which to begin, and successful experiments will then follow without the operator's exercising any positive will or control, or imparting anything like a subtle magnetic fluid. In a manner somewhat similar, spirits seek to establish confidence with mediums, open communication, and impart influences acting on the individuality of their mediums. There are double reasons for our taking this ground, in seeming conflict with the position often assumed by believers. First, we here discover that mesmeric operators are not the authors of the powers so often ascribed to them. They are impelled to acknowledge laws, powers, and intelligences beyond their control. Second, to admit that either mesmerizers or spirits have anything like absolute control over mortals, would be to rob us of our individuality and responsibility. Man's will must be left inviolate. It were mischievous and dangerous to place us beneath the arbitrary control of beings either in or out of the form. If it is said that mesmeric subjects and mediums are often influenced in spite of their own wills, we reply, it is only seemingly so. There is an outer and inner consciousness, an outer and inner will. Persons may sometimes seem to exercise an external resistance, but after all there is a yielding of the internal will under the influence of higher spiritual powers. The man in the Gospel at first refused to go and do the bidding of conscience, but conscience at last conquered, and he went. Saul started out for Damascus in opposition to Christian Spiritualism, but his external will was overcome on the way, by powerful physical and spiritual appeals, and he at last yielded to the Christ-principle of his nature. Sometimes skeptical persons sit down in circles with the most persistent opposition. But there are spiritual needs and spiritual elements in their natures, and before they are aware they find themselves coming under spiritual influences; their skepticism is overcome; their better natures are called into activity; they come into conscious communion with spirit friends; they are prepared to witness the most astounding manifestations; they yield to those silent, subtle influences which must be experienced to be realized and believed, and are ready to exclaim, "Lord, I believe; help thou mine unbelief!"

Many persons seem to seek the most difficult causes to account for the phenomena, rather than fall back on the simplest laws which spirits themselves are endeavoring to unfold. Nothing is more common than to attribute spiritual manifestations to electricity. We were in company with three other men and two women, besides the little girl medium, who was about thirteen years old. A large table was in the centre of the room, and two large fluid lamps were burning brightly. We could all see clearly; could see over and under the table; we were all sure no machinery, no human hands or feet were in contact with the table. In answer to various questions, the table was moved entirely free from the floor, and gave unquestionable manifestations of a power and an intelligence entirely beyond all human agency. Every person in the room, with the exception of one man, was satisfied that spirits were the authors of the phenomena. This man endeavored to dispose of the whole thing by exclaiming, "Oh, I believe it's electricity!" And yet he knew little or nothing about electricity. It is the same with most of those persons who are continually seeking to evade Spiritualism by referring its phenomena to some unknown electrical laws. Those who have experimented most and studied most profoundly are the least inclined to boast of proficiency in being able to solve all mysteries by referring to magnetism, galvanism or electricity. What is electricity? Prof. Faraday says, "There was a time when I thought I knew someting about the matter; but the longer I live and the more carefully I study the subject, the more convinced I am of my total ignorance of the nature of electricity." What a rebuke to the uninitiated multitudes who are so loud and positive in their assumptions concerning the causes of the spiritual phenomena! *They* know all about these things, and yet, perhaps, have not spent an hour in study or investigation. The eminent Prof. Hare spent a lifetime in the investigation of electricity and other subtle forces in nature, and yet, when he sat down at the table of Mrs. Gourlay, a single moment sufficed to overthrow all his theories of material science, and he was compelled to admit the existence of spiritual forces mightier and more wonderful than all material things. The celebrated Grecian orator and philosopher, Demosthenes, through a modern medium, is represented as having said, "Had you asked me concerning God, a thousand years ago, I could have told you all about him; but now, after I have walked the highway of celestial worlds for more than two thousand years, I am so far lost and overpowered amid the splendors of Infinitude, I can say nothing. Height on height beyond the penetration of finite vision, I see the dim outlines of a deitific universe; I feel the flood-tides of Divinity flowing down through all the avenues of my immortal being. I hear peal after peal of archangel eloquence ringing through the endless archways of the empyrean, evermore sounding into my ears the name of God, God, God! I am silent, dumb!"

If such are the wonders, the glories and mysteries appearing to the vision of those who have walked the eternal world for centuries, with what humility may man walk in this finite sphere of existence. Search as profoundly as we may in the arcana of nature, still we know little or nothing of the primary elements or forces with which we are surrounded. What is mind, what is soul, what is spirit, what is electricity? Take the simplest rapping, table-tipping, or the moving of the smallest ponderable body without human contact, and we can find no law or element in nature to account for the manifestation, without admitting the agency of spirits. Rutter says: "Some of the conditions which we call the *laws* of electricity and of magnetism are known. These may not improperly be viewed as their habits or modes of action, the ways in which they manifest themselves to some of our senses. But of what they consist, whether they possess properties peculiar to themselves and independent of the ponderable substances with which we have ever found them associated, or in what respects they differ from light and heat and from each other, is beyond the range of our experience, and probably of our comprehension."

These concessions of the profoundest students of nature may serve to check our conceits and assumptions. After the spiritual phenomena have been subjected to all the severest scientific tests, they still remain as indisputable facts, in no manner accountable without conceding the agency of spirits. "Try the spirits."

Objection 5. It is objected that Spiritualism is at war with all social, civil and religious laws, and advocates unrestrained lust, liberty, anarchy, individual sovereignty, a reckless unconcern for the rights of others, and an entire disregard of all the rules of morality and religion.

Answer. This objection is not stated in the precise language commonly used by our opposing brethren, but we believe this is the substance. Doubtless there are many honest persons who really fear Spiritualism has the above tendencies. But before considering this objection in detail, our first business is to know what is truth. Are the facts of Spiritualism well authenticated? Are its witnesses reliable? Is there a spirit-world peopled by departed human spirits who now hold tangible intercourse with mortals? Are those spirits, myriads of whom are supposed to have been on the road of progress for ages, now able to impart influences and inspirations to aid man in unfolding his spiritual nature and in leading a true, pure, noble life? Are these celestials endowed with power to sympathize with mortals, and to open views of man's true nature, duty, dignity and destiny? Are they the messengers of God, sent to inaugurate the kingdom of heaven on earth, or rather to open a new dispensation of that kingdom, in order that man may realize his true relations to his fellow-man, his relations to God and the universe and the celestial worlds, and thereby learn obligations which rise higher than those growing out of false, temporal and transient relations? These are the most momentous questions with which to begin. If Spiritualism be true, according to the millions of current manifestations and several millions of living reliable witnesses, then we need have no fears as to its tendency; for truth cannot otherwise than tend to good, however radical and alarming certain changes and revolutions may appear. When the fact was first announced that the world was round instead of flat, and turned over on its axis once in twenty-four hours, the multitude, unacquainted with the law of gravitation, and accustomed only to the idea that all things stood still on a dead level, grew exceedingly alarmed, and declared if the world was to turn round, according to the teachings of the new astronomical innovators, everything on the surface of the earth, houses and inhabitants, rivers and oceans, would speedily spill off into space and cause universal chaos. But nobody, after all, was injured. The globe kept on its course as from the beginning. Some of the inhabitants were temporarily frightened, but the order of the universe remained undisturbed.

So with the newly unfolded truths of this spiritual dispensation. Radical changes in belief and practice are announced as we come to learn anew, in the light of Spiritualism, that the moral world does not stand still, a dead level cut off from other worlds, but is moving onward according to the law of progress, and that man is called on to arise anew in recognition of laws and relations higher than those recognized by the multitudes in the past. Our opposing brethren are fearful of dangerous results. Why? Because they judge from false, old, conservative stand-points. Despots are fearful of republicans, because they judge from the stand-point of despotism. Catholics are fearful of Protestants, because they judge from the stand-point of Catholicism. Evangelical, Orthodox Christians are fearful of Universalists and Unitarians, because they judge from the stand-point of Orthodoxy. Anti-Spiritualists are fearful of Spiritualists, because they judge from the stand-point of theological and material conservatism. Demagogues are fearful of reformers, because they judge from the stand-point of demagogueism.

Now we do not deny the radical and revolutionary tendency of Spiritualism. It lays the axe at the root of the tree of all existing evils, errors, and falsities found in churches, governments, institutions, laws, and customs. It recognizes the individual man, every human being bearing the impress of God, as superior to all these last-named externals. But it does not ignore anything good or true in the existing order of things. There are eternal principles at the foundation of all existing laws, religions, customs, and institutions. We seek to fathom and preserve these principles, while we ignore their abuses as seen in the church, state, and society. We assert the doctrine of individual rights and liberties; but we ignore political parties which cater to corruption, and abuse their powers. We recognize the obligations of religion, of our relations to God and man, but we ignore all priestly authorities which seek to dictate and lord it over the conscience. We recognize true conjugal laws, and the holy relations existing between the sexes, but we do not regard all the present marital laws as perfect. There are spiritual opponents who appear utterly reckless in their accusations, though charity would impel us to believe them free from any wilful evil or misrepresentation. Judged from their stand-point, we may seem to be involved in awful errors, and in danger of present and everlasting ruin. But in all seriousness we ask, What are the principles and the practices of Spiritualists? We do not claim to be perfect in either, but we *do* claim freedom from the grossest charges brought against us.

It is charged that many mediums, lecturers, and believers are utterly reckless of social laws and obligations; have broken up old relations; run counter to popular customs, conventionalities, and laws; while husbands, wives, children, and whole neighborhoods, have been involved in scandalous evils. It is possible that some such cases have been known among Spiritualists. But have not such cases been common among all classes? Popular church members, and even ministers and their families, have been frequently involved in social scandals of the most outrageous character. But we do not regard it just to attribute these evils to Christianity, nor would it be just or generous to hold all church members and all ministers responsible for the guilt in which some have been involved. It is said that Spiritualists attempt to gloss over and apologize for these things, and uphold mediums, lecturers, and believers. In reply, we remark, our philosophy teaches us to look into causes, search out the secret springs of all action, study human nature with all its passions and affections, and pronounce no uncharitable judgment, no withering curses, no anathemas on the heads of alleged offenders. If we seek to shield our brothers and sisters from reproach and slander, it is because we know God and ministering spirits enjoin this duty, and bid us remember we are all more or less exposed to imperfections. If we do not pronounce judgment on those whom the world esteems guilty, it is because we have been taught to remember how utterly incapable mortals are to judge their fellow-mortals. If we do not adopt the world's standard of law and morality, it is because higher and purer laws are unfolded in the light of the opening heavens. But how is it when scandalous social and sexual evils are found in popular churches and society? Are there no efforts to conceal these evils? Fashionable society seeks to throw the veil of concealment and conventionalism over the most enormous corruptions. Licentiousness runs riot in hot-beds of luxury and aristocracy, and glittering gold covers the Stygian sty from the gaze of the world. Good heavens! could we only lift the veil, and look into society, and see it as it is! And could we only lift the veil that covers the sanctuaries of religion, what scenes would startle the world! If any foundation for scandal can be found among Spiritualists, the alleged details are unblushingly blazoned to the ends of the earth, and are cited as positive proofs of the dangerous tendency of Spiritualism. But if a popular clergyman is suspected, all possible efforts are made to conceal the facts; and if facts are established and proclaimed to the world, it is poor human nature that is at fault, and not the clergyman's religion. Were a Spiritualist involved in the very same things, Spiritualism would be responsible as the cause.

In all these cases of social evil it will be found that causes lie far back of all religious faiths or professions, and arise from bad organizations, imperfect educations, and unfortunate conditions. It is certain that Spiritualism does not teach men and women to violate the laws of chastity, but rather to cultivate pure and harmonic affections in communion with the holy dead who have passed beyond the sensuous veil. It teaches the sacredness of sexual relations, of all true marriage, and permits no licentious violations of conjugal bonds. It insists that no true marriage can exist, and no sexual intercourse can be tolerated in the sight of Heaven, unless pure mutual love is the basis, and parties are congenially mated. Are these teachings dangerous or licentious? What are the teachings of society, of custom, of human laws, of the conservative churches?

The writer once fell into conversation with a popular clergyman who not only denounced Spiritualism as a whole, but especially deprecated the free discussions it tolerated in regard to social questions, maintaining that social and sexual relations had nothing to do with the spiritual. We confessed unfeigned astonishment, as well as deep shame and mortification, at a position like this taken by a man claiming to be an apostle of the immaculate Nazarene, and a spiritual teacher and pastor over a large, popular city church, on a salary of over two thousand dollars. In view of all the licentiousness found in false marriages, all the sexual abuses and corruptions found outside of marriage, the unrestrained lusts and indulgences into which thousands are running rampant to ruin, this clergyman had no voice of warning to lift, and no efforts to put forth in behalf of social or sexual regeneration! Great God! and is this the position of the thousands of salaried priests who claim to be shepherds of humanity? No marvel that ravenous wolves of lust are running riot amid their flocks, and society is rent with the despairing cry of bleeding and dying victims. What are churches, what are ministers, doing? Is the position of this popular clergyman an illustration of the loose position occupied by the masses of the clergy and the laity? Let their words, deeds, and publications answer.

Spiritualists and other reformers are agitating these social questions, and they insist on the need and the possibility of spiritual regeneration. They insist on the necessity of recognizing spiritual laws and adaptations in all sexual or conjugal relations; and they pronounce all marriages and all sexual cohabitings as false and infernal, unless they are based on spiritual affections and are under the purer influences of celestial harmony. But churches and ministers seem united in denouncing the agitation of these momentous themes, and they raise the mad and slanderous cry of "Free love! free love!" only for the purpose of disguising the corruptions over which they stand blushing with mock modesty and dumb with cowardice. It is folly and madness, is it, to lift the voice of reform? So thought the scribes, Pharisees and chief priests, ages ago, when Jesus came rolling thunders over Jerusalem. And modern priesthoods and synagogues are slumbering over the same volcanic fires of gehenna. And when any outbreak of social evil is manifested, what is the course adopted, and what is the remedy suggested, by these modern Pharisees? They lift up their hands and roll their eyes with holy horror, and deal out the direst damnation on all who are suspected of the least deviation from conventional standards. Little or no effort is made to redeem the unfortunate, or to strike at the root of their alleged evils. It is virtually contended that the sexual relations are merely sensual, and must be regulated by mechanical laws, restraints, and popular conventionalities, and cannot be reached or controlled by moral, religious, and spiritual influences; and so the multitudes are left to rush on in the blindness of lust, lost to all those higher laws which should govern men and women as immortal beings. God knows we have need of some startling revolutions to break up this wide-spread state of apathy and corruption, and we believe the angel hosts are now inaugurating a dispensation of radical agitations preparatory to radical social reformations.

We dislike everything in the form of wholesale charges against the church, the clergy, or any other class of humanity. None are totally corrupt, either in or out of the church. Some ministers are among the purest, noblest reformers and philanthropists, and many church members are praying and laboring with Christ-like devotion for the eradication of social evils and the establishment of that celestial kingdom in which men and women shall become true and holy in all their intercourse and relations. Yet, after all, the position of the popular church is such we are compelled to hold it responsible for the most glaring falsities and corruptions of the age. Measurably regardless of honest private convictions, established principles, and true relations, it is the present policy of all these popular churches to influence men and women to come in and take their place and position among the fashionable throngs. It is of but little consequence what they believe or how they live, if they maintain a respectable appearance, assume the form of religion, preserve a politic silence, and pay up for their pews. Heretics, infidels, atheists, libertines, prostitutes, misers, skinflints, whitewashed hypocrites and knaves, can pass with impunity beneath the garb of sanctimony. Now, what is the tendency of this policy? It is in direct encouragement of spiritual adultery,—a sin which Jesus denounced as worse than sexual adultery. The scribes, Pharisees and priests were guilty of this religious adultery, and he denounced them as hypocrites and whited sepulchres, filled with all manner of corruption, while he pronounced no woe on the woman of Samaria, or the woman taken in sexual adultery. The popular church claims to be the holy church of God, and if so, its covenant should be regarded as the most sacred and solemn; and whoever becomes connected with the church should enter it as though entering the most holy marriage covenant; their faith should be firm and clear, their love pure and true, and their lives exemplary. If they enter the church, or stay there under any other conditions, their relations are false; they are practising a lie; they are living in spiritual adultery; they are prostituting the soul, and are guilty of a crime more heinous than the prostitution of the body. And all who are involved in this false, unholy alliance, priest and people, are held more or less responsible. If any party is more guilty than the other, it is the party acting the part of the brazen-faced prostitute, who goes out into the streets and seeks to entice and allure those who are outside: "Come into our church; join our fashionable and respectable throng; assume the form of marriage with the church; no matter whether you are truly one with us or not, take your place and position in our midst; and no matter whether the relation is true or not, it is politic, it is expedient, it is reputable." Is not this the alluring church logic of to-day? Who dare deny it, as profligate as it is? And thousands are wallowing in this cesspool of spiritual debauchery, perfectly conscious of the falsity and corruption of their relations. And when anything is said about breaking up and coming out from these false relations an awful alarm is raised; the church is in danger; it will not answer to disturb the existing state of things; the peace of society and the church will be broken up, and what will become of all the old obligations, interests, and associations? And this same alarming logic is carried out and applied to social, sexual, or marriage relations. Old covenants must be maintained at all hazards, though they are as false and rotten as Hades. God save the church! God save the sexes! Now, as spiritualist reformers, we insist on the need of revolution and reorganization in all these relationships. Whoever lives in a false church relation is guilty of adulterating the holy spiritual temple of Almighty God, and whoever lives in false sexual communion prostitutes the divinest functions of the human soul and body.

All the social evils existing for ages, and becoming more and more apparent in the light of to-day, are caught up by the corrupt prejudice and suspicion of spiritual opponents, and flaunted in the faces of Spiritualists as indications of the dangerous tendency of Spiritualism. Some of the secular papers in central New York, some years ago, took up the social misfortunes of several persons in Utica and vicinity, with mean insinuations about "free love," "affinity," etc., as though gloating in glee over the least shadow of a chance for scandalization. Now, in the name of justice and humanity, we ask what Spiritualism had to do with the unfortunate incompatibilities of the once married persons in question? We knew something of the antecedents of these individuals. The men most prominent as Spiritualists were married according to orthodox law, and not under the auspices of Spiritualism. The difficulties leading to separation from their wives were not caused by Spiritualism. We do not claim the right to judge as to whether those difficulties were adequate to justify a dissolution of the marriage relation. In one case, however, we know the husband might have obtained a divorce according to the most rigid law, but his Spiritualism taught him to shield the unfaithful partner, and, according to the Jewish law, "put her away privily." The most flagrant and shameful marriage disruptions are constantly occurring outside of the spiritual ranks, but no notice is taken of these to throw the awful responsibility on a corrupt state, church and society; yet when Spiritualists are involved, an attempt is made to cast reflection on the whole body of believers, and to impeach our sentiments. This course of vilification and slander is too outrageous for endurance. And some professed Spiritualists are egregiously at fault in joining the scandalmongering multitude in unqualified denunciation, and in manifesting an unwise anxiety to exonerate our cause from blame. It is hypocritical nonsense to pretend that all professed Spiritualists are perfectly happy and harmonious in their marriage relations, and entirely exempt from marital disruptions. Many of them assumed marriage under the falsities existing for ages, and those falsities often appear so infernal in the light of new unfoldings of life and love, endurance becomes impossible, while there is no hope of reformation in view. But Spiritualism teaches them to bear and forbear as long as there is the least ray of hope, and thousands of unhappy partners have become harmonized after all other means have failed, while thousands more are continuing to bear their burdens with heroic fortitude, in spite of all discord. But there are those whose condition seems beyond all hope. There are husbands and wives, good men and good women in their own way, perhaps, whose natures are so illy adapted, heaven only knows in what domestic hells they live, and heaven only can judge their cause. It is the most solemn and fearful ground in which mortals can stand. We abominate everything like "free love" as it is popularly understood; we hate the term "affinity;" we would warn men and women against either hasty unions or dissolutions; and yet in heaven's name, and in behalf of bleeding humanity, would we raise our loudest protest against this sitting in scandalous judgment and dealing out unmitigated damnation over hearts and homes already crushed beneath insufferable agonies. As spiritual reformers and philosophers it becomes us to stand aloof from the denouncing multitude, and rebuke every word uttered with any other spirit than that of fraternal sympathy for the unfortunate; and when a brother or sister is assailed, whether in our ranks or not, let wisdom guide us in seeking to understand all the causes and conditions involved, all the trials and struggles endured, all the hidden springs of action which lie open only to angel eyes; let love prompt words and deeds of sympathy and protection, and charity hush our lips into eternal silence! Unless this is the course adopted by Spiritualists, as there is a just God in heaven, and his angels are ministering spirits of mercy, the spiritual cause will sink down into the deepest cesspools of infamy, and become an impotent auxiliary to these corrupt standards dealing slander and death.

Spiritualists would have been utterly routed, and Spiritualism annihilated, had a hundredth part of the alarming rumors which have gone abroad proved true. Every prominent medium, lecturer, and believer in the land has been reported as guilty of things most startling and astounding, if not outrageous and infernal; and some have, doubtless, proved themselves culpable of violating conservative ideas of right and propriety. But why take any alarm? "Offences must needs come," in order that we may learn lessons of wisdom and humility, and stand on our own merits and on truth alone, without depending on the reputation of others or even on the opinions which the world may entertain of ourselves. An eminent reformer has said that men and women are not prepared for the work of progress until their reputation has become blasted and they have gone through the fiery ordeals of suffering. We may not seek to make ourselves martyrs, nor glory in aught that seems offensive in the eyes of the world; but if we are accounted worthy to suffer for conscience sake or in obedience to the divinest intuitions of our own souls, the blessings of God and humanity shall fall on us, and legions of angels shall encompass our pathway, though thorns pierce our feet, and thunders break over our heads in alarm.

We are often beset with scandalmongers and gossip-whisperers who are everlastingly on the scent of some fancied sins and enormities, of which nobody ever cares a farthing, or finds any tangible foundation. They fatten on fancying they have found something to be fastened on persons who are before the public. They delight in raking up the past, and hang with ecstasy on the skeleton of a rumor which had the ghost of an existence years ago. They shake their heads and heave dolorous sighs of sorrow. Poor mortals! how oppressed they are; and they show how bad they feel by running off and retailing their feelings to everybody they meet. Shame! Hold that member which is set on fire of hell. Judge not. Who cares how many devils Mary Magdelene had once, if they were only cast out at last. Take men and women for what they are to-day, and for the divinity within them which promises more to-morrow. If any wrong is done, help right it, but do not run and bore anybody with your blab. Heaven save us from sneaking Judases and sin-scenting Pharisees!

We do not ask you what you have heard, suspected, imagined or conjectured, or somebody has reported, whispered or hinted; but what do you know about it? Suppose you do know some things which seem not in accordance with your standard of the right; do you know all the causes involved? Have you gone down deep into the souls of those whom you censure, and are you fully prepared to sit in judgment? Oh, brothers and sisters, let us put ourselves in each other's places, and ask Heaven to judge us as we judge others. If in our sorrows and sufferings we would call on angel friends to sympathize with us, let us first sympathize with those who are around us.

What is the relation between Spiritualism and the so-called radicalisms and reforms agitating the age? Without setting up any sort of authority over others, to abridge their liberty, to silence their convictions of the right and true, or to suspend their reason, we regard Spiritualism as unfolding those laws of human progress which underlie all true reform, and aim at a radical revolution of all that is false in the existing condition of church, state, and society. But we advocate no violence, no ruthless aggression, no carnal warfare, no pulling down of the old until some preparation for the new is made, no upbuilding of new sects, parties or societies to compromise the soul, but the unfolding of the divinity of the individual man and woman as more sacred than all false, external institutions. While we grant to all their rights, we insist that individuals alone shall be held responsible for the use and application they make of Spiritualism. We mean to be conservative enough to retain everything of the good and true in the past and present, and radical enough to keep up with the most progressive ideas and agitations of the age, while we seek to exercise all possible wisdom and discretion as to what conscience and humanity demand. Let us not become unduly sensitive in regard to certain reforms, though we may guard against an undue radicalism which is in danger of running a good cause into the ground. Paul spoke of those who had a "zeal not according to knowledge." We should call such persons "fanatical radicals." We have samples of "fanatical radicalism" in every department of human progress; yet, after all, they have a use. Seething brains are better than conservative, besotted numskulls. Extravagance is vastly better than laziness. A crazy man is preferable to a dotard old fool or a muddled Pharisee. Men had better die of cracked brains than of a dry rot. Give us any kind of radicalism rather than the stench of stagnation. Heaven save us from a set of men and women who are in danger of turning to powder-post and blowing away.

The widest and deepest agitation on social and other reform questions has only commenced, and yet an intense interest is felt everywhere. The discussion on marriage and divorce between Horace Greeley and Robert Dale Owen in the New York Tribune, some time ago, excited attention throughout the country. Conservative pulpits and presses are loud and alarming in warnings against Spiritualism as the leading cause of all the radical and revolutionary tendencies of the age. If disruptions ensue between husbands and wives, Spiritualism is at fault; while the well-known facts are, that those disruptions are wholly referable to pre-existing antagonisms and incompatibilities concerning which the parties alone may have been able to judge. If persons form passional attachments independent of the laws, customs and order of society, and fall into the lowest depths of sensualism, anything but the real cause is assigned. Again and again have Spiritualists protested against being held responsible for any tendencies of a licentious nature. Spiritualism advocates no freedom in sexual relationships except that which is based first on spiritual purification and the law of conjugal harmony. All the loftiest spirits communicating with mortals, and all the leading writers, representatives and mediums, are uniform in denouncing everything like freedom in miscellaneous sexual intercourse. They advocate the monogamic idea of marriage, or that true marriage consists in the harmonic union of one man with one woman; that such unions are sacred, inviolable, indissoluble; that all violations of this conjugal law are fraught with incalculable mischief and loathsome abominations. In regard to discordant legal marriages, they are slow to pronounce judgment. They believe, however, that our conflicting laws, customs and institutions are unable to remedy many of these evils, and in the name of humanity they call for reforms allowing some rights and liberties beyond those now granted. They contend that some of the worst forms of licentiousness exist under the cloak of legal marriage; and where such false marriages exist, compelling either party to a life of sexual and infernal degradation, all heaven and earth demand some remedy. But they advise no dissolutions except those which are inevitable, and are urged by all the most solemn obligations involving the life, liberty and happiness of the parties involved. They advocate no freedom of the affections tending to miscellaneous affinities, or the formation of loose passional attachments, or the license of any kind of merely sensual gratification. While they recognize a free, fraternal love based on spiritual laws, they are distinct in repudiating everything like sexual freedom, and insist on the law of conjugal, monogamic purity and continence. Spiritualists seek to prove faithful in proclaiming none but those lofty sentiments inculcating the need of true marriage, pure conjugal love, monogamic continence, a rigid chastity between men and women, the sacredness of all genuine marital relations, the exclusiveness of sexual intercourse, and the inauguration of that spiritual kingdom in which men and women shall be prepared for the freedom of a holy angel life. Where the calm, the rational, the religious, the philosophical and Christ-like spirit prevails, with no passionate, personal, pharisaic or railing disposition, the agitation of these momentous themes must inevitably tend to the elucidation of clearer perceptions of duty and reform, and the exercise of a broader charity in behalf of those who are now liable to fall under the ban of a false popular proscription.

While the love-relations between the sexes are regarded as the basis of all the divinest joys and hopes of man and woman, we may not wonder that the marriage and divorce controversy excites the broadest and deepest interest. The discussion in the New York Tribune; the Key and Sickles tragedy in Washington; the Gurney case in England; the Burch scandal in Chicago; the numerous suicides, elopements, intrigues and marriage disruptions in every grade of society; the wife and husband murders filling the public prints; the wide-spread hue and cry about "free-loveisms," "affinities," and "passional attractions;" the mobocratic mania manifested in Utica and Syracuse; the systematic slander seeking to fasten all these social outbreaks on Spiritualism; changes in the divorce laws of New York and other States; the agitation of Women's Rights; the movements of socialists, associationists and advocates of individual sovereignty; the decrease of marriages, the increase of sexual incontinence; the discords turning thousands of homes into hells of horror; the sighs and groans of bleeding hearts crushed beneath altars on which blinded love once plighted vows of eternal fidelity, — all these are signs significant of the intense interests involved in sexual and conjugal relationships. Some of these are the topics coming up in almost every social circle where conversation is permitted to take a free turn. Agitation seems inevitable, however unwise and untimely some conservative minds may deem it. Men and women are becoming alive, open and free to discuss whatever relates to human weal or woe. And who shall seek to abridge their rights and liberties? There are proper times, places and persons, and these may not always be selected aright. There are dangerous and unseasonable excitements, but even these, on the whole, are better than stagnation and death. Winds and waves, storms, thunders and lightnings may sometimes topple over feeble fabrics and dash the frailest barks against fearful rocks, while tottering foundations are swept away and wild crashes are heard amid the contending elements. But the air will become purified, and all that is built on solid foundations will stand firm amid the conflict. So with all that is sacred and sound amid these agitations of our age.

Agitation and revolution are inevitable, not only in the political and religious, but in the social relationships of life. The true philosophy of spiritual reform inculcates the duty of seeking first a harmonic unfoldment of our better natures, and then comes the duty of seeking our true relationships to each other; our relations in civil, religious, secular and social life. But Spiritualism teaches us to ignore no obligations we have voluntarily assumed, nor to violate or rupture any solemn compacts within our power to maintain sacred.

We may join a political party or church, or enter into a business copartnership, and at last meet with changes impelling us to withdraw our relationship and see our way out, without incurring any reasonable censure or violating any known obligation. But the case becomes more difficult with men and women entering the marriage compact. More sacred responsibilities are involved, embracing the divinest affections, hopes, joys and interests of a whole life-time, and it may be the offspring of the wedded pair. And who shall determine what cause is adequate to produce a disruption of this solemn compact? Some have contended that the marriage compact when once entered should remain indissoluble without regard to whether the relation is true or false. It is said to be the duty of men and women to suffer, bear, wait, and the reward will at last come, and sometime in eternity they may chance to find their true conjugal relationship. The same counsel might be given to men and women found in other false relations. Should the drunkard and the prostitute be exhorted to maintain resignation in their false course of life? No. And what rule shall apply to those who find themselves in false marriage? State laws specify as to what causes or crimes are adequate to divorce, but no laws, no judges, no mortals can designate certain causes seen and understood by the married pair alone. No crime may be committed by either party; each may be pure, noble, loving, temperate, and to all external appearances happy and well-mated, yet their conjugal adaptation prove so imperfect as to make a hell of their homes, and their false relation anon transform them into demons. Is it the duty of such to remain in this false relation, suffering, sinking, dying, prostituting their divinest sexual natures and conjugal affections, in order to maintain a show of propriety and sustain the reputation of an external institution? God and angels have mercy on all those who dare thus make mock of marriage, and barter soul and body in the shambles of a legalized prostitution!

We may have no specific counsel to offer in regard to cases like these, and yet we cannot avoid certain reflections. Observation and experience are constantly revealing facts which startle us into the duty of taking some decisive ground in advocating the obligation under which men and women are impelled to seek a true life and relation in harmony with the divine conjugal laws of earth and heaven. If they find themselves in false relations which can possibly be improved, harmonized and reconciled in conformity with the obligations they owe themselves, their offspring and the world, or which can be borne without compromising the divinest offices, aims and affections of their being, let them cling to each other like holy martyrs, content to bear, suffer and wait. But if everything is otherwise; if their offspring are being bred in domestic hells; if their own souls and bodies are perpetually subjected to a fruitless martyrdom; if all their holiest affections and aspirations are crushed out amid excruciating and remediless tortures, then let us pray that God, angels, all earth and heaven, lend helping hands and sympathizing hearts to aid them in standing forth freed from the awful manacles of marital incompatibility. And let no mortals judge or condemn them, unless they are first able to penetrate into all the inmost causes of disruption. Angels pity and compassionate, and angels may bless and applaud thousands of such martyr hearts on whom the world pours scorn, scandal and condemnation. The time is fast coming when all these social and affectional relations will be seen in a light higher than they are now seen by the vulgar rabble, who gloat over every rumor of bleeding hearts and ruptured homes; and when men and women who dare to be pure, true and free according to the laws of God and nature, as unfolded by the philoscphy of the spheres, shall stand forth enrolled among the heroic souls of the age.

Spiritualism, understood aright, repudiates the loose passional philosophy attributed to the so-called "free-lovers," and maintains that no attractions are legitimate unless they are based on fraternal or conjugal laws holding supreme control over the sensual and recognizing the monogamic relationship. The contract of marriage is the most sacred and solemn contract on earth, and it should never be ignored for any slight cause or transient "affinities;" should be maintained under the most trying circumstances so long as there is the least prospect of peace and harmony, and so long as the parties can possibly see any good results in view, involving themselves, friends and children. But there are good men and women so unfortunately mismated, and subjected to so many remediless discords, they are under the most solemn obligations to consider what course should be pursued to improve their condition. Their usefulness, happiness, liberty, even life, and, what is more sacred still, their divinest affections, demand a change from that false relation in which they become transformed into demons and find nothing but a domestic hell. There are cases like these where it were impertinent for any other mortals to interfere, counsel, dictate, or condemn. Heaven alone can bear witness to all the anguish hid behind false marriages, and all the holiest aspirations and affections sometimes animating men and women in dissolving the false and seeking the true conjugal relationship. But God and angels forbid that we should ever sanction any dissolutions or changes ignoring obligations within the possibility of human discharge.

There is everything so sacred in the sentiment called LOVE as existing between the sexes, we almost shrink from the attempt to utter our thoughts. The very name of love carries us back to the first, fresh rosy ideals with which life became peopled when youthful hopes shone radiant over all the future. Every true man and woman begins existence with deep heart-longings after some ideal companion of the opposite sex whose entire being shall blend in the harmony of a love, blissful, beatific, complete. The sentiment at first may seem undefined, but sooner or later it unfolds, and seeks after the conjugal mate, with aspirations insatiable and divine. We say divine, because this sentiment originates in the very essence of man's being, and is an element of the All-creative, All-unfolding Spirit which we call God, whose essence is love, in whose image man is moulded. As an evidence of the divinity of love, we know it seeks for nothing short of perfection in the object of its adoration. The immature youth forms his ideal of a mistress. The first girl he meets is fancied to be the one after his own heart. He finds himself mistaken, and perhaps one after another passes before him, each supposed the one destined to fulfil the richest hopes of his being. At last, he is quite sure the ideal is found, and whatever misgivings arise he fancies will readily disappear on entering the marriage relation. But alas, in the multitude of instances, a few months or years of serious experience in marriage serve more to reveal incompatibilities which had been concealed during courtship, than to reveal the ideal perfections thrown by each party around the other. It is a lamentable yet undeniable fact that comparatively few, in the earthly marriage relation, ever realize the perfect harmony and happiness at first anticipated. They begin with a false estimate of the relations of the present life and the state of wedlock. They fancy perfect love, perfect bliss may be realized; forgetful that the perfect can come only after long labors, trials, suffering, and if attained to any degree in this state of existence, is only a foretaste of the future and eternal.

Now, were love merely a sensuous, animal instinct, with nothing divine and infinite in its nature, it might become satisfied with sensual possession, as in the case with brutes. But not so with the true man and woman. There are manifold needs demanded by love; needs embracing the entire being; and unless all these are perfectly satisfied, there is an inevitable yearning. It is the divine and infinite element of Godhood in man seeking after the ideal love needed to make existence complete. It is the great prophecy, the beautiful dream, the godlike aspiration, the roseate hope beginning in the inmost heart of all human souls, and reaching out over an entire universe, peopling eternity with Edens of primeval glory, beauty, beatitude and perfection.

Spiritualism inquires into the legitimate offices, the uses of love. We can find no satisfactory answer in the current socialistic reforms and agitations of the day.

The "free-love" philosophy covertly developed in French socialism half a century ago, imported to New York, and culminating in Mr. and Mrs. Drs. Nichols, if understood at all, is deemed too sensualistic. And yet no men and women have been so much slandered and misunderstood as those of the Brisbane, Andrews, Lazarus and Nicholas school. As unwise and radical as they may have been considered, they never advocated miscellaneous sexual indulgence. The substance of their philosophy is that there should be a condition of purity and culture in which men and women might live perfectly natural and free, without the intervention of external laws, institutions, and false conventionalities. We believe Stephen Pearl Andrews and Dr. Nichols were among the first to identify this philosophy with Spiritualism, which has no more to do with it than Solomon's several hundred wives had to do with primitive Christianity. Since the effort of Dr. Nichols and wife to saddle Spiritualism with free-love, and their signal break-down and backing off into the Papal church, various other attempts have been made with similar success, though some of them appeared exceedingly insidious. Certain men and women, unfortunate in their marriage relations and angular in their proclivities, have found the spiritual name and some spiritual ideas very convenient for them to use as a cloak to cover other purposes inexpedient to reveal except to the initiated. They talk largely of "freedom," "individuality," "rights," "social reform," etc., all of which may sound well enough, but when you come to learn their meaning, if you are so successful as to worm it out of them, you find they are where you little thought at first. Ask them if they are free-lovers, and you will get an equivocal answer. Some of these persons are prowling over the land like vultures and vampires, and the spiritual public scents them out. Some of them, in male attire, have been "the abomination of desolation," and the slime of the serpent has marked their track.

We have nothing to say against any legitimate social reform. With our whole heart we bid God-speed to the many noble men and women who are seeking to redeem humanity from the accursed wrongs arising from our false social, civil and sectarian institutions. Let the false church, with all its hollow forms, horrible dogmas and infernal practices, rock beneath the thunders of the reform rostrum. Let the state tremble in view of its Draco laws and its corrupt demagogueism. Let woman's rights be agitated, and her wrongs be redressed. Let false social customs, opinions and prejudices, and oppressive marital laws and relations, be discussed. That there are glaring evils and errors in all these, is fast coming to light, and never more clearly than in the light of modern Spiritualism. But Spiritualism does not create these evils, it only reveals them. The more spiritual minded men and women become, the more sensitive they grow; and unless they are well balanced, they are liable to rush into extremes of lawlessness worse than their first estate. The evils and errors of which we complain in our social, civil and religious institutions, do not originate in institutions; they only culminate there; they arise from the individual imperfections of humanity. Let all our false codes, creeds and customs be abolished to-day, still evils and errors would exist, unless the individuals composing state, church and society become radically reformed. That these institutions stand in the way of many who might otherwise reform, is an undeniable fact; yet, on the other hand, these institutions are temporarily expedient to check the multitude who need external restraints, and are not yet prepared for the highest plane of freedom and progress. The few who are prepared must therefore become martyrs before the outcries of the unprepared many. The remedy, then, for existing evils and errors is not in the immediate abolition of institutions, but in individual effort; and when the majority of individuals shall have attained a plane of freedom and progress above the need of institutions, then the latter will become either abolished, modified or superseded by the higher divine law written by the finger of God on the tablets of the human soul.

While the question of individual freedom is widely agitated in the church and state, it is not surprising to find it likewise agitated in the social circle. The evils and errors found manifest in laws and creeds have crept into the heart, the holiest relations of life, and have prostituted love on the unholy altars of lust, mammon and oppression. At this hour there are more sufferers groaning beneath false social relations, laws, customs and opinions, than beneath civil and sectarian codes. Uncounted thousands are suffering in a silent sorrow and an agony the world never knows; for the heart is a sacred thing, and will often break with unutterable woe rather than reveal its secrets of crushed love, blasted hope, unrequited affection and stifled longings after the soul's ideal. It is terrible to contemplate how many hearts lie bleeding beneath the social altar, whose fair outside is nominally consecrated by church and State, and the unnumbered hearts of the unloved whose sighings can neither seek nor find in popular society those congenial responses essential to the divinest needs of human nature. It is a common custom to allude to these things in a trifling manner, perhaps with a jest, sneer, laugh, curse or contempt. The loving yet unloved, who have found no heart-mates, are too often ridiculed, while their very souls are dying as though stifled within cold, damp sepulchres. Those who are unhappily wedded are almost uniformly condemned without any qualification, and everything that can possibly be conjectured is tortured into the severest reprobation, and made matter of private and public scandal. If open disruption ensues, one party or both are branded with infamy and shame. Yet who really knows anything of the causes at the foundation of all these difficulties? Who is prepared to judge or condemn? We must know the hearts, the entire nature of the parties, and enter the sanctuary of all that pertains to home and the most private, sacred relations of life, before we are qualified to sit in judgment; and when we come to know all and see clearly into the inmost causes, we shall judge as Jesus did the woman of Samaria and the Magdalen whom the Jews would have stoned.

But where is the remedy for these evils? Certainly not in either an immediate change or abrogation of all the laws, customs and opinions regarding our social relations; for a worse state of lust and lawlessness would inevitably ensue, if worse than the present can be imagined. Some of the socialistic schemes of the day doubtless offer important suggestions, and may provide refuge from popular societary wrongs, but they are generally predicated on theories of human perfection scarcely attainable in the present state of existence. Besides, they propose to take the better men and women out of the world where they are most needed; and when thus removed from the evils of the world, the evils must go on uncorrected, and the come-outers enjoy an easy, cosy little heaven, with nothing against which to contend. Too much association weakens individual responsibility and absolute individual sovereignty, contracts fraternal sympathy and benevolence, rendering self-love stronger than love for the neighbor or the conjugal companion. The physiological schools fail to offer an adequate remedy for these social evils. Their scientific and philosophical rules look more to the animal and intellectual development of the race than the affectional, spiritual, immortal. Their aims are laudable as far as they go, but we need something more than a fine breed of animals. Let it not be understood that we are seeking to disparage the labors of physiological reformers like Gall, Spurzheim, the Fowlers, and hosts of others. Their books, pamphlets, periodicals and lectures are doing a primary work of matchless importance. We agree with them as to the necessity of a true physical development, and can have little or no hope for the improvement of humanity without a due regard to the laws of generation and physiological culture. Men and women must have sound, healthy bodies in which to develop true souls. "First, the natural, then the spiritual." But the fault with nearly all existing schools and reforms, is mainly in overlooking or failing to discover the uses, the offices of true love between man and woman. The marriage relation has been regarded one of gain, lust, sensuous pleasure or mere propagation. Now if physical health, sensuous pleasure, and the propagation of the species, are the chief offices of love, then man rises no higher in the scale of being than the brute. If love be divine in its origin and nature, the individual growth and unfolding of the soul towards the divine plane must be among its highest offices, while other uses, however sacred and indispensable, must be regarded subordinate. The Christian world holds Christ as the perfect exemplar, the divine type of humanity. And yet we have no knowledge he was either a father, husband, or sexual lover in any popular sense. He recognized these relations as important, essential, obligatory, yet enjoined a love and sacrifice above all these. He taught a spiritual philosophy pointing to the angel-world as a state beyond transient marriage relations. With Mary, Martha, and Lazarus, he found congenialities his own kindred failed to afford him. His father, mother and brothers were appreciated, but held over him no authority so high as that divine inner consciousness bidding him to do the will of his heavenly Father. His birth, Matthew and Luke say, was under circumstances ignoring formal laws and customs; his life and example were in defiance of popular opinions of decorum and conformity; his gospel radical against existing codes, creeds and conventionalities, and the kingdom he sought to inaugurate was celestial, and in repudiation of all the models offered by earthly states, churches and societies. On these grounds the Bible Communists of Oneida, N. Y., build their faith and practice, and enjoy the reputation of pure-minded, honest people. Let Christ be interpreted and imitated literally, and the orthodox world would find him the chief of a certain kind of free-lovers and radicals. But a spiritual understanding will find significance in his life and teachings, without prostituting them on the plane of lust, license and lawlessness. "Unto the pure all things are pure."

In closing, then, we again briefly recur to the remedy of social evils, without claiming the discovery of any new universal panacea. We can offer no counsels, no systems, no rules susceptible of uniform application; for the specific remedy for every individual case will differ as widely as individuals differ.

We can do no more than advert to general principles, and recommend persons to use their own God-given reason and affection as their guide, seeking first of all to become assured of the purity of their hearts and the integrity of their consciences in the sight of the All-Seeing and the celestial host. The cure must begin with each individual soul. In this age of agitation, we may expect occasional excesses; and those who run into reckless, unwise extremes, breaking over all the bounds of common law and morality, may be regarded with commiseration, as pointing a moral against leaping from the evils of conservatism into those of a rampant radicalism. We may denounce none, but take lessons of wisdom and charity from all. "Offences will come," and come as warnings against unwise courses in seeking to rid ourselves of existing ills, while we may fly to "others we know not of." The lesson has a fearful application to those who are prone to haste either in making or breaking marriage relations. This relation is a unit, and has eternal issues. If mistakes are made in the choice of companions, let the highest wisdom, love and truth seek for harmony where the errors can find no other just remedy or rectification in accordance with the laws of God and humanity.

Spiritualism bids us seek within ourselves for the ideals, and in the angel-world for the types, of a true, social, affectional life. Communion with the beatified and beloved, the good, wise and holy who have passed into the divine land, may aid in unfolding the loftiest ideals of conjugal relationship, and in keeping the heart and life as pure and peaceful as the love of the skies. Let no unhallowed lust or lawless liberty seek shelter beneath the outspread wings of Heaven's descending hosts. Nothing but a fabulous hell or a mundane demonism shall be held responsible for the licentious spawns with which Spiritualism has been besmearingly slandered. True love is no mere animal passion sweltering in sensualism and ending in satiety. Born of heaven, it pours its baptismal tides of divine life into the human heart, till all is pure and clear as the crystal waters of Paradise, on whose placid bosom is mirrored the face of God and angel beauty. Oh, it is a sacred thing to love truly, with all the depth of human tenderness; and sacred are the truly beloved! There is a fraternal, an angelic plane on which all men and women may and should love freely and purely. And when Spiritualism shall have accomplished its mission, this fraternal plane will be recognized, and men and women be trusted as brothers and sisters, regardless of the sham and heartless conventionalities enslaving popular society, and without being exposed to the corrupt and suspicious slanders now so rife against Spiritualists. But let none seek to pervert fraternal love into mere lust. The love we owe all our brothers and sisters is neither sexual nor conjugal, and whoever attempts to play the libertine beneath its mantle will finally become unmasked. The love seeking its ideal companion is special, central and eternal. The beloved one becomes an embodiment of the most perfect conception of earthly and heavenly attractions. All that is lovely, beautiful, adorable and divine, is centred there as the star of duty and destiny. God is incarnate as another Emmanuel in the form, the soul, and heart of the beloved, and we worship in beams of beauty, holiness and bliss, bathing the entire being with transfigured beatitude, and peopling all the universe with scenes and images of seraphic glory. Oh, holy, holy is the altar on which the harmonic man and woman kneel and plight the love of God and eternity! And happy are they whose affectional natures have found their congenial mates for time and forever! But though time bring not the meet companion of your souls, O ye unloved, know ye there is another land where freed spirits shall walk no more entrammelled by the false and fleeting, and the beloved ones wait to crown you home with the bridal chaplets of everlasting love.

Objection 6. It is objected that Spiritualism leads to insanity.

Answer. There are individuals whose organizations predispose them to insanity on whatever subject comes uppermost while they are in certain states of body and mind. Persons have gone mad on money, lands, houses, love, law, religion, everything; yet none propose to abolish these because they are liable to abuse. We have heard of persons said to have been made crazy by Spiritualism, but most of them were reported by foes. We have known of scores made insane and driven to suicide by orthodoxy. The writer had a cousin, a graduate of Yale College, a brilliant, promising young man, who went mad while preaching a future judgment. We performed the mournful duty of accompanying him to the Bloomingdale Lunatic Asylum. He was partially restored, but at last went down desolate to a premature grave. We well remember, in early life, of being aroused at midnight by the wailing despair of a young man, who went wild under the influence of a Methodist hell-fire sermon preached that very night. And we recall the case of a young lady in Lowell, who came to us in the night-time with the mournful story of her reason wrecked under the teachings of orthodoxy. She grew hopeless for a season, and we went with her to the asylum in Concord, N. H. She is now living and resides in Chicago, restored to her right mind by Spiritualism. Throughout the country, in asylums and out, are innumerable victims of insanity, wrecked by popular orthodoxy. No man or woman can really believe the doctrine of endless torment without being made crazy. To realize a God of almighty wrath ruling in thunder-clouds over head, with bolts of perdition uplifted to hurl millions of shrieking souls down deep into abysses of flaming damnation, there to howl on forever amid torturing fiends, were enough to dethrone the mightiest reason, and send its victims to rave in maniac chains or plunge despairingly into the suicide's grave, in spite of the "canon against self-slaughter fixed by the Everlasting." And yet the advocates of this dogma, which for ages has been slaughtering its thousands of human beings, have the effrontery to stand up in their pulpits and deal denunciations against the alleged tendencies of Spiritualism, without giving one solitary reason to sustain their slanders. Well, "let the heathen rage, and the people imagine vain things."

Strange reports are constantly current concerning Spiritualists. Mediums are stark mad, and believers are shattered in intellect or the subjects of demoniac possession.

Various signs are observed as indicative of the lunacy of Spiritualists. We have an anecdote in illustration. In Niles, N. Y., a good friend, named James Beegle, for some time had been subject to powerful spiritual influences, but they were always of a harmless, though sometimes of an eccentric character. Mr. Beegle was never ruffled in temper. He would endure the most pharisaic batteries of abuse, and smile as placidly as the moon at the bark of a juvenile cur. A violent opponent once pounced on him and exerted his fury in endeavoring to excite Mr. B.'s anger. But the brother remained perfectly calm and unmoved. His opponent at last left in rage, and was afterwards heard to say that Beegle must have gone insane, for he was unable to make him *mad*.

Two instances occurred in Oswego county, N. Y. A young man became developed as a writing-medium, and was strongly influenced to write communications to some skeptical friends. But his parents opposed him with such violence, he was deeply grieved, and at last grew excited. His enthusiasm to discharge his duty, and his determination, in spite of all opposition, was taken for insanity. We knew a young lady in Pennsylvania who was sent to an insane asylum for no other reason than that she persisted in exercising the gift of spirit mediumship. Her friends assumed she was insane because she was a medium, while she was regarded as perfectly rational and intelligent on all other topics.

A woman in Hastings, N. Y., went out in the public highway and began such an unearthly howling, a large company of neighbors soon assembled to learn the cause. She flung her arms aloft, and shrieked the awful intelligence that her son was lost, lost! And how? He had attended spiritual circles, and became interested! The poor, honest, ignorant mother believed him ruined for time and eternity, and for a season she was wild, hopeless, and thought to be insane, and Spiritualism was charged with the responsibility. Now, in all cases like these, it is evident the responsibility belongs to orthodox ignorance, error and superstition, and nothing but a belief in Spiritualism can prevent such lamentable results.

Objection 7. It is objected that Spiritualists are infidels, and opposed to the Bible and Christianity.

Answer. This objection, in part, has already been anticipated and answered. Both in public and private, we have invariably insisted that the Bible laid the foundation of Spiritualism, and embraced all its primary elements; that they were inseparably united. But the Bible as a mere book of ink, paper and binding, containing a record of what was said and done ages ago, is valuable only so far as it serves to guide us to the knowledge, demonstration, reception and practical realization of facts, principles, inspirations, spiritual manifestations and communications of a corresponding nature. The Bible is composed of various Hebrew and Christian writings, embracing a history of doings and sayings claimed under the direction of God and angels. Spiritualism demonstrates corresponding manifestations today. Bible believers who reject Spiritualism have only the *history* of inspiration, while Spiritualists have the *fact* demonstrated.

The Bible, spiritually interpreted, with its mis-translations and interpolations expurged, affords an indispensable record of unfoldings more remarkable than found elsewhere in history; and the teachings of the New Testament, whether original or not, embrace a matchless code of divine morality. Jesus Christ, — as a Mediator or medium of hitherto unequalled spiritual powers, as a teacher, an exemplar, living in spotless purity, laboring with unselfish philanthropy, and dying, as Rousseau's hero said, "like a god," — we may love, honor, revere, and regard as a divine type of God and humanity. But, according to the Protestant idea under which we profess to live, every man must be allowed to interpret the Bible for himself, and frame his own creed. The orthodox sects have their interpretations; the liberal Christians theirs; the Rationalists theirs, and the Spiritualists theirs; and all must be permitted to enjoy their conscientious opinions without being denounced either infidel, heretical or time-serving. No human interpretation is infallible. It will be a long time before we all arrive at the absolute truth, and it were unwise for any to assume the authority to pronounce absolute judgment in wholesale condemnation of any class of our human brotherhood, because they are not on our plane of understanding.

However, there are those who seem so perverse in their dogmatical interpretations of Scripture, it becomes difficult to withhold the thunderbolts of denunciation Jesus hurled at the hard heads of Judea. Wrapping their creeds around them like coats of mail, they resist everything like appeals, unless it comes like the thunders shaking Sinai and jarring down the walls of Jerusalem. We must give them their Bible as a literal book, until some idea of its spiritual significance is literally knocked into their materialistic sconces. But not so with the masses of religionists who cling to the Bible with uninformed reverence. Their religious nature is weak, sick, diseased. It were humane to remember this, and to go to our brothers and sisters, who, with sickly, diseased and misguided natures, are in vain seeking to satisfy their souls with the false creeds which they believe are drawn from the Bible; and, instead of rudely assailing the only citadel on which they stand, and dashing the Bible from their grasp, unfold its pages with a gentle hand, point out its teachings and manifestations, and let the descending light of Spiritualism fall on their weak and unsealed eyes with all its soft and winning radiance, until at last they are enabled to open their beatified vision in the full effulgence of noon-day joy and glory.

One class denouncing Spiritualism takes the ground of materialism, and denies the existence of spiritual beings. This is atheism. Another class admits the existence of such beings, God and angels, but assumes their revelations and manifestations forever closed with the Bible history. Another class concedes the phenomena of Spiritualism in the main to be genuine, but refers them to agency of *demons*, or evil spirits once belonging to planets other than the earth. Those who adopt the latter theory must prove it, by demonstrating the spirits are other than they claim to be, viz., spirits once wearing the human form on earth; and must likewise show wherein their deeds and teachings are *demoniac*. "Try the spirits." "By their fruits ye shall know them." We know their fruits are good. Hundreds of thousands can rise up to-day declaring they *know* Spiritualism to be "the power of God unto the salvation" of their souls from the thraldom of fear, doubt and despair. Those who admit the existence of God and the spirit-world, but who limit all manifestations to other ages, virtually take atheistic ground; for neither God nor angels have any practical, living, communicative existence to the inhabitants of our globe at the present day. And this position throws doubt into all past revelations; and those who take it in order to oppose modern spirit-manifestations, before they are aware find themselves fighting against the Bible, and laboring to show how those manifestations recorded in the Bible which are like modern manifestations, may be accounted for by referring to trick, psychology, electricity, odyle, or some *unknown* law of nature of which they know nothing.

Now, whoever takes this ground virtually ignores the ancient Biblical phenomena. Christianity was preached solely on the ground that Christ rose from the dead, reappeared, manifested himself, promised a continued manifestation of himself in spirit and power; and it was under the influence of his spirit the apostles went out startling the world with signs and wonders, making Jerusalem tremble on Pentecost, and in less than a quarter of a century shaking the seven-hilled city of Rome from its idolatrous centre. Christ was preached as a pattern, exemplar, guide; and as he came from the glorified spheres, leaving along his track streams of divine radiance, they who follow his example must likewise descend on errands of mercy and love. Jesus did not, in precise language, tell his disciples they should hold direct personal intercourse with their departed spirit-friends, but he *did* teach them this by inference and example, himself, in presence of Peter, James, and John, holding communion with Moses and Elias on the mount, and assuring them, in the kingdom then at hand, they should "sit down with Abraham, Isaac, and Jacob."

We ask Christians, and especially the clergy, to consider these things, and beware how they are found standing on anti-spiritual or infidel ground. Every blow the clergy aim against Spiritualism must rebound on themselves. There are some who remind us of Samson shorn of his strength. Shorn of their spiritual strength by the great harlot of the generation, blinded by the glitter and glare of whited sepulchres, in which the bones of dead men once inspired are canonized, while living apostles are scouted; like Samson, they are wandering wildly among the God-forsaken ruins of sectarianism, and hurling themselves with impotent rage against the pillars of their own temples, are seeking in their wrath to pull down that very temple of inspiration in which all revelations centre, though in its fall they themselves would be crushed and pulverized. Let them pull away, and though their divided house shall fall, and the inrolling waves of eternal truth wash away the last vestige into oblivion, the spiritual temple shall stand, —

For the eternal years of God are hers.

Notwithstanding the variety of sacred books or Bibles among different nations in the past, it is interesting to know that, in substance, they all teach, 1. That there is one God, just, wise, and good. 2. That the soul is immortal. 3. That virtue and happiness, vice and misery, are inseparably connected. 4. That the wicked are punished in the future state. 5. That angels minister unto them. 6. That good shall finally triumph over evil. 7. They all speak of divine incarnations. 8. They all speak of miraculous births. 9. They all speak of signs and wonders. 10. Those of each religion have been regarded, by those who received them, as the only Word of God. 11. They have been received as infallible. 12. They have been held to be the *last* Revelation; 13. And destined, ultimately, to be everywhere received. 14. All the sacred books have been interpolated, or corrupted, to a greater or less extent. 15. They were all written in languages now dead. (The Koran is not an exception; its classic language is not spoken by the people.) 16. Each has given rise to numerous sects, which have warred against each other. 17. And on each voluminous commentaries have been written.

Spiritualists do not shrink from owning the fact that among the heterogeneous hosts recognizing spiritual manifestations, there are various phases of opinion and belief, notwithstanding all may unite in certain primary, practical principles. The spiritual test relates to the heart and life, not merely to the head, or the theories it may elaborate, any further than those theories affect the heart and life. We can judge only for ourselves. Among Spiritualists there are those whose views of the Bible are such some call them "infidel." Others accept the Bible in a reserved sense as the *Word of God*, and Christianity as a living, reliable gospel of inseparable harmony with Spiritualism; and they are called, or call themselves, "Christians." Now, we do not regard it in taste for one class to call the other "infidel" in any sense implying an infidelity of the olden stamp, nor to call any "Christian" in any sense implying an old-fogyish, bat-blind, priestcraft, creed-and-conscience-bound sectarianism. There are many "infidel" *Christians*, and many "Christian" *infidels*, who swagger like Peter for Christ, one moment, and the next, like Peter, swear against him, in heart and practice. If there are any who come into Spiritualism bringing with them old forms of infidelity, or any who come with old forms of theology, Spiritualism is not responsible for either, for the same infidelity and theology existed ages before modern Spiritualism, and were born out of the materialisms and mythologies of the past.

Objection 8. It is objected that the doctrine of spiritual intercourse, as well as many of the sentiments identified with Spiritualism, are in direct conflict with numerous texts of Scripture and the doctrines of the Bible.

Answer. This objection has already been answered in several of its phases. We are to discriminate between what the Bible really teaches, and the teachings which sectarians ascribe to it. Is it said that the Bible teaches that all revelations were to end eighteen hundred years ago? We insist that not a single passage can be found of any such import. Jesus said: "I have many things to say unto you, but ye cannot bear them now. Howbeit, when He, the Spirit of Truth, is come, he will guide you into all truth; . . and he will show you things to come." John xvi. 12, 13. No writer in the Bible claimed to be perfect, or to set up any final authority. To understand the Scriptures aright, we are not to be governed by the creeds or interpretations of the past, but read in the light of the present, remembering that the English translation now in use was the work of fallible men, not free from all sectarian bias, though doubtless they did their work as well as could have been expected. We are likewise to remember that many of its prohibitions and commands were especially adapted and addressed to persons and peoples living ages ago, and have no reference to the present age, any farther than certain general principles are involved. Much that Moses addressed to the Israelites, and Jesus to the Jews of his time, has no application to mankind to-day. The Mosaic dispensation in part forbid the common people to hold intercourse with spirits; but, as we have already shown, the new dispensation insisted on spiritual intercourse. In ancient times the masses of the people were not as well prepared as the masses are to-day; the conditions have improved.

If it be objected that Spiritualism is not "orthodox" in regard to certain doctrines, the same objection is adduced with equal force against several large, liberal, Christian sects which question old statements of the doctrine of total depravity, vicarious atonement, the Trinity, future general judgment, and endless punishment. While we admit that no mortals are perfect, we maintain that none are totally depraved; none beyond the reach of divine benevolence; none so evil but their evils may be overcome. Ps. cxlv. 9; Rom. xii. 21. We admit that Jesus Christ and all noble souls devoted to the cause of humanity offer a sort of vicarious atonement, the "just suffering for the unjust," as the good parent suffers for the unfortunate child; but justice as well as mercy insists on retribution as necessary to discipline. Prov. xi. 21–31; Heb. xii. 11. While we question the mystical doctrine of the Trinity, we admit a sort of trinity, and insist that all men are endowed with a divinity in harmony with the divinity of Christ. John xiv. 12–28; xvii. 21; Mal. ii. 10. While we admit that all men cannot be fully seen or judged in the light of heaven until they pass into the eternal world, we maintain, at the same time, that all are now more or less judged, and justice is present and active in its administration. John ix. 39; xii. 31; Prov. xi. 31. While we deny the dogma of endless punishment, we admit that punishment or chastisement may not be confined in all cases to the present life; yet we insist on its temporary nature; and we insist on the triumph of good over evil, the ultimate end of all discord, and the final progress of all souls in holiness, happiness, and harmony. Isa. lvii. 16; lv. 21, etc.; Acts iii. 21; Rom. viii. 21; 1 Cor. xv.; Eph. i. 9, etc.; Phil. ii. 9, etc.; Col. i. 20; 1 Tim. ii. 1, etc.; Heb. xii. 11; Rev. xxi.; v. 13.

Now, without our insisting on the infallibility or final authority of any records, either ancient or modern, we *do* insist that when all genuine records come to be compared in the light of history, science, philosophy, and the opened heavens, they will be found in entire harmony. It were folly for theologians to seek any conflict between the ancient and modern, and a greater folly still to insist that the ancient records are to stand unquestioned, and certain dogmas be accepted as final and infallible. The great controversy now agitating Christendom is on this ground. It began in Germany many years ago, and has recently broken out anew in Great Britain, while American theologians are now preparing for a fearful conflict on this continent. Some of the most pious and learned clergymen of England have publicly endorsed a book which insists on placing the Bible on grounds of rational interpretation; and Bishop Colenso's work on the Pentateuch, questioning plenary inspiration, has caused new consternation and alarm among theological conservatives.

When a rational interpretation of the Bible comes to be adopted, the greatest stumbling-blocks to infidelity will be removed, and Spiritualism will be found in harmony with all the authentic records of the past and present. Whatever texts of Scripture may be adduced in seeming conflict, will no longer be arrayed against the gospel of to-day. Whatever may be said about *devil, Satan, devils, demons, demoniac influences, etc., death, hell, everlasting punishment*, etc., will be understood without clashing with the doctrine of spiritual intercourse, and the glorious prospect of ultimate harmony, happiness, and eternal progress. (See Balfour's First and Second Inquiries; Jahn's Archæology; Paige's Commentary, etc.)

Other objections will be anticipated in the ensuing chapter of ninety-five questions.

CHAPTER V.

NINETY-FIVE QUESTIONS TO BIBLE RELIGIONISTS AND SKEPTICS.

THE following questions will suggest their own answers, and anticipate many doubts and objections not already stated: —

1. Is there a first great Infinite Cause of all things called God? Psalms xix. 1; Gen. i. 1.

2. If God is a spirit, how does he create, control, and manifest himself in all forms of existence, in man and the material universe? John iv. 24; Psalms civ.

3. If the God-spirit has controlling manifestation over all the elements of the universe, and man is "made after the similitude of God," may not the spirit of man likewise have control in proportion to his development? Ps. cxxxix.; Gen. i. 27.

4. If mind or spirit is superior to matter, is it not immortal, and must it not retain an immortalized individuality after the material form is cast aside? 2 Cor. iv. 16–18.

5. How can God, the Infinite, reveal to man, the finite, a knowledge of the infinite and eternal, unless through the intermediate agency of angels or spirits occupying a plane between the Infinite and finite, and adapted to the appreciation of man? John i. 18; Heb. i. 14.

6. Can man on the finite plane receive a perfect and complete revelation from God, the Infinite? 1 Cor. xiii. 12.

7. In communicating with man, would God select messengers from some foreign realm, or the spirits of departed human beings in sympathy with man, and best capable of interpreting between God and man? Rev. xxii. 9.

8. Though some of the angels named in sacred history may never have worn the human form, is it not evident that most of those communicating with mortals were once earthly inhabitants? Heb. xii. 1; Gen. xxxii. 24, etc.

9. If it was lawful for Moses, Elias, Samuel, the spirit who came to John on Patmos, and even for Jesus himself, to come back from the spirit-world, is it not lawful now for other spirits to come on similar missions? Matthew xvii. 3.

10. Have the laws of God changed in relation to inspirations, visions, dreams, healings, and communications between earth and heaven? Mal. iii. 6; Joel ii. 28; Mark xvi. 17.

11. On what ground are the necessity, the possibility, the probability, and the certainty of present spiritual intercourse denied? Eccl. iii. 15.

12. Did not Christ's coming in human form on earth render him a more befitting mediator or medium between God and humanity? Heb. iv. 15.

13. As Christ commanded his disciples to invoke his spirit, and as he came back manifesting himself, is it not lawful to invoke the spirits of his followers to follow his example in likewise returning to earth? John xiv. 18.

14. Did Christ and his apostles limit to their age the signs, wonders, healings, and spiritual manifestations which attended them? 1 Cor. xii.; Eph. ii. 7.

15. Are there not as many reliable living witnesses to modern spiritual manifestations as there were to the facts recorded in sacred history?

16. If the witnesses of to-day are repudiated, may not the scoffer repudiate the witnesses of ancient times?

17. If the Bible is believed on the testimony of dead men living centuries ago, should not Spiritualism be believed on the evidence of men now living? 1 Cor. xv. 6; Matt. viii. 16.

18. If psychology, illusion, collusion, electricity, odd

force, odyle, magnetism, biology, ventriloquism, legerdemain, demonology, the devil, or anything else, can account for modern manifestations, may not everything of a similar character recorded in the Bible be accounted for on the same grounds?

19. Is there any middle ground between utter atheism and modern Spiritualism?

20. If these modern manifestations are the work of the so-called devil, demons, and damned spirits, is not the character of hell and its inhabitants changed; Satan no longer chained; the impassable gulf passed; spirits doomed to incessant fire and torture released in the cool air of our earth, and allowed better company than that of tormenting fiends?

21. Is it consistent with the character of God to suppose he would allow the infernal world to let loose all its demons to allure and destroy his own children on earth, and close the gates of heaven against angels coming on errands of mercy and salvation? Heb. ii. 14; 1 John iii. 8.

22. Would not this be a virtual abandonment of his government over humanity, and a consignment to the kingdom of diabolical darkness and damnation?

23. If there be an eternal world we are all destined to inherit, why may not those who have already entered that world come back and aid us by their experience in living this life and preparing for that which shall never end? John xiv. 1–3.

24. If Spiritualism is rejected because its teachings are not understood alike by all, must not the Bible, and all scientific and philosophical systems, be rejected on the same ground, since there are hundreds of conflicting sects and systems? 1 Cor. xii. 4; xiv. 26.

25. If Spiritualism is rejected because some alleged Spiritualists are not perfect, must not all religions and systems be rejected for like reasons, since many priests, re-

ligionists, and skeptics have fallen far short of perfection? John vi. 70.

26. If Spiritualism is to be known by its fruits, what judgment must be pronounced in view of the fact that it has converted thousands to a belief and knowledge of God and immortal life, comforted the mournful, quieted the disconsolate, saved the doubtful and despairing, reclaimed the wandering, healed the sick, blessed the afflicted, strengthened the weak, given to the lonely the angel companionship of celestial guardians, and cheered the dying with opened visions of glory beyond the tomb? John x. 21; Matt. vii. 16.

27. If religionists insist that God, nor the Holy Ghost, nor the Lord Jesus Christ, nor the Triune Almighty, can impart the saving influences of the Divine Spirit without man first complies with certain conditions, why complain that modern spiritual manifestations cannot be induced regardless of conditions? John v. 40.

28. If no scientific experiments can be made without the observance of certain laws and conditions, why should spiritual phenomena be expected to occur independent of all laws and conditions? Matt. xiii. 58.

29. If persons of peculiar organism and culture are requisite to make orators, teachers, poets, artists, why object that spirits cannot communicate except through mediums who possess peculiar organisms adapted to the manifestations? 1 Cor. xii. 29, 30.

30. If all are not mediums for like manifestations, why are not all persons orators, teachers, etc.? Rom. xii. 6; 1 Cor. iv. 7.

31. Do not history and tradition afford evidence that some phenomena like modern Spiritualism have occurred in all the past ages? Rom. i. 19, 20.

32. If these manifestations did not become more general till the present age, why were not railroads, tele-

graphs, reforms, many inventions, and all the advanced ideas of the day, in more general vogue before?

33. Can imperfect mortals expect perfect communications from God, angels, or departed spirits, while imperfect mediums are of necessity used as the agents? 1 Cor. xiii. 12.

34. If all spiritual communications are rejected because some prove fallible, must not all communications between man and man on earth be alike rejected, since no man is infallible? 1 Thes. v. 21.

35. If we can judge as to the reliability of men on earth, may not the same reason and intelligence enable us to judge as to what purports to come from the spirit-world? 1 John iv. 1.

36. If we are to receive anything as absolute, infallible authority, laying aside all reason, are we not made blind slaves? 1 Cor. x. 15.

37. Can any man be as well satisfied with historical faith in things spiritual and eternal, as though he had faith and knowledge based on demonstrations given to-day? John iii. 11.

38. Are not the multitudes spiritually dying and dead for the want of living manifestations from God and the eternal world?

39. What save Spiritualism can reach the masses who are living "without hope and without God in the world?"

40. Has not all Christendom been praying for celestial manifestations to usher in a millennial morning of communion between earth and heaven?

41. Do not Christians as well as infidels need something like Spiritualism?

42. Can any man become a Christian without first coming under the "Spirit of Christ" or some kind of spiritual influence? 2 Cor. iii. 6.

43. If the early apostles were not qualified to preach

until they became developed and "endowed with power from on high," can men become truly qualified at the present day without coming under similar influences?

44. What proofs can anti-spiritual ministers give the world that they are commissioned "from on high?" Mark xvi. 17; Luke xxiv. 49; John xiv. 12.

45. If objection is raised against Spiritualism on account of the alleged reputation of some of its mediums, does not the same objection apply to Christianity for Christ's selecting as his mediums, fishermen tax-gatherers, publicans, sinners, Judas, Mary Magdalen, the woman of Samaria, and others?

46. If it was lawful for Christ to grant Thomas some conclusive test, is it not lawful for the doubting Thomases of to-day to receive some convincing demonstrations? John xx. 25.

47. Is not humanity now as sacred in the sight of God as it was ages ago?

48. Have the revelations of the past saved the world to-day, or guided all men in the way of unerring truth and righteousness?

49. Can the letter of past revelations be understood without present inspirations? 2 Cor. iii. 6.

50. Can man, as a spiritual being, live on the experiences of other ages, any better than he can sustain bodily health and strength on believing and reading of what men ate and drank ages ago?

51. If manifestations of spiritual influence and power were necessary to convert men ages ago, as on the day of Pentecost, are they not necessary now? Acts ii.

52. If men to-day can rest on the manifestations of the past, may they not likewise rest on the conversions ensuing, and live entirely on the experiences of the past, without experiencing anything for themselves?

53. Outside of Spiritualism is there any school of science, philosophy, or religion, able to give men to-day

a single particle of tangible knowledge or demonstration of things spiritual, divine and eternal, since all the schools are hostile to Spiritualism on the ground of its claiming to give such knowledge and demonstration?

54. If men are now unable to receive any tangible light or influence from the invisible world, why do Christians command them to seek and call on God, Christ and the Holy Ghost?

55. If blasphemy against the Holy Ghost consisted in attributing the spiritual powers of Christ to false and infernal influences, what kind of sin is committed by those who deny the manifestation of all such powers today? Matt. xii. 24.

56. If spirits manifest themselves with teachings constantly enjoining harmony, wisdom, truth, purity, and love, how can evil or error result? Matt. vii. 16.

57. If mortals desire the companionship of the loved, the great, the good, why repel those who come back laden with messages from the spirit home? Rev. iii. 20.

58. Why should Spiritualists be called infidels, while they believe not only in past revelations, but in present inspiration and spiritual intercourse?

59. Is it not more essential to live the commandment of love to God and man, than believe in mere forms and creeds? John xiii. 35; Mark xii. 30, 31.

60. If "there is joy in heaven over one sinner that repenteth," is it not evident that celestial beings are in direct sympathy and communication with mortals, and must rejoice in ministering to them? Luke xv. 7.

61. If it is said that angelic beings would be made unhappy by a knowledge of the sad and suffering conditions of mortals, may not the same be said of all wise and noble souls here on earth who witness human suffering? 2 Cor. iv. 17.

62. As the wise and good on earth and in the spheres are permitted to see the use of all sorrow and suffering,

may they not rejoice in seeing how all shall at last end well? Rom. viii. 18, etc.

63. If, as religionists admit, angels are hovering around us, why not permit them to manifest themselves?

64. If, in modern times, spirits cannot manifest themselves to all persons alike, why did not God, angels and Jesus Christ manifest themselves to all alike in ancient times? 1 Cor. ii.; read whole chapter.

65. Why were Peter, James and John alone permitted to see Moses and Elias on the mount of transfiguration? Matt. xvii. 1, etc.

66. Why was Christ, after his resurrection, seen only by about five hundred persons besides Paul, unless it was because he arose as a spirit, and could be seen only by those who were spiritually prepared to see? 1 Cor. xv. 6.

67. If it is objected that the spirits cannot convince the whole world at once, we may ask why Christ did not succeed in convincing and converting the world?

68. If living in the light of heaven, and under the guardianship of angel friends, is not calculated to make mortals holy and happy, what is?

69. If this gospel of angel light shining beyond the night of death, and opening to view the glories of another and a better world, is "not good to die by," where shall we find a gospel better adapted? Rev. xxi. 1, etc.

70. How is it possible for man to live a spiritual life without some demonstrations of the spiritual?

71. How is it possible for us to realize we are immortal, unless immortals give us some direct evidences of immortality?

72. How can angels become "ministering spirits" to "them who shall be heirs of salvation," unless they can manifest themselves in some tangible manner? Heb. i. 14.

73. If Jesus had "more than twelve legions of angels"

at his command, may not all who have the "spirit of Christ" likewise enjoy a similar angelic guardianship? Matt. xxvi. 53.

74. If certain "signs" were to follow Christian believers, who now are believers, unless they are spiritual mediums? Mark xvi. 17.

75. If "greater works" than those which attended Christ were to be done by his successors, who were or are those successors? John xiv. 12.

76. If angels have "charge" over mortals, are "encamped round," and are a "great cloud of witnesses," must they not have tangible intercourse with mortals? Ps. xci. 11, 12; Ps. xxxiv. 7; Heb. xii. 1.

77. If there are difficulties in discriminating between the true and false in modern Spiritualism, did not similar difficulties arise with reference to ancient prophets, apostles, and Christs? Matt. xxiv. 5, 6. 1 John iv. 1.

78. What save Spiritualism can "swallow up death in victory" "and wipe away tears from off all faces"? 1 Cor. xv. 54. Rev. xxi. 4.

79. How can we, like Paul, "know" we have an inheritance, "eternal in the heavens," unless like him we have direct spiritual evidences? 2 Cor. v. 1; 2 Cor. xii.

80. If "no man hath seen God at any time," must not the ancient seers have seen angels rather, when sometimes they believed themselves communicating with Deity? John i. 18. Rev. xxii. 9.

81. Did not Jesus teach that the "dead" live, "are raised," and "are as the angels of God"? Luke xx. 36–38; Mark xii. 25; Matt. xxii. 30; 1 Cor. xv. 16.

82. How can ancient prophecies be fulfilled unless spiritual intercourse becomes inaugurated? Joel ii. 28; Rev. xxi. 1–5.

83. How can the "kingdom of heaven" become inaugurated without heavenly communion? Matt. iii. 2; Heb. xii. 22.

84. "He that loveth not his brother whom he hath seen, how can he love God whom he hath not seen?" 1 John iv. 20.

85. Were not Jesus and his apostles as infidel and radical to the popular religions of their age as Spiritualists are to the religions of the present? Luke xii. 49–53.

86. Was not Christianity just as alarming to the church, state, and society of Judea eighteen centuries ago, as Spiritualism is to conservatives of to-day? John xii. 19; Acts v. 17, 18; Luke xii. 49, etc.

87. If angels could release Peter and the other apostles from prisons, why may not angelic beings effect similar deliverances to-day? Acts v. 9; Acts xii.

88. If the friends of Peter believed it consistent for "his angel" to come knocking at the gate, why should Christians scoff at the idea of angels knocking in modern times? Acts xii.; Rev. iii. 20.

89. If it was consistent and essential for Jesus to be tried by what was called an evil spirit, may it not be necessary for men and women sometimes to be tried in a similar manner in modern times? Matt. iv.

90. If we complain becanse spirits do not always seem to interpose in our behalf, may we not ask why the "twelve legions of angels" did not interpose to save Jesus in Gethsemane? Matt. xxvi. 53.

91. If we are perplexed with doubts and anxieties, may we not ask if all these are not essential to our discipline? 2 Cor. iv.

92. Are not all the "spiritual gifts" and manifestations specified by Paul to be found in our age? 1 Cor. xii.; xiii.; xiv.

93. If all modern mediums and believers are deceivers, or under some diabolical or illusive influences, may not the same be conjectured of all ancient seers and saints? 1 Cor. xv. 15.

94. If the great fact of spiritual intercourse be denied,

are we not left to wander, dark, desolate, lonely, lost, despairing? 1 Cor. xv. 32.

95. Reader, wilt thou ponder on these questions, and answer them to thyself, within the sacred temple of thine own soul? Rom. xiv. 22.

CHAPTER VI.

THE PHILOSOPHY — PHASES OF MEDIUMSHIP — HOW TO CONDUCT CIRCLES, DEVELOP MEDIUMSHIP, CULTIVATE SPIRITUAL GIFTS, INDUCT MANIFESTATIONS, AND ENJOY CELESTIAL COMMUNION.

However novel may be some of the phenomena of modern Spiritualism, we insist that its philosophy lies at the basis of all science, all philosophy and all revealed religion. It is conceded that God as a Spirit is the Father of all spirits; that the elements or essences of his being are the essential elements of man as an immortal; that these elements of divine and human existence, though unseen, are the mightiest elements of the universe. "The things which are seen are temporal, but the things which are unseen are eternal." 2 Cor. iv. Those imponderable elements in the material universe, which science and philosophy recognize, are admitted to be the mightiest forces in the material universe; and these are akin to those more ethereal elements which we regard as spiritual. Man, as the image of God, is a miniature, a compound embodiment of the universe, material and spiritual, terrestrial and celestial, human and divine. Or in him are represented on the finite plane all the attributes ascribed to Deity. Just so far as these attributes are cultivated and unfolded in keeping with the laws of nature, just so far he becomes a medium for all the elements in the natural world; just so far as he lives in harmony with the laws of the spirit-world, just so far he becomes a medium for the influences and inspirations of that world, and attracts spiritual beings to his aid; just so far as he lives in keeping with the laws of God, he becomes God-like in power, and an angel or messenger of God, a medium for the reception and impartation of the divinest influxes. "Be ye followers of God, as dear children;" "perfect, even as your Father in heaven is perfect." This was the standard Jesus held up, and up to which he lived, thereby becoming a medium constantly attracting the loftiest angelic aids, and working wonders of a God-like nature. But he did not claim this power as exclusively his own. "Verily, verily I say unto you, he that believeth on me, the works that I do shall he do also, and greater than these shall he do; because I go unto my Father." John xii.

With this philosophy in view, all miracles, all mediumships cease to be mysterious or miraculous. Man, as a being endowed with the attributes of his Creator, has within him all the powers capable of being manifested on the finite plane of being. All the instruments, utensils and machines which man invents, manufactures and brings into use, enabling him to have command over objects and elements in nature, — all these are only outer manifestations of the spiritual and divine attributes which are wrapped up in man himself; and when he comes to attain the highest plane of unfolding, and comes into right conditions, under right influences, he will manifest powers transcending all those ever embodied in human, external mechanism, — for he is an embodiment of *all* mechanisms! As men and women are organized and unfolded aright, they become used as mediums by spirits, — the spirits, in the use of unseen elements, playing on the human mechanism, and producing manifestations without the aid of any external machinery. A Prof. Morse, in the spirit-world, no longer able to use the material electrical machine, plays on the mechanical elements he finds in and around the medium, and, lo! heaven telegraphs to earth the gladsome news of immortal life.

We might adduce numerous illustrations in support of

this philosophy, but they will occur to the mind of the intelligent reader. Keep this philosophy in view, and you will understand many phenomena deemed wholly inexplicable. We must remember that the *elements* of all the powers we ascribe to God and the spirit world are latent within our own being; but for their unfoldment and manifestation we are more or less dependent on higher worlds. Mediums are frequently troubled to know what manifestations and influences are their own, and what may be ascribed to the sole and direct agency of spirits. Now, we may never know exactly where to draw the line of discrimination; the two worlds are constantly blending and exchanging, and we are constantly receiving more or less from the celestial hosts evermore guarding over us as the angels of God, without our ever becoming entirely robbed of our individuality or the divinity enthroned within. With this fact in view we never need fear any arbitrary control of spirits. Persons may sometimes, for a while, seem subjected to unpleasant influences, but let the soul rise up in its dignity and divinity, and call on the loftiest ideals of the eternal world, and all seemingly demoniac agencies will depart.

As already intimated, the phases of spiritual mediumship are so numerous and so constantly blending, it is impossible to give any reliable classification. 1. The rapping medium was the first developed in this age of spiritual manifestations. We name other phases without regard to order or gradation. 2. The tipping medium. 3. The medium for raising ponderable bodies, sometimes with and sometimes without hands in contact. 4. The musical medium, with instruments and without. 5. The medium for spirit voices, without using the vocal organs, and sometimes with. 6. Writing medium, sometimes by impression and sometimes mechanically. 7. The trance medium, sometimes conscious and sometimes otherwise. 8. Vibrating medium, sometimes shaken and convulsed, and sometimes lifted or impelled without any seeming volition. 9. The transfigured medium, thrilled, exalted and enchanted under celestial influences. 10. Personification medium, imitating words, looks, tones and actions of spirits. 11. Sensation medium, made to feel signals and touches by spirits. 12. Clairvoyant medium, describing persons, spirits, diseases, etc. 13. Healing medium, for the laying on of hands. 14. Painting medium, producing pictures and portraits. 15. Hieroglyphic medium, executing strange scrolls. 16. The medium for unknown tongues, sometimes writing and sometimes speaking. 17. Impressional medium, liable to take on impressions from mortals and from spirits. 18. The clairaudant medium, for hearing spirit sounds and voices. 19. The vision medium, dealing in tropes, symbols, etc., like the Apocalypse. 20. Seeing medium, describing spirit-scenes and forms. 21. The telegraphic medium, sending messages to absent persons, without writing or speaking. 22. Developing medium, imparting influences to develop other mediums. 23. Prophetic medium, giving warnings and predictions. 24. Illuminatti medium, presenting spirit lights. 25. Itinerant medium, sent out after the sick, suffering, tempted, fallen, dying, etc. 26. The psychological medium, liable to be influenced by persons in the form, and subjected to impositions, counterfeits, etc. 27. The psychographic medium, reading persons at a distance, with letters, locks of hair, etc. 28. The speaking medium, speaking under influence, some conscious and some unconscious. 29. The inspirational medium, thinking, feeling, acting, writing, and speaking under a vivid consciousness of the reality of things spiritual, divine and eternal, yet in full possession of all the senses. 30. The improvisation medium, giving music or poetry without premeditation, under spirit influence. 31. The normal medium, without any external signs, realizing the all-pervading atmosphere of the spirit-world with a calm, deep consciousness of angel guardianship.

We come now to the important subject of spiritual culture. Those who investigate Spiritualism should begin endeavoring to realize its importance. It is a solemn as well as joyous thing to communicate with spirit friends. In forming circles, urge none to join who regard the subject with levity, or whose minds are filled with opposing influences. Those who would "find" must "seek" with sincere and earnest desires. Let your circles be composed of congenial minds seriously seeking to know the truth for themselves. It will avail nothing to importune those who are rigidly opposed. Such persons invariably repel spiritual influences and counteract manifestations, unless you have mediums of a remarkably positive nature already developed. If your circles are for the development of mediums, they need to be free from the embarrassing effects of the presence of scoffers. It is not necessary persons should believe in order that they may be admitted, but they should have their minds free from antagonistic influences. This is just as necessary as for one to have his eyes unbandaged if he would see the light of the sun.

Let those who join your circles endeavor to realize what it is to hold intercourse with the spirit world. It requires some preparation of mind, heart, and life. If your desires are not above the ordinary plane of selfishness and sensuality, you will find nothing of a satisfactory or elevated nature. If you would attract elevated manifestations and influences, let your aims be of a corresponding character. To commune with the beloved and beatified is to enjoy privileges of priceless value, and we cannot expect to enjoy such without some cost, some sacrifice, some trial, some earnest and persevering effort. If we would attain such holy intercourse, above all else we must "seek first the kingdom of heaven." "*Strive* to enter!" Our loftiest achievements come only through struggles and conflicts with opposing elements.

Select your company of persons most congenial, harmonious, patient, quiet, persevering, and confidential; the number from three to twenty, with an equal number of each sex; join hands; sing, have music, engage in devout exercises, or keep silence, as shall best accord with the predominant feeling of the circle; seek to put yourselves in sympathy with those with whom you would communicate, elevate your thoughts and emotions to the plane they occupy, and invoking the divinest influences; then let each person freely yield, willing to become an instrument for the manifestations of the spirits under the guidance of that supreme Spirit whose government is over all.

No arbitrary number of persons is requisite to form a circle. The number may be according to convenience. An equal number of males and females is usually preferable, though not indispensable. Each person should join the circle not merely to witness what may come through others present, but to test his or her own mediumship, and look for nothing save that which may come through himself or herself. It is the first business of each to test himself, and not rely on others alone. All have the elements of some kind of mediumship. If persons are continually depending on what comes through others, their own development is neglected, they make little or no progress, and learn to feel just as dependent as though they were under the guidance of an arbitrary priesthood. Each one should come to a consciousness of his or her own spiritual nature, its powers and capacities, and remember the spirit world is open for all to commune directly without the agency of other mediums; though most persons, at first, may need the aid of others that they may become initiated into a knowledge of the reality of Spiritualism.

If the circle, on opening, is agreed in uniting in some

kind of religious or musical exercises, a condition of harmony is induced favorable to manifestations, though no rigid form should be prescribed. Let the company take that course which is most likely to induce oneness of thought and feeling. Each mind should seek a lofty plane, conscious of the presence of angel friends, and always invoke the wisdom, love, and truth of the highest ideals, whether in the name of GOD or CHRIST or the sainted dead coming in nearest sympathy with the soul's needs. If physical manifestations, like rappings, tippings, movings, writings, etc., are sought, form your circle around a table of suitable size, place the hands thereon, and wait from twenty to thirty minutes. Be sure the conditions are such that no one can manufacture manifestations. Allow no conditions to be imposed on you which deprive you of the use of all your senses as well as your intellect. Beware of imposition, yet do not entertain any unkind suspicions. Let each person be willing to be questioned and tested, if anything is doubted. If no physical demonstrations come, then wait for other forms of manifestation, like speakings, visions, impressions, entrancements, vibrations of the physical system, etc. Let no person resist whatever impulse or influence may come, unless the conditions are bad and something palpably injurious is likely to ensue. Persons are frequently controlled at first in an unpleasant and apprehensive manner, but no evils may be feared in the end. The greatest danger almost invariably ensues not from yielding to the influence, but from resisting it. No hesitation or timidity may be felt when persons yield freely with pure and earnest desires for the highest and holiest influences. Guardian angels are ever watchful over their medium friends, and if they, at first, permit anything of a seemingly violent nature, it is for the purpose of developing a mediumship at last resulting in good.

As soon as circles or individuals begin to receive any

manifestations or communications, if they need further directions, they can ask the spirits whatever questions they please, and receive the answers needed. But everything received should be tested by reason, intuition, and common sense, and nothing be taken as absolute authority unless it be proved. The highest spirits seldom, if ever, seek to lead men blindly, or to give particular directions in regard to every step in life, but rather to impart influxes, to enlighten and expand the individual mind and heart, that mortals may receive reliable impressions for their own guidance in all things. And all mortals who are in the right condition may receive influences and impressions more or less. Sometimes, when spirits communicate through reliable and well-tried mediums, their counsels and teachings must be heeded in spite of what would seem to be the best judgment and reasons of mortals in the form. Directions and instructions often come from the spheres which are based on wisdom higher than mortals know, and old opinions, prejudices, convictions, and relationships, may be shocked and startled in opposition. Ordinary reasons and feelings arising from a false foundation or education must frequently yield to those inspirations which come from the congregated generations of the spirit world, sanctioned by superior intelligence. Admonitions may come hard to heed; as hard as to forsake all that was once loved, take up a Christ-cross, and follow on in the face of a frowning world. But oh, what compensating glory shall crown the heroic soul, and convoys of gladsome angels shall bend over the highway of spiritual progress, beaming with the love of the everlasting, and bearing palms of triumph plucked from the plains of immortal life!

Circles for invoking and imparting the elements of healing are recommended as practical and important. Healing mediums have become so successful in treating the sick, that there is a perpetual demand for them. But those who are most successful are not yet sufficiently numerous to answer all the calls coming from the afflicted in various parts of the country. Clairvoyant and spiritual physicians are fast multiplying and becoming very successful, but they are not yet sufficiently numerous to meet the demand. Those who are in need of healing mediums can form circles for the purpose of calling out the latent mediumship with which almost every normal individual is endowed. Let the afflicted sit in circles composed of none but harmonic persons, and beneficent results will almost invariably follow.

Some years ago, one morning, on rising quite early, the writer found himself attacked with most violent pains, indicating a malignant disease with which he suffered severely some two years before. He took no breakfast, drank some fresh, cold spring water, sat in a rocking-chair, and began to make manipulations, invoking invisible aids. In a few moments he felt soothing, somnolent influences stealing over him; threw himself on the lounge; fell into a deep trance-state, and remained unconscious for about two hours. On waking out of the sleep he was entirely relieved, and from that time he experienced not the slightest symptom of the disease. He was positive that the elements of nature were imparted under spiritual control. Let those who are attacked with any symptoms of acute disease make the experiment, and they will find marvellous virtue in the method of spiritual cure. Let the mind become entirely composed; let all care, anxiety, and fear be ignored; as far as possible abandon all selfish thoughts; seek to realize the existence of the imponderable elements permeating all space, and on which we are reliant for life, health, and strength; seek to realize that all these elements act according to certain laws, and that invisible intelligences understand the operation of those laws; open the soul in communion with those superior beings who come as the ministering angels of the Father, and invoke their aid in imparting the elements needed to restore the equilibrium of body and mind. The aid of some positive healing medium may often add to the virtue imparted direct by spirits; but when we become unfolded in harmony with the natural and the spiritual worlds, we shall need no intermediate agents.

We have named various phases of mediumship, without any arbitrary classification, or recommending any particular phases as preferable to others. Of course, there are essential differences, but persons must "covet earnestly the best gifts," according to their own best judgment, as well as their organization and adaptation. Some persons may have an undue ambition or desire for that which may be difficult to obtain, and they wonder why they cannot receive just what they ask. It is because they are not prepared, or because they are not adapted, or because the conditions are not right. They marvel why their spirit friends cannot communicate at once in the most satisfactory manner; and they are inclined to have serious doubts and anxieties. We may remember it is not the fault of spirits. We may have wise and good friends in the form, who are in other lands, or otherwise separated from us; and we, as well as they, may be exceedingly anxious to communicate; but there may be a variety of unavoidable obstacles which delay all communication for a time. Just so in our intercourse with the spirit world. But we may rest assured that when we are in the right condition, and our end of the celestial telegraphic line is all right, we shall receive all the messages, influences or impressions we need.

There are some phases of mediumship concerning which caution is necessary; though all phases, when rightly used, are not only harmless, but beneficent. Some persons are influenced in such a manner as to lose their own external individuality in a measure, for a time, and to assume the appearance, the air, the tones and other indications peculiar to the spirits influencing them. These are called personating, speaking and trance mediums. We have a most striking illustration of this phase of mediumship described in 1 Sam. x. 6. Samuel, in addressing Saul, says: "The spirit of the Lord will come upon thee, and thou shalt prophesy with them, *and thou shalt be turned into another man;*" or, as the passage might be more properly rendered, "thou shalt be turned into the seeming, the appearance of another man." Mediums often assume this seeming or appearance in resemblance of the spirits influencing them. We allude to this phase of mediumship more for the purpose of illustrating facts than to encourage persons in seeking and perpetuating it. For temporary uses in behalf of select friends, it may be well to allow spirits thus to personify themselves for a time; but mediums of a negative nature should be exceedingly cautious about yielding themselves very often to these influences, unless all the conditions and the persons present are of the most harmonious character. It is not well to yield our own individuality or wills to any influence or power outside of ourselves. It is seldom if ever possible to thus yield ourselves entirely, and is not required. The wisest and best spirits only require us to come into sympathy with them; and, instead of desiring to control us in any mechanical manner, they seek only to cöoperate with us and impart aids and influences to quicken the divine energies of our being. Instead of seeking to guide us in any arbitrary manner, they seek to quicken the monitor within, and call on us to stand up on our own accountability.

Skeptics and inquirers often grow disheartened because they are unable to receive all they seek without delay. But they should remember that all spiritual manifestations and communications depend on certain laws and conditions, and truth is gradual in its unfoldings. Many persons need the discipline of patience and perseverance before they are prepared to receive the facts and philosophy of Spiritualism. "Seek and ye shall find," is the law. Every step taken in the course of investigation, every hour spent in reading, hearing, meditating, conversing and sitting, becomes necessary in disciplining and unfolding the spiritual nature, preparatory to the reception of spiritual influences. As our own souls are moulded in the image of the Divine, and the spiritual universe is infinite, it is a work not only of all time, but of eternity itself, for us to become harmoniously unfolded in full communion with celestial worlds. Mediums, just beginning to receive some manifestations, and anxious to unfold the loftiest gifts, often impatiently wonder at the tardy progress of their development. The least feeling of impatience should teach them the need of discipline, and that they are not yet prepared for higher unfoldings. They need delays, trials to test and strengthen them, lest they become "exalted above measure." So with laborers who are already in the field. Sordid ambition is frequently checked and pride wounded. They wonder why the world is not convinced and converted at once. And many devoted believers partake of the same feeling, and at times seem nearly discouraged. But let patience possess their souls, and perseverance mark their prayers and purposes. No aspirations rise, no word falls, no deed is done, no step is taken in vain. Angel watchers are over the field of humanity watering the seed thou art sowing in tears. Faint not. The harvest time shall come. "Learn to labor and to — *wait.*"

"Could ye not watch one hour?" How often in our petulance and impatience may we hear this appeal made to the weary disciples in the garden of Gethsemene! It was on the dark and ominous night before the tragedy of Calvary, and Jesus groaned and prayed in view of the coming crisis. But his disciples grew weary and slumbered. "What, could ye not watch one hour?" Ah, how often do even the strongest of us need to hear this same touching appeal! We grow weak and weary amid the duties of day and the watchings of night, and would fain fall into supineness and discontent. Our hopes are deferred and our affections go unanswered, till we sicken at heart and would lie down disconsolate. We would have all the loftiest boons of existence realized at once or we despond. We gaze over the field of humanity; we go out on our mission in behalf of the lowly, the benighted, the fallen; but, alas, how little we seem to accomplish; and we anon grow disheartened. We forget a Jesus, a Howard, a Fenelon, and the hosts of heroes and martyrs who faced life-long battles, who wept in Gethsemanes, groaned in Golgothas, and bled on Calvarys.

And thus it is in the work of spiritual culture and communion. There are many who grow weary in waiting only one hour for their angel friends to come, seeking to manifest and communicate themselves; and then they are tempted to abandon all effort. But not so with our angel friends; they come again and again. They follow our path by day, and seek to exert over us a benign influence, to shield us from harm, and win our affections heavenward; they watch over us by night, and drop on our pillows the dews of peace; all the night long they stand at our doors and knock; and can we not wait one hour? O messengers of the Father! forgive our mortal weakness. O beatified ones, bend in compassion. Unseal our eyelids and give us strength. Shall we grow weary during but an hour now and then consecrated to communion with the immortal myriads peopling the eternal worlds? What were an hour each day, compared with eternity? We can spend a lifetime in hoarding up the gold destined to perish, but not even one hour a day can be devoted to the unfolding of the imperishable treasures of heaven. We can spend night after night with frivolous friends here in the form amid scenes of false tinsel and fading glory, but envy even one hour spent in communion with the glorified throngs of God walking worlds of fadeless splendor and waving palms of victory to beckon us homeward to the highway of eternal progress. O ye doubting, trembling, skeptical, seeking souls, "can ye not wait one hour?" And ye sad and mournful ones, look up, and behold how your angel watchers wait and weep. Ye weary ones, listen; for lo, the invisible beings of the Father are near, as over the garden of Gethsemane they hovered waiting for the prayer of Jesus.

Some persons become interested in Spiritualism for a season, and then lapse back into indifference, or fall into the ranks of an easy, fashionable sectarism. Some begin, perhaps, with the largest expectations, and desire spirits to accomplish everything at once, without any efforts on their part. Hence, they become easily discouraged, on learning they have an earnest work to perform in cöoperation with the invisibles. Others are governed more by curiosity than by any deep and profound interest in regard to spiritual culture and the weal of humanity; or they seek for self-gratification and the advancement of sordid ends and aims. No marvel that individuals thus influenced should grow easily disheartened, and go back to the "beggarly elements of the world." And what is the condition of such in their lapsed or backsliding state? Can the idle, scoffing world or the dogmatic church compensate them for the loss of the light, the hope, the joy, the glory of spiritual intercourse? Never! One smile from the angel world of God is worth more than all the smiles and pleasures of the passing throng. If there is no truth in Spiritualism, then there is no God, no spirit world, no immortal life, no beloved ones living beyond the charnel house; and soon all these scenes and moving multitudes will forever pass into the shadows of an eternal night.

But Spiritualism *is* true. It is attested by millions of phenomena in all ages up to the present. Every household, home and heart may find evidences, either external or internal. And those who have once realized this celestial communion can never go back to the soulless creeds and materialisms of the world. After they have once drank at the fountain of angel intercourse, it becomes in their inmost being a "well of water springing up into everlasting life;" and with the woman of Samaria they exclaim, "Evermore give us to drink of this water!" Oh, in this hot and dusty highway of life, amid the heat and burden of each day's care and turmoil, how refreshing to catch breezes wafted from Eden lands and songs sung by the triumphal hosts waving palms of victory on

> "That silent shore,
> Where billows never break nor tempests roar."

Faint not, ye who are sometimes weary and wayworn! Every thought, word, and deed shall tell for time and eternity. Though all may anon look dark and dispiriting around you, keep your feet firm in the pathway once trod by those who have gone heavenward, and light shall come streaming down from those angel lands to dispel the cloud and storm, and gladsome companions breathe into your souls the heroism of the skies. The momentous issues involved in spiritual intercourse are but feebly appreciated by those who have only a smattering knowledge of its facts and philosophy. The existence of a living God, the verities of an eternal world, the endless destiny of man, and all those problems which relate to the divine needs of humanity, are to be placed on the ground of demonstration and knowledge. Systems and forms of belief must pass away before the light of heaven, and become as gathered scrolls, no longer obstructing the vision of man; and the fraternal bands of the celestial empire shall come and walk side by side with the brotherhood of earth.

During long evenings, as friends and families gather round the social board, no enjoyment can become more genial and benign than that of seeking communion with those who have passed on to the land of eternal springtime and perennial summer. How many have faded away like flowers before an autumnal frost and fallen like the leaves rustling before wintry winds. And where are they? Do they yet live and love, and linger around us, seeking to breathe over our drooping hearts the airs of that paradise land where the loved and lost shall one day mingle in beatified communion, and part forever no more? The busy throngs of life move on, and the millions are hurrying along to join departed generations. A few more seasons will come and go, and then over our graves the flowers will bloom and fade, the grass grow green and then sered, the leaves will fall, and the winds sigh in requiem with the wail of weeping friends; but the sun will shine on in the heavens, the stars gleam down over our burial-places, and rainbows smile on thunder-clouds and beyond storms whose roar shall no longer be heard. As mournful and melancholy as are these reflections, they are befitting, since all these physical forms of ours are mortal, and destined to crumble back to the mouldering vaults of time. And what mockery are all these human hopes, affections, aspirations, if there be no elements of immortal life within us. And how are we to know? How know and realize the departed still live? How come in communion with them, and feel their presence overshadowing us as the guardian angels of God come on errands of mercy to quicken our affections into spiritual life, and enable us to sit, as it were, in heavenly places? In our closets alone, in the fields or workshops, or wherever we are, the soul may lift its thoughts in consecrated intercourse with the dead; but if we would enjoy the most social and congenial communion, and receive the most tangible external manifestations of invisible power and intelligence, we may convene friends, neighbors, and families around the altar of home, remembering the needs of holy harmony as most essential to harmonic visitations from angel companions. No evidences can be so satisfactory or reliable as those which come through yourselves or friends and acquaintances with whom you are familiar. Sometimes you may find it expedient or necessary to visit mediums and circles where you are unacquainted. But never allow your expectations to become too high, or disappointment may ensue. Always make some allowance for honest exaggerations in regard to manifestations, and likewise for conditions; and be sure that you comply with all reasonable conditions. Sometimes you may receive nothing, and then again be favored with the most startling evidences.

A word of caution may be demanded in regard to motives and influences thrown on mediums. From familiar acquaintance with all kinds of mediums during the observation of several years, we are confident no class in society is more justly exempt from charges of moral evil. Exposed as they are to the criticisms of skeptics and inquirers, it were marvellous if they entirely escaped all slander and suspicions. Had they not been sustained by higher powers, a consciousness of virtue, but few could have withstood the ruthless assaults they have suffered. The professedly pure and pious, as well as the openly vulgar and sensual, have loaded them with contumely and suspicion, and assailed their motives and deeds as base and infamous. Hence, there are men, and women too, who seek interviews with mediums, professing to be anxious to investigate Spiritualism, while in reality their motives are of a character which have been falsely and foully attributed to mediums. There are certain men, especially, who are very anxious to investigate, and solicit sittings whenever they can find lady-mediums, attractive young ladies, no matter how many other opportunities they may enjoy or may have enjoyed. We have known scores of such very anxious investigators, and known some of them served with lessons of rebuke which sent them home to investigate their moral nature and blush with shame over their infamous designs. We warn such lecherous hypocrites to beware how they seek to approach women-mediums, for these mediums are endowed with intuitions which can penetrate the masks of sensualism, and shrink back with loathing from the very touch, yea, even the atmosphere of the libertine, however sincere and specious his professions, his manner, his exterior may seem. And they are constantly guarded by angel guides who can see still more clearly into all the recesses of the soul, and give premonitions of approaching danger and contamination. Experienced mediums are constantly fortified against the exposures to which we allude; and we need do no more than throw out a hint as sufficient to the younger and less experienced. Women who are truly pure and intuitive need no warnings. They can anticipate the motives of those who are assuming the garb of "investigators" while in reality they are governed by the basest curiosity or sensualism. Let no airs or flatteries or specious pretensions ever blind women-mediums into any undue confidence in those men whose characters and whose very natures exhale an infernal magnetism whose presence is contaminating, however subtle, unseen, or unrealized for the time being. True virtue is safe, even in the society of the most subtle and infamous; but no possible benefit can result from such society, to compensate for the useless exposure. Such men must begin the work of regeneration at home, before they seek the mediumship of angel women.

Notwithstanding the airs assumed by some progressed

and highly developed philosophers, who claim for themselves and the masses of the people such an astonishing growth as to be entirely beyond the need of all external phenomena, there is a constant demand for manifestations adapted to the condition of seekers, skeptics, and those who are not yet fully confirmed in the faith of angel ministrations. Men and women who have enjoyed sufficient opportunities to satisfy themselves beyond a doubt as to the facts and philosophy of Spiritualism, may sit down in their cosy chairs or complacently mount platforms, and write and talk on the comparative insignificance of raps, tips, trances and other tests of spiritual power and intelligence; but let them go out and mingle with the people; the material multitude absorbed in external things; the crowd on the street, the highway and the market places; go into lanes, hamlets, desolate and darkened homes, dungeons, fields, workshops, places of worship, and dens howling with wickedness and woe, halls glittering with hollow gayety and gold, and the vast majority, not only in public but in private life, will be found living with no vivid consciousness of immortality and the overshadowing presence of angel hosts, and are either spiritually dead or dying for the need of those very spirit manifestations which some easy would-be philosophers affect to regard with indifference and contempt. If we have gone beyond A, B, C's, we are to remember where we once were, and what we then needed; and we shall then realize what thousands of others still need. While we are soaring away in loftiest flights, it may anon answer a good purpose to look back and down a little, in order that we may keep our reckoning and realize the multitude beneath. We may shout Onward, upward! and that is well, but do not let us fancy ourselves so far onward as to be out of sight of everybody else, or so far upward as to lose our balance, and, while aiming at stars, find ourselves at last floundering in the mud. We may occasionally turn somersaults far up into the cerulean vaults of the celestial empire, swing on rainbows, drink dew-drops on mounts where gods quaff nectar, chip off starry scintillations from universes blazing in the unknown heights of the boundless blue empyrean, and fancy ourselves inflated with inspirations so stupendous as to astonish Deity himself, yet, after all, what we need most, and what the people need, is the daily, substantial bread of life. Your theories are very plausible, your speculations are fine, your philosophy is beautiful, your schemes of reform sound very feasible, your predictions of the millennium are very grand and hopeful, but the people demand facts and demonstrations designed to unfold and enforce practical principles for daily use.

Let it not be understood that we deprecate the need of taking high ground in regard to the speculative, the scientific, the philosophical, the moral, the religious, the intellectual, the ideal, the eclectical and the reformatory. Nothing is more disheartening to progressive Spiritualists than to find persons wholly absorbed in the phenomenal, the curious, and the superficial, incessantly calling for marvellous manifestations, with no disposition to seek for practical principles, or make a practical application, or take any advance steps. Spiritualism is good for nothing only so far as it becomes practical, and makes men and women happier, wiser and better. But while we are advocating principles, we cannot ignore the need of primary facts. All our philosophers who now claim a high sphere of attainment, came up step by step on a basis of facts. They came up the ladder on one round after another. And now some of these highly-progressed souls would kick the ladder down, and treat it with contempt, and allow the multitude beneath to get along as best they can. They are like fast, over-grown boys who are not content with merely leaving the old school-master behind, but propose to go back and give the old fogy a thrashing, turn him out of doors, tear down the school-house, and bid the rising generation dispense with their A, B, C's and A, B, abs. They call spirit manifestations baby baubles; denounce circles as superfluous nonsense and nuisances; denominate mediums as mere machines of a toyish nature, useful only to amuse and astonish the undeveloped rabble of gulls and flats who are unprepared to appreciate the loftier unfoldings of a supernal philosophy which begins in the mud and ends in moonshine. We once met a very sensitive and an intelligent young woman who was regarded a superior and highly promising trance-speaking and writing medium, but she informed us that, for a time, she gave up her mediumship, because a well-known reputed philosopher had spoken discouragingly of her cultivating her gifts and had even ridiculed mediumship. Now, such men ought to know better than thus to throw contempt on gifts on which the masses of mankind must, for a long time, depend for the foundations of all spiritual faith, philosophy, and progress. If these gifts have been abused, what then? Everything has suffered abuse and perversion. Are mediums and investigators sometimes liable to be deceived and led astray, or to pass through severe disciplines? All these things are essential to true growth. Spirits may often lead us through strange and fearful experiences, but if our aims are true and pure, in the end we shall rejoice in triumphing over all seeming evil and error, and bless the ordeals through which we have passed.

Let no noble minds therefore fear the cultivation of spiritual gifts. All have a use. Fear no devils or psychological imps lurking beneath tables or hovering with infernal missions around our circles. Calling on the dear departed, in the name of the Highest, with pure hearts and elevated minds, we shall receive no manifestations which may not in the end be seen in harmony with the ministration of the wise, the beloved and beatified angels of the Father, come back to convince the unbelieving, to strengthen the weak and wavering, to gladden the lonely and despondent, to take the hand of the poor wanderer drooping along the highway of the world, to inspire the heroic with new hopes in behalf of humanity, to call back the prodigal lost in strange lands, to cheer the despairing with new gleams of joy, and sustain the dying through the last change of nature.

CHAPTER VII.

QUOTATIONS FROM REPRESENTATIVE SPIRITUALISTS.

In these selections many first-class spiritual writers are unavoidably omitted; the citations are given more for the purpose of presenting a variety, rather than the best specimens of style or thought, or anything like a complete embodiment of Spiritualism:—

Men are doubting whether the American Union will be preserved. Men say that ages ago there existed a freedom something like ours, and our "experiment" may perish like theirs. It may as likely perish as that the sun, which has sunk, will in a few moments reappear in the western horizon, and retrace its steps. Be sure humanity will work out its destiny. This nationality will live, and live not only to accomplish its destiny, but to be the potency by which the world itself is to be regenerated. Other nations have attained perfection in some single department; it is reserved for America to achieve a universal excellence. We are still in a state of transition. This process is to go on for years; and when it is completed, there will begin to work back and out in every direction, from this great centre, a new influence of life and of power. Greece succumbed to barbarian Rome. Rome became civilized and Christian, but fell before the northern barbarians. That was the era of brute force. But brute force is no longer the power that rules the world; and these reverses in the progress of the race can no longer occur. Science, and not strength, now decides the battles of the world. We shall be the focal centre to which the desire of all nations shall tend, and from which this light shall expand. Asia, receiving back its sons and daughters inoculated with the new blood of a new nation, shall begin to feel its sluggish life stimulated, and its ancient glory shall return to it again. The Brahmin, as he walks the plains of Hindostan, begins to doubt the truth of the religion which has ruled his land so many ages. The missionary unfolds to him the scheme of the Christian religion, and he says, "All this my ancestors knew before Jesus was born, and before Israel fled from Egypt." He does want something new, but he does not wish his old doctrines brought back to him in a new form. But when he shall be shown that all these have a common origin away back in the distance of time, and that origin was real spiritual demonstration of immortality and a future state, the nations of the East will begin to listen, and to see that, while they have kept alive this idea, it has been perverted to all the forms of idolatry in which it has been abused. Thus will come on the great progress of the race in the years to come. In the revelation to our age of the truths of immortality, by means of spiritual manfestations, the race shall see a new and fuller development of those intimations of religious truth which in the infancy of the race gave birth to that ancient religion which has been the foundation and the essence of all the theologies of the world's history; and seeing in this clearer light the truths of our spiritual being, the world shall be led into that higher plane of thought and action in which may be attained the final ends of human existence. — *J. S. Loveland.*

Tables rise into the air, speak by the alphabet, musical instruments play; spirit hands appear and write, as plenty of us know from repeated observations; people who never learned, draw and paint wonderful and beautiful things; spirits appear, and there are certain persons who see spirits as commonly as they see bodies, and give the most undeniable proofs of it. Well, these do convince, and have convinced many atheists and materialists, and, therefore, whether they be wise or foolish, let common sense decide. — *Wm. Howitt.*

The time is coming when children shall be taken from the cradle and moulded by spirits to their organic inspiration, shall grow up to be seers, prophets, and interpret the speech of God in the celestial and spiritual, as in the natural conditions. Every man to a certain degree may be an inspired man, if he does not so shut up his faculties that no divine truth can penetrate into him. Thank God, the vast spirit world has opened its doors, and its inhabitants are pouring down floods of inspiration. Let every man take the truth thus offered, and, more than that, let him live up to it, graduating it to his present plane of being, and projecting it into spheres of use. Inspiration is the expression of the Divine himself, not limited to any place or time, but extending over all ages and all space, and embracing all mankind. Open your minds to receive this inspiration of God through his spirits, and you will not have to go to sacred books and special teachers, but each man will be unto himself a teacher — a recipient of divine truth day by day. As he receives and lives out these truths does he thus become sanctified in practicalities before the Father. — *L. Judd Pardee.*

I am a Spiritualist, again, because I regard Spiritualism a great help in the promulgation of free discussion. There are thousands of questions on the subject of religion, science, and philosophy, which must be discussed, but could never be solved by any method mankind possessed prior to the birth of modern Spiritualism. These subjects, we say, must be discussed. The thousands who have been shut up in the caves of dark and gloomy theology did not dare look beyond the bands which bound them down. Man's eternal destiny was a mere fancy; the essential religious truths were mere baseless whims. The time has come when religion and reason must be married. Heretofore, religion has damned reason, and reason, in turn, has damned religion. The people were narrow-minded and superstitionized, and reason could not laugh nor argue them out of their condition. Reason urged her voice upon them, and tried to persuade them that the religion that denounced the exercise of their own faculties of thought and judgment could not be a finality. — *Rev. Adin Ballou.*

Mediums are our fathers, mothers, sisters, and brothers, neighbors, and friends; most of them have become mediums contrary to their wish and will, and, in spite of the opposition of themselves and friends, the phenomena have appeared wherever they chose, and have, in each case, commanded attention and enforced conviction of their spiritual origin, until now, in the comparatively short space of ten years, Spiritualism has its millions of mediums and believers scattered over the wide world, in every nation and with every race of people. There has been no collusion between mediums, and yet there is a remarkable likeness in all the manifestations wherever they occur, with whatsoever race of people, and in whatsoever language, and through the several phases of the manifestations. Beside, wheresoever they occur, and in the presence of persons who do not believe they are spiritually produced, the phenomena *claim* for themselves a spiritual origin. We submit that the history of the phenomena fully vindicates the integrity of their mediums, and the hypothesis of deception offered in solution of them has ever been weak, malevolent, insufferably unjust, and we submit that it should forever be abandoned. — *Charles Partridge.*

This great spiritual power cannot be stopped, or prevented from renovating humanity. The human family must have a higher standard. The ideas of the past have brought us, in our social relations, to monogamy, and into legalized libertinism. A higher standard of morals will lead us to true virtue. Marriage has been legal, instead of spiritual. We have to become individualized, and to come out of all custom, and to come into truth. This has no reference to any action against our laws, for, were we all unmarried to-night, we should marry just as badly to-morrow morning. The angel world is going not to interfere, particularly, with our marriage relations, but to individualize us, to enlighten our souls. The question of marriage very much agitated the Christians in the days of the apostles. In these days, many people seem to suppose Spiritualism comes to unmarry us all. But we need supporters; let us have them. When we are grown up to true individualism, we realize the oneness of the sexes, and shall find that male and female are alike, until the soul finds its mate, whether in this world or the next. Our laws are right, for every man that is under the laws needs them. — *Amanda Britt Spence.*

The necessity for a personality as a central point for man's worship arises from the inability of man to measure infinity. Man on the religious plane must have something that he can grasp; his object of worship must be visible, so to speak, to his comprehension; must be able to manifest himself in God-like love, wisdom, and action. On the philosophical plane he conceives of principles and forces. His God is the grand aggregate of natural law. But while this may satisfy the mere philosopher, it does not meet a universal need, which demands not alone attributes, but a personality to whom they belong, and through whom they can be made manifest. Man cannot worship his philosophical God; necessity has no affection, and can beget none. He thinks it a sound philosophical conclusion that Jesus is the highest representative of natural principles in a state of the most perfect equilibration that man can conceive of, and representing thus all the principles of nature in himself, is all of God that man can comprehend. In him all human philosophy and theology are brought to a focus, and in this sense there is philosophical propriety in saying that Christ is God. . . . His superiority was all principles in equilibration. "Love thy neighbor as thyself" was a new doctrine, and all of value that we enjoy to-day is a birth out of that love. Men, before and since his time, have manifested scintillations of greatness, but in him greatness culminated. It is doubted whether a Newton or a Fulton would have been possible, but for Christ's promise to be ever with us. To be able to love one another is greatness itself. This love is the Christ principle, the Christ doctrine, and the Christ life. It produces, comprehends, and governs the universe of matter and of mind.—*Prof. Mapes.*

The affectional phase of Spiritualism is dear to us all, for our orb of love is not yet fully rounded. Dear friends leave us; eyes once beaming courage in our souls shine on us no more; we feel the sun of life has set; our hearts are homeless; we are weary wanderers on life's way. Spiritualism bids us realize the broad wings of their love spread over us, and we feel we are sheltered from without, have entered the quiet haven within. Brows radiant with light bend over us; soft voices speak, and our heart-chords vibrate to a strange, rich music, waking a world of thought that slumbers not again. Our being trembles with its weight of tenderness. Thus are we nerved anew for the battle of life; we know that souls set with the seal of purity are above and around us. These spirit voices, coming to us in the still midnight, are sweeter than murmur of woodland brook, softer than the melody of forest bird. Yet they sound the depths of the soul, as the leaded line the sea.—*Mrs. U. Clark.*

If the story of Prometheus was once a fable, we are sure that in an important sense it is fabulous no longer. Invisible hands have rekindled immortal fires on our own altars, to warm the great heart and to light up the face of humanity. The relations of great thoughts and noble deeds to the realms of spiritual causation are daily becoming more perceptible. Through all the inherent forces and essential laws of the celestial, spiritual, and natural worlds, a divine energy is infused, and powers unseen speak in the inspired thoughts of living men, who sit like stars at the celestial gates. — *S. B. Brittan.*

The spiritual theory and spiritual communications maintain all the great and leading doctrines of Christianity. In regard to the Bible, I cannot better express my views than in the language of the Rev. Adin Ballou: "Whatever of divine fundamental principle, absolute truth, and essential righteousness there is in the Bible, in the popular religion, and in the established churches, will stand. It cannot be done away. On the contrary, it will be corroborated and fulfilled by spirit manifestations." — *Hon. N. P. Tallmadge.*

However far back we extend our researches into the depths of antiquity, we find no period so remote that this method of communicating with invisible intelligence does not seem to have existed; and its universal prevalence among the ancients seems indicative of a necessity, by a law of human nature, that some channel of supernal wisdom should be constantly open to man through which he might receive instruction adapted to the ever-varying circumstances and exigencies of individual, social, national life. — *Wm. Fishbough.*

No one need fear the sovereignty of individualism — the right of each to act in accordance with his highest intuitions. For should one man transcend his boundaries, another will let him know it. We need to practise the gospel of self-government. The conservative may cry aloud for the safety and sanctity of institutions. But heed him not! His cries proceed from the wilderness of crime and the marshes of despotism, which are tenfold more dangerous than the everglades of Florida. — *A. J. Davis.*

As respects myself, I am much happier since my conversion. I no longer regret the supervening of old age. Each step toward the portal of death is an approximation to that of heaven, and consequently of a state of happy rejuvenation as respects body and mind. I am now a true Christian, so far as devotion to the morality and theology which was really taught by the founder of Christianity, and personal fealty to that founder, can entitle me to this designation. — *Prof. R. Hare.*

No deep spiritual law can be evaded or disobeyed, as sure as the Almighty Father and Mother are present everywhere to administer them. And if men generally would aim to secure just that amount of material wealth and good for which their spiritual parts had use, and only that, they would soon find that they had come into that divine relation, both with themselves and one another, which is the secret of all harmony and happiness in this world or any other. — *Banner of Light.*

This new dispensation comes to supply the want of the countless thousands who are now slumbering in indifference or toiling in infidelity; to convict man of his immortality, and instruct him how to make it happy; to open to his view the great doctrine of progression, involving an eternity of action, and the supremacy of his reason over the besetting propensities of his material nature, and to impress upon him forever to love God and his neighbor. — *Judge Edmonds.*

Enough that the Great Father loves *all* his children with an undying, inexhaustible affection, which many waters cannot quench, nor floods drown, and which sin itself has no power to diminish. Enough that all his providences tend invariably to some kind and degree of good, forever and ever. Our soul is made glad within us, and shouts with an interior joy for what unknown mercies must eternally be measured out, and what more than puny human thoughts are in the GREAT EVERLASTING LOVE. — *W. H. Fernald.*

Every individual must make his own soul the standard of authority in determining what is true or false in principle and right or wrong in action. If we aim to do right, if our motives are approved by the highest convictions of the soul, although we may err in judgment and run into trouble, we shall never fall under self-condemnation. The God within us shall bring us into judgment, and if we stand acquitted before that inward tribunal, no other "judgment seat" shall have power over the happiness and destiny of the soul. — *Leo Miller.*

God's pitying angels stand at your bedside, and watch over you — poor stray children of the Father — with yearning tenderness, bringing you sometimes a dream of home and your dear ones, sometimes a hope of pardon and heaven. Oh, take heart! A pure and honorable life is *possible* for you all — God has not lost his hold of you yet. — *Grace Greenwood.*

Spiritualism requires for its ranks men who are willing to brave the world — who are firm in truth, and yet liberal and generous to their opponents. — *E. V. Wilson.*

I do not desire to see a creed formed for Spiritualists to believe, but I do believe in a free platform, on which Spiritualists can discuss everything, and thus make themselves strong in their own moral and intellectual power. — *H. B. Storer.*

Spiritualism will ring out its CLARION notes in the battle of the destruction of the old and the triumphs of the new, and her BANNER shall float in triumph over a world conquered, not as Alexander, Cæsar and Napoleon conquered, but by love and kindness. — *Miss A. W. Sprague.*

When the spirit of man, disengaged from the body, passes to another state of existence, its thoughts and affections may still revert to earth; it occasionally makes itself perceptible to the living, whether in dream or in the light of day — sometimes to the sense of sight, sometimes to that of hearing or of touch, sometimes by an impression which we detect in its effect but cannot trace to its origin; these various spiritual agencies wearing in this instance a frivolous, in that a solemn aspect, now assuming the form of petty annoyance, now of grave retribution, but more frequently brightening into indications of gentle ministry and loving guardianship. — *Robert Dale Owen.*

In using spirit manifestations as a means of instruction, we are to exercise the same judgment and wisdom we do in using anything else. We must not expect a medium to be able to tell everything we wish to know, or even to be impressed with an opinion upon subjects respecting which we are decided and dogmatical. — *G. Beckwith.*

I have unbounded faith in genuine Spiritualism; the promulgation of its truths has been my most earnest prayer, and though every friend forsake me, I will be true to it, because I know it concerns humanity. — *Mrs. A. M. Spence.*

The more we learn of the laws governing spiritual intercourse, the more perfect appears the harmony between modern manifestations and those of which we have record in the dawning era of Christianity, as manifested through Jesus and his disciples. — *C. D. Griswold.*

We are engaged in a movement which is ultimately to overturn the fabric of the world's present moral, social and intellectual philosophies, a movement wide and deep as infinitude, and the least sandgrain which momentarily obstructs the rolling wheels should be removed. — *Hudson Tuttle.*

He who stands in the light of genuine spirit-illumination, seeing the scheme of human existence and providence as it really is, can by no possible means denounce, condemn or vilify any human being. — *J. S. Loveland.*

The soul demands a faith which can look into the spirit-world and there recognize friends prematurely summoned from their labors here, and entered on that state where neither fire nor flood can arrest their progress forever. — *R. Hassal.*

In spiritual as in natural science, we must ever be on our guard against premature theories and hasty generalizations. The best views we can herein attain should still be held only as provisional, partial truth, perhaps, but not the rounded and absolute truth to which a higher light and a consummate and perfect knowledge of the subject would conduct us. — *London (Eng.) Spiritual Magazine.*

Woman! take courage to elevate thyself; for the true-hearted of this century are already laboring in thy behalf. Strive to free thyself from fetters, and great-souled men will haste to the rescue. Honor thyself, and the nations will honor thee. Know thy greatness, and the very heavens will bend to thee in kindly recognition. — *Mrs. Mary F. Davis.*

There is a vast uplifting power in the belief that good kindred angels are present to guide our feet in the paths of truth and peace, to breathe around and through us a purer charity, a brighter hope, a serener joy than belong to our clay-bound souls. — *Hon. A. Putnam.*

Oh, the glory of a spirit crowned with the consciousness of immortality, who feels no death because it has life, and knows no darkness because it has constant light. — *Mrs. C. L. V. Hatch.*

Men and women of all classes and in all countries, physicians and men of science, ministers of all persuasions, and men of literature and art, all have sought for the proofs of this great and absorbing question of the possibility of spiritual causes acting on this world of nature. — *D. D. Home.*

The stability of the physical universe depends not more on the truth of physical harmony of its parts, than the integrity of the moral universe depends upon moral truth; the harmony of its parts with the whole, and of the whole with the universal cause. — *Mrs. C. Bebee Wilbour.*

The human soul is a grand microcosm of the spiritual realm, for there is nothing that exists in the spirit world but has its counterpart in the human soul. Yet the individual soul differs from every other soul in the universe, because it is an immortal thing, an individuality, and contains within itself the kingdoms of heaven and hell. — *Mrs. J. H. Conant.*

Whenever we learn a new truth, or strengthen our affections for that which is pure and good in any object, we are feeding our souls with that which shall endure forever. — *Joel Tiffany.*

The age is transitional. The seventh angel has sounded. The angelic dispensation is upon us, the "door in heaven," as the apocalyptic John declared, is "opened." — *J. M. Peebles.*

The truths of a spiritual philosophy, whether to be termed religious or not, lie within man's spirit, and their confirmation can only come from his spiritual recognition. — *Mrs. L. M. Willis.*

Where one's consciousness is his law of life, religion, and all outward authority, are of minor importance. I will worship the God within me, and no God of human organizations. — *H. C. Wright.*

Though we do not accept, as belonging to Spiritualism, many things laid upon it, neither will we condemn those who are the parents of these monstrosities, but with meekness will correct them. You who are Spiritualists, do you live up to the highest light within your souls? —*Mrs. A. M. Middlebrook.*

I do not believe in an organization that shall form a creed or establish a church. I recognize every individual's duty to form his own standard of right and wrong, so long as we occupy different planes of development and growth. — *Dr. H. F. Gardner.*

To know that we are immortal, ever-progressive beings, who through eternal ages must grow in goodness, wisdom, and glory above our highest conceptions, must take hold of our natures and lead us to respect and aid the lowest and humblest of the race. — *Hon. F. Robinson.*

Oh, my friends, let the thought of the houseless, the dying, and the outcast children of sorrow sound in your midst, not like a requiem note of mourning, but a sweet Sabbath bell, calling upon every soul to join in this cathedral of nature's own erection, and upon the altar of sweet flowers and fragrant summer grass offer up the only worship which the common Father requires, — the incense of pity for the wretched, help for the helpless, strength for the fallen. — *Miss Emma Hardinge.*

Let the people know they can adopt or create their own theology, and their minds will expand to wider growth; all evil will be eradicated from the earth, and good will take its place. — *F. L. Wadsworth.*

Love is the inner door that leads to heaven's joy. It is the glorious morning of the eternal day of the immortal soul of man. Love is the harmony of the soul whose strain of melody ceases not when begun throughout eternal ages. — *Dr. A. B. Child.*

All desire to live in a higher life after the dissolution of the external form. All desire to feel conscious that departed friends are still near and loving as when in the external form. That is our faith. — *S. S. Jones.*

Our bodies are but travelling garments which nature kindly takes in her arms when we are done with them, and bids us join the white-robed angels. —*Mrs. Fannie Davis Smith.*

Men and women, prepare yourselves for stirring times. Be true to God and the right, and let come what will. There is a God who speaks out over the voices of all the people. — *Lizzie Doten.*

Spiritualism teaches whatever is written in the moral constitution and spiritual needs of the human soul. — *A. E. Newton.*

The people are starving for the true "bread of life;" who will supply the demand? — *Rising Tide.*

Be infidel to every selfish and mean act, to everything unjust, to policy when made the rule of life, but do not be infidel to your true character. — *Mrs. M. A. Wood.*

Over the rainbow bridge of faith mortals have passed and entered the gates of friendship's paradise. — *Cora Wilburn.*

All the light the Bible sheds on immortality was the result of spirit intercourse. — *I. V. Mapes.*

No kind word, deed, or smile bestowed on the humblest of God's children, shall pass unnoted by the invisibles. — *Mary J. King.*

How glorious, then, does the doctrine of Spiritualism come to the suffering hearts of humanity, bringing the breathings of angels from the happy homes of spirits who have passed beyond us to the point where they, while progressing upwards in their endless march, can lead us with them in the path of all that is good, true, and noble.— *Mrs. M. S. Townsend.*

We believe this is the second coming of Christ, or the spiritual era in which his spirit will descend, by power of his Father, into every heart, and all will be born anew, and become as little children. — *A. P. Pierce.*

If a peaceful, calm death be the test of true religion, then truly is Spiritualism divine. The knowledge which it gives of the "hereafter" ennobles life, elevates the affections, robs the grave of its gloom, and death of its sting. — *W. F. Jamieson.*

"The good time coming" is not far distant, when creeds and dogmas shall exist only in name, and that name be but a keepsake to remind us of our infantile efforts to walk. — *Mrs. S. L. Chappell.*

Inspiration is the essential method by which God educates all his creatures, and nature is the grand medium of inspiration in all its varieties. — *George Stearns.*

As different circles in the body may converse together, so different circles in the spirit world may do the same. — *Charles Hammond.*

The doctrine of Spiritualists has love, charity, nature, reason, philosophy, science, and facts to sustain it, and to me it is beautifully true. — *Warren Chase.*

We (reformers) are charged with being Spiritualists. Some of us are, and some are not. But if we all were, still might not we all be Christians? — *Gerrit Smith.*

If the inspiration of the present age be rejected by the churches, how can they believe in the inspiration of the past? — *Dr. J. H. Robinson.*

Man's lips shall yet be touched by the angels, and he shall utter the inspiration of God. — *Mrs. De Force Gordon.*

Mind or spirit is above all, and absolutely disposes of and controls all. — *Dr. J. B. Dods.*

God has constituted us individually to differ, in order that we might harmonize as a whole. — *Dr. O. H. Wellington.*

Spirit is the pivotal fact in nature, being the soul and essence of all things that move and have a being. — *J. H. W. Toohey.*

Our greatest hope is in the development of the heavenly germ within us.— *Lyman C. Howe.*

What soul has not an inborn need of "somebody to love," and some one to love in return? — *Francis Brown.*

Our spiritual creed is, one God, one belief in immortality, and one common destiny in the great To Come. — *P. B. Randolph.*

All are teachers to each other, and the spirit world works through mortal instruments.— *Mrs. E. A. Bliss.*

The greatest virtues are found in the littlest things of life. — *Rufus Elmer.*

All things indicate the coming of a new wave of the divine spirit into man. — *T. L. Harris.*

CHAPTER VIII.

ORGANIZATIONS — FORMS, ORDINANCES, ETC. — PRACTICAL ACTION — MEANS OF PROGRESS — LECTURERS AND MEDIUMS — IMPOSTORS — SUNDAY SCHOOLS — MARRIAGES AND FUNERALS — THE CLERGY — COUNSELS AND WARNINGS.

AMONG Spiritualists there is no tendency to organizations seeking to bind the conscience or prescribe ordinances, ceremonies, or rigid forms of belief or worship. But a need is felt for such organizations as are expedient to form orderly circles, obtain places for public conferences and lectures, procure suitable speakers and mediums, raise means for meeting expenses and maintain certain legal rights. In many places these things have been left with none to assume the responsibility; and the result has been unfortunate to the people, to the cause of Spiritualism and laborers in the public field. The time will come when believers will avail themselves of the advantages to be gained by adopting some unobjectionable organization. In many places some legal form is already adopted, and acceptable lecturers are granted letters which entitle them to the rights of ministers. No good reason can be offered against Spiritualists taking their legal rights, though we may object to everything that looks like dictating or dogmatizing. But we are not obliged to dogmatize, or to dodge direct issues. We can assert the existence of Deity without insisting on an orthodox code of divinity, or setting up an army of arbitrary D. D.'s. We can recognize the religious element in man, without harnessing him up in sectarian forms and creeds. We can maintain the practical principles of Christianity, without believing the orthodox trinity or vicarious atonement.

We can take an eclectic view of the Bibles of all ages and nations, without accepting plenary inspiration or infallibility. We can recognize the essential relationship between ancient and modern Spiritualism, without compromising our reason, our individuality or the independence of our consciences. As Spiritualists, we can give expression to certain distinct facts and sentiments, without asserting a rigid creed, or assailing the rights of others; and we can meet together in large or small bodies, for fraternal interchange and mutual protection, without being suspected of sectarian or sinister motives, and without subjecting ourselves to the charge of seeking the organization of some infernal inquisition. We are heartily sick of canting suspicions of sectarian designs; just as though Spiritualists should never dare say or do anything under heaven that looks or sounds anything like what has ever been said or done before, lest we may run into the most foul and diabolical abuses. We dislike this running into extremes. We see no need of repudiating everything that has been adopted before this spiritual era, simply because men have run into excesses and abuses. On the same ground, we might ignore the air and sunlight of heaven.

There are no desires or efforts among Spiritualists towards sectarian organizations. Their conventions indicate nothing in that direction. The preambles and resolutions they have passed in conventions are the farthest from sectarian; covering the broadest ground, asserting the sovereignty of the individual conscience, and embracing principles of the most catholic harmony. As a body of believers we quote no large council or convention as our authority, nor do we allow any particular individuals, however great or notorious, to be our leaders. Yet, when we are assailed from without, it is perfectly right and natural for us to seek self-defence and protection by coming together and acting as a band of united brothers and sisters. When certain authorities are thrust on us, it is proper we should protest; and when false sentiments and practices are attributed to us, it were ignoble and cowardly on our part not to arise and assert our honest convictions. Should we keep back silent in the dark, and allow ourselves to be pelted down by slander and falsehood? No! unless we would be branded as poltroons. If it is right, proper and safe for us to defend ourselves and our sentiments in our houses and select circles, it is equally so for us to come together in our conventions, and stand out open before the world, firm, united, unflinching. If we are Spiritualists, we may show our hands, our hearts, our faces.

Let it be distinctly understood, then, that while we are no advocates of anything like a Spiritualist sect or creed, we contend for the right of some sort of an external organization designed to facilitate the work of reform and subserve purposes of self-defence, and also the right of defining those principles of our faith and philosophy which leave all consciences unfettered and free for higher unfoldings. Where any legal organization is needed, the friends interested can consult legal authorities, and learn what course to pursue in obtaining a charter which will enable them to do business and enjoy the rights and privileges belonging to corporate bodies. But due caution will be exercised against forming any organization liable to run into abuses of a sectarian, aristocratic, despotic or political character.

Spiritualists repudiate all combinations of church and state as tending to inquisitorial abominations. Some years ago, a scheme was projected to combine all the orthodox sects into a political party and carry our government by storm, but the scheme was strangled in its birth by the overwhelming voice of the people. Any effort in that direction put forth by Spiritualists would meet with the most infamous defeat. Our "kingdom is not of this world." Spiritualism seeks to unfold the individual soul, and lift us above all governments and institutions. The moment we abandon our confidence in the power of the moral principles entrusted to our keeping and inculcation, and fall back on the ballot-box or any other merely external aids, our influence is gone, and we put ourselves on the level of shoulder-hitters and brawling demagogues. While the temperance reform relied on moral power, it rolled on in triumph; but when its advocates turned politicians, and pulpits were transformed into caucuses, the cause of reformation began to degenerate, until rum reigned over the land in spite of priest and magistrate.

As Spiritualists we may participate in the affairs of government, and remain indifferent to no movement involving the weal of humanity; but for the ultimate triumph of our principles and the achievement of our rights, we must rely on those moral influences which reach beyond the caucus and ballot-box, and take hold of the individual heart and life. We depend less on external circumstances and institutions than on those omnipotent energies which slumber within the soul, and can be called out into the field of heroic action under the quickening influences of the angel world. Our mission is not to call the roll for any merely outward organization, but to go out into the highways, the hedges, the lanes, the lowly hamlets and the wide fields of humanity, seeking first to enlist the reason and affections of the lost millions; and when the minds of the people are enlightened and their hearts are warmed into spiritual life, we shall need no external laws or officials, for the kingdom of God will have come and his "will be done on earth as in heaven."

The only kinds of organization existing among us are those for the purpose of managing financial and external affairs. We ignore all attempts to embody the religion of Spiritualism in anything like a society, sect, institution, creed, form, or ordinance; it were like attempting to organize the sun-light, the air, or the elements of life. We recognize the central importance of individual freedom; but the moment we attempt anything like an external organization, insisting on forms, creeds, and restrictions, the souls of individuals become cramped, confined, subjected to authorities and standards outside of themselves, and must submit, no longer called upon to feel their own accountability, no longer thrown back on their own responsibility, no longer stimulated or permitted to exercise their own reason or religious intuitions. Spiritualism begins by recognizing God and the spirit world opened with freedom for all to communicate, receive and apply according to their individual needs. Each must seek, find and appropriate for themselves. God and angels must be revealed to individuals according to their planes. To prescribe any sectarian organization, with forms and creeds, would be like prescribing ordinances to govern our communications with each other on the social plane; like manufacturing rules to guide us in the exercise of love and friendship, and all the social sympathies of life. This folly has been attempted long enough. Sectarian organizations, seeking to dictate the soul, have resulted in enslaving millions of the weak, while they have failed to entrammel the minds of the strong, the bold, the free. No man of rational enlightenment or large liberty will allow any class of men to mould him into anything like stereotyped sects, creeds or ceremonies. The same is obvious in social and affectional affairs. Laws and customs may be instituted, but the diviner affections of the human heart can subsist only in the atmosphere of freedom, and at times they will break over all the bounds of ordinances and conventionalisms. Law-makers, phrenologists and physiologists may manufacture codes, charts and creeds to regulate marriage and the affections, yet, after all, men and women will fall in love and marry, regardless of all these external paraphernalia, notwithstanding the expediency of the latter.

The central element of all life and religion is Love; love flowing down from God, through angelic beings, thence manifest in the human heart, and flowing out over the plane of humanity in deeds and desires of divine goodness. And freedom is the essential condition of this divine, angelic and human love. So far as individuals can become perfectly united in organizing some methods of action, the result may prove favorable, but the spirit of life and religion can never find true, spontaneous expression in any external organization. It anticipates a perpetual growth in the individual soul, while a sect, creed or form must perpetually cramp and warp its energies Certain religious forms, ceremonies, ordinances may doubtless afford some minds important aids to spiritual culture and impress the senses in a manner to reach the soul, but if they are insisted on with regularity they will inevitably become irksome, dull and a mere drudgery. For ten years the writer had some trial in this line, while officiating as a minister. When the time came round for us to go through the prayers and benedictions of the pulpit, the administration of baptism and the Lord's Supper, the saying of grace over fancy tea-tables and epicurean festivals, we always tried to feel the spirit of the occasion, but the task was utterly impossible, and sometimes the spirit would not move. But now, as a Spiritualist, we feel at liberty; and when conditions are favorable and the spirit moves, we may indulge in forms of invocation, praise, thanksgiving and inspiration. But we can recommend no rigid forms. Worship should be the perpetual outgushing of the soul. The external ordinance of baptism can be of little service compared with a baptism into the Christ-like spirit. The true sacrament of the Lord's Supper is to heed his precepts and examples, and endure the martyrdom of a noble life and death. To receive the right hand of fellowship, and true ordination or confirmation, we need to come in communion with "the general assembly and church of the first born which are written in heaven" (Heb. xii. 23), and realize that we have "received the spirit of adoption, whereby we cry, Abba, Father; the spirit itself bearing witness with our spirit that we are the children of God." Rom. viii. 15, 16.

There are many cautions and counsels essential to the cause of spiritual progress. Some practical hints in regard to meetings, lecturers and mediums may here come in place. Numerous places are in need of public meetings and popular lectures, but sometimes those who are best able to furnish means perhaps lack zeal or the spirit of liberality, while those who are most devoted find themselves in limited circumstances. Many of our wealthy friends are ready to make generous contributions, yet the heaviest responsibility often falls on those whose hearts are willing but whose means are humble. Under such circumstances it becomes expedient to adopt a variety of methods. In many places social circles are formed, regular meetings are called, members or visitors each contributing a stipulated sum per week or month, and parties, fairs, levees or festivals are held. Many who are not Spiritualists are attracted, and congenial associations are formed. It is impossible to dispense with these means in advancing the cause of truth. Men and women, especially the young, are governed much by social influences, and unless we can present some genial and attractive associations, they will seek them elsewhere, and will lavish their means in other directions.

In New England these methods have been already quite extensively adopted, and have become very efficient in establishing reserved funds. Women are the most efficient workers in these enterprises. In any place where three or four believers can be found to unite, their efforts may be crowned with results enabling them to begin public meetings and employ occasional speakers.

There are many places where spiritual friends are few, and their means humble, while opposers are numerous and strong; yet there is an earnest desire that something be done for the advancement of truth. But too often all opportunities are neglected. Complaints are often made that lecturers and mediums are negligent in visiting certain places. But where is the fault? It is usually understood where most of our lecturers and mediums may be addressed, and most of them are in the habit of publishing their pioneer routes. If they are needed, let them be sent for, and let some persons assume the responsibility. There are thousands of needy places of which pioneer laborers know nothing. And but few if any of them are able to assume the responsibility of visiting, laboring, spending time and money, unless they are assured of some co-operation on the part of friends. If it is said they ought to be willing to make some sacrifice, our reply is, the friends ought to be likewise willing. If believers are unwilling to make sacrifices in behalf of the cause among their own friends and neighbors, how can laborers, who are entire strangers, be expected to feel much of a self-sacrificing interest? Besides, it must be remembered that no laborers have any time or means they are able to sacrifice. To meet their expenses and sustain their families, they are entirely dependent on the people; they are continually in need, and can seldom, if ever, labor without receiving more than their travelling expenses and their keeping. To offer them just enough to eat and drink and pay their fare, is to demand their labor for nothing, to treat them as beggars, to bring their families on public charity, and rob them of the means requisite to sustain their credit for honesty, justice and common decency. And how is it with many places in need of spiritual laborers? Mediums and lecturers sometimes send word, offering their services, and receive no sort of encouragement. "We are few and feeble, and fearful nothing can be done," is the too common plea. And the fact is, nothing ever will be done, until the few and feeble ones take hold with all their might, put forth their best efforts, and manifest a willingness to make some sacrifices. Suppose the attendance is small? It will never be any larger until repeated experiments are made. Suppose some time, labor and money are required? Nothing can ever be accomplished without some expenditures. No matter whether any great results are expected or not. Let the friends do the best they can, and trust the results with God, angels and the future. "Despise not the day of small things." Do your part towards encouraging devoted laborers, and benedictions will surely follow.

How shall the skeptical and inquiring public be reached? What mediums can be obtained for the right kind of tests? What lecturers or trance speakers can be had to present Spiritualism in the most acceptable manner? These questions are rife in every part of the country. In the first place, we may not be over-anxious to reach those who are unprepared to seek for themselves or to make any sacrifices in behalf of spiritual truth. If persons feel no need, but are rather indifferent or hostile, however their condition may be deplored, it were not wise to run after them with importunities. Receptive souls will seek, and then find. Those who persist in prejudice and opposition must wait their own time. To urge them against their will usually proves unavailing. We have no desire to force Spiritualism on any minds, nor hasten to make it popular among those now considered its opponents. Some Spiritualists are zealous to make converts and build up a reputation for the cause, in order that they may be relieved from the duty of standing out alone and bearing the individual, unpopular responsibility now resting on them. Most believers, however, are governed by higher motives; they desire men and women should realize the unspeakable blessings of Spiritualism, and are solicitous to use all means at their command for the diffusion of light.

In places not accessible to known mediums and lecturers, let those who are anxious to investigate form circles composed of none but honest, candid inquirers or believers. Let social meetings, either public or private, be called regularly, and books, pamphlets and periodicals be read and circulated. If you are not able to decide as to the most appropriate works needed, send your means to some responsible spiritual editor or lecturer, and he will furnish you with what is adapted to your necessities. In sending for books, be careful how you are influenced by catch-penny advertisements, or by the reputation of great names. The same caution may be heeded in regard to procuring lecturers and mediums. Developing circles and conference meetings are highly profitable in all places where a few earnest minds can harmonize; and let each person feel an entire liberty to speak, to present written essays, or addresses, etc., yield to the influences and impressions they feel, however humble may be their efforts. Let an earnest desire for truth predominate over all curiosity and prejudice. Minds must be open, free, unbiassed, and prepared to grapple with things new and old. After a few social circles or conference meetings are held, harmonious conditions will be sure to develop some facts, phenomena and teachings of peculiar interest pointing to the spirit world; for the very attitude of seeking always induces spiritual aids and influences from angel friends. If genuine mediums are found in your midst, whether they are highly developed or not, encourage them, and in many cases they will be able to accomplish more than strangers who are regarded far better mediums. We are to remember, all persons are more or less mediumistic, and whenever the right course is perseveringly pursued, efficient mediums may be developed without sending for distant strangers. Prejudice may sometimes exist against home mediums, but this should be overcome, and everything be tested by its own intrinsic value, regardless of preconceived impressions.

Sustain home mediums and home speakers, if you have any; for it often happens that many of those who are regarded with but little interest at home enjoy a useful reputation abroad. In many places laborers from abroad are indispensable. If their services are sought, let their temporal needs be remembered. Most of them are entirely dependent on their spiritual labors, with no regular salary or income, and are unable to live without something more than travelling expenses. Paying these expenses will not supply their home needs and incidentals. Mediums and lecturers are often asked to labor and sacrifice without any regard to material recompense, and they are generally very willing, where they can possibly afford it. Hundreds have suffered, and nearly starved, while unselfishly devoted to the cause, and very few have yet received a comfortable living for their labors. These responsibilities should be shared by those who call for their services. Spiritualists are coming to understand these things, and many laborers are now nobly sustained. The time will come when all mercenary considerations will cease, and no lack of means will hinder the advancement of truth. Those who have been prospered in temporal things will cheerfully minister to the needs of those who are devoted to things spiritual.

Friends in neighboring places should unite their energies in attracting laborers. When a sufficient amount of means cannot be raised by private contribution, let it be understood that each person calling on the medium for services, if able, is expected to offer some gift, and at public lectures let each one able contribute a small fee at the door. A door fee, however, is usually objectionable, and in the end will probably be entirely abolished, though in some places it may be deemed most appropriate for a while. The poor, however, should always be remembered and served without money and without price. When no fee is taken at the door, and a collection is taken up from the audience, the friends should consider the delicate position in which the speaker is placed, and make up the requisite sum which a voluntary contribution seldom affords, to say nothing of the unpleasantness of passing around the hats.

In seeking mediums and speakers, the public can seldom be governed by the newspaper notoriety given certain persons, however superior are the claims of many of these. Nor can the largest cities be always relied on as affording the best tests of superiority. Large allowance must be made for newspaper reports, personal favoritisms, fictitious attractions, and false judgments. Hundreds of public lecturers, equally efficient, may not have been published, and hundreds more may already be in the process of development, waiting to be called out and encouraged. Spiritualism seeks to idolize no particular class of teachers or leaders, like the priesthoods, but recognizes all possessed of equally divine gifts waiting for higher unfoldment. In some places trance speakers alone are desired for a time, and the novelty of this phase of teaching attracts many who would not otherwise hear. But trance speaking in the abnormal state is necessarily transient, and speakers of this class are fast advancing towards the normal plane of inspiration. No single class of laborers should be called to monopolize the whole field. All are aiming towards the same end, — the inculcation of a Spiritualism which opens every human soul to the light of heaven and the inspiration of God and angels. Good normal lecturers are often the most serviceable in preparing the way for trance speakers, and many of them are favored with inspirations of the most eloquent and efficient character. In providing for the public, no effort should be made to cater to a particular class of hearers, or minister to a morbid curiosity. Nor is it advisable to strain every nerve to produce a great effect at first. Stars of the greatest magnitude are not always the most efficient in shedding the light needed by the humble multitude. Let the people be fed, and not merely pleased, startled, astonished. In the spiritual kingdom there is no small nor great, but all are one in equal fraternity. Mediums and lecturers have each their place, each their gifts, and all are working towards the same great harmonic end. "What lecturer or speaking medium do you like best?" was the inquiry one spiritual friend put to another. "The last one I hear!" was the reply. Exactly so. The majority of Spiritualists are enthusiastic, warm-hearted, spontaneous; and their hearts are open to all. But sometimes the enthusiasm of the moment carries them away; and on hearing some new messenger, they grow so wild with joy and delight as to declare they never heard the like nor ever expect to hear its equal from any other lips. But another messenger comes, and they are equally delighted and elevated. "Onward, upward, higher, and still higher," is the motto; and just so it should be. Only the people should be cautious in their laudations, lest some speakers are disheartened, and others are injured by over-laudations.

How shall we discriminate between true and false spiritual laborers? It becomes exceedingly difficult to adopt any standards like those adopted by the sects or by conservative society. We have in mind a Spiritualist Association which proposed to publish to the world that no lecturers or mediums should be employed unless they could show good certificates as to their antecedents; but the proposition was dropped when it was suggested that *no* spiritual laborer might be able to bring certificates entirely satisfactory to all, for every lecturer and medium in the land had been denounced or suspected either by bitter enemies or jealous friends, and most of them had been driven to overstep the bounds of church or society, or adopt sentiments deemed radical and dangerous by conservatives. But there are individuals in our ranks so palpably false to the principles and practices of genuine Spiritualists, it is dangerous to trust them, unwise to encourage or sanction them. We must have some positive knowledge that the individuals are persistently dangerous, corrupt, and false, and temporarily beyond the desire or reach of reformation. But few such cases are found. And even then it is hard to ignore and denounce them. Jesus clung to Peter and Judas even to the last, and then administered only a sorrowful, sympathizing rebuke. As spiritual reformers and philosophers, we may grow wise and considerate in regard to these things, and launch no thunderbolts on the heads of even the most fallen and unfortunate.

The spiritual public has been exceedingly long-suffering and tolerant with a class of individuals who have been wandering through the country, filled with vague ideas of some lofty "mission" which the very loftiest spirits had to perform through them. They abound in "impressions" which seldom happen to correspond with that kind of common sense belonging to the normal plane of practical life. They drop down, here and there, all over the land, under the plea of having been "sent by the spirits," for some "object" which neither they nor anybody else ever finds out. They are always going to do some "wonderful things," which are never done. Their "mission" turns out to be a fizzle, and common-sense people are prone to consider them as being not far from fools. They are proverbially improvident; don't care about money; the spirits will provide for them, *providing* they can find good easy friends on whom to sponge, and who can fork over a five, ten, or twenty dollar bill with which to close. They are lazy louts, but set up the pious plea that the spirits won't let them work; stopped them; broke up their business, and sent them off to work wonders designed to astonish the inhabitants of earth, if not heaven itself. They are "wandering stars," all save the starry part, and their bungling attempts to fly off into the celestial firmament usually terminate in finding them stuck in the mud. They are a very ethereal class of beings, and very particular about their diet. The spirits won't let them eat or drink certain horribly contraband anti-celestial things; but give them a chance at pork and beans, or a good round of beef, and they are death on the same; the spirits "permit" them an occasional gratification in that line,—occasional whenever occasion offers. They are great magnetic subjects, and seldom get out of "condition" till the housewife gets out of patience waiting to clear off the breakfast table. In short, they are vagrants, vagabonds, vampires, and ought to be introduced to wood-saws, spades, or wheelbarrows, and be made of some service. Pass them along. Whoever recognizes the portraiture as their own will apply the moral.

We occasionally hear complaints of persons passing themselves as clairvoyant, healing, and spirit mediums, their extravagant claims, pretensions, failures, charges, impostures, and so on to the end of the catalogue. But these complaints are rarely well founded. Genuine healing mediums are modest, successful, moderate in their charges, and, above all other classes before the public, are eminently self-sacrificing, laboring freely for the poor, and often exhausting their last energies in relief of the suffering. But there are itinerent physicians outside the spiritual ranks, whose pretensions and charges far outstrip all those ever attributed to mediums. They carry pockets full of self-concocted puffs, ply the press with extravagant advertisements, spread out glaring bills and circulars, blow loud blasts in every public hall and on every corner, open their temporary offices, propose to cure everybody of everything except "hard times," and when it comes to that point, they are ready to relieve you of your last dollar, and leave you to whistle after they have taken their departure to some new and distant field of quackish speculation.

There are several classes of anti-spiritual lecturers perambulating the land, who have a most specious way of seeking to ingratiate themselves into favor with Spiritualists and extract their dimes. We refer to itinerant lecturers endeavoring to make capital out of the prejudice and opposition to Spiritualism. These mercenary speculators seek not only to obtain the favor of opponents, but are peculiarly gracious in their professions towards Spiritualists. They sometimes profess to believers that they are helping along "the cause" and doing it more good than hurt. They are profuse in invitations for Spiritualists to attend their lectures, and are willing to lavish free tickets as an extra inducement. They invite free discussion, and are pressing to have some persons come in and take part, in order that the crowd may be attracted at the prospect of a little excitement. But if any Spiritualists attempt to ask questions or take part, they are laughed, hissed, hooted, stamped or ridiculed down, by the lecturer or his rabble. Our unqualified advice is to keep away from these men. Let them depend on the opponents of our faith, and not make capital out of us. If they can obtain responsible endorsers, and can be induced to settle on any honorable terms of discussion with some experienced spiritual controversialist, then let them be met; but it is utter folly to patronize their catch-penny performances or to go into their meetings under any circumstances. Let us convince them and their abettors that we are prepared for fair controversy in an open field, but that we have too much respect for ourselves and our sentiments to be caught where we are robbed of our rights and needlessly exposed to vulgar abuse.

Some persons are too liable to fall into the weakness of idolatry and flattery. They may be perfectly honest and sincere in motive, but they forget the injustice they are doing not only the persons they idolize, but other laborers equally worthy, and those great principles of equality recognized by Spiritualism. Their praises are wholesale and indiscriminate, and lavished without that wisdom which is sometimes needed to administer counsel and kindly criticism in place of fulsome praise. No lecturer or medium is perfect; and all, at times, need the warmest commendation, encouragement and sympathy, in order that they may feel themselves strengthened and appreciated; yet now and then they may be profited by words of kindly counsel and hints towards improvement. Many youngerly persons, as well as older ones, have been seriously injured by undue praise and attentions. Receiving nothing but smiles, cordial greetings, pressing invitations, officious attentions and loud commendations, they have fancied themselves stars of unequalled attraction, and have put on airs of a corresponding character, or been overwhelmed with sincerest gratitude, realizing but little how indiscriminately the same honors may have been bestowed on those who came before them, and may be lavished on those who shall come after them. They forget how very natural it is for persons to pet and praise those who are placed in public positions, and how often the most popular applause may arise from vanity, selfishness, and other motives of a superficial character. True apostles of Spiritualism need no noisy or officious homage. An audience hushed into intense interest until heart beatings can almost be heard, and bosoms heave, and brows bend, and faces glow, and tears moisten the eye — these are the most eloquent encomiums mortals can bestow in encouragement of the inspired medium or lecturer. The most genuine praise is not heard in loud words or seen in ceremonious attentions. Let those who are seeking for genuine approbation, find out the poor, the lowly, the modest, the humble, and learn how they are affected, and whether they feel themselves blessed. It is idle to rely on the applause of the multitude ever swarming around every public individual and seeking to share in the honors or favors they would feign seem to bestow. We remember a touching illustration of the kind of praise and honor we would commend all to seek. A young medium was being received with the most cordial flatteries and attentions. Her performances were lauded by all. She left the company for a time, and when she returned her eyes were moistened with tears. We afterwards learned that she had gone into the kitchen to offer a few words of hope and comfort to a poor hired girl who had been excluded from the parlor. The poor servant-girl's heart was touched with gratitude; and the young woman medium wept with joy, and told us that the little good she seemed to do that poor girl was a richer boon than all the favor and applause bestowed during her visit among those who were continually petting and praising her. Hollow, indeed, is all the praise of a loud-sounding world, compared with the deep gratitude gushing from humble and lowly hearts long suffering in obscurity. The widow's mite and the Magdalen's box of ointment spoke to Jesus with eloquence louder than the clamorous multitude thronging his triumphal entry into the Holy City. The silent Mary crouched at his feet, bathed in tears of love and sorrow, was a spectacle more touching than the plaudits of millions.

Humility becomes the apostles of an angel ministry. Ministering spirits seek no praise or applause, but come all silent and unseen, dropping their benedictions on the meek and lowly who offer no idolatry but that of grateful hearts. We pray the time may hasten when no more idolatry shall be bestowed on either priests, mediums, spiritual apostles or any other class of public characters. Of this superlative folly we have had enough already. We have in mind one of our most brilliant inspirational speaking sisters, who, on making her first appearance on the spiritual platform, requested editors to offer nothing like the compliments which had been bestowed on others. She had seen enough notices announcing new speakers as among the most eloquent, attractive, thrilling and all that sort of thing, and she regarded such notices worse than worthless. Every reader or hearer has his peculiar idea of what is eloquent, and when he sees or hears a notice, he forms an opinion from his own individual idea, and in nine cases out of ten becomes disappointed in the end. In the spiritual ranks we know neither high nor low. Some of our humblest laborers may accomplish the highest amount of good, and may merit the warmest encouragement. The prosperity and progress of Spiritualism must not depend on itinerant stars alone, but on the calling out of apostles from among people at home. The sects have suffered from the idolatry of certain popular priests, Spiritualism may suffer from idolatry for certain lecturers and mediums. We insist on the democratic idea of talent and spiritual gifts, and seek to inaugurate the era of universal unfolding, that all may become priests and kings. We need no lords, masters or orators to rule over us, however much we may at times seek aids from those who are highly gifted. In our idolatry for others we are liable to forget the divinity, the dignity of our own natures, and bow down in abject humility, disheartened at all efforts to become truly great, good and noble. We are in danger of becoming dazzled and bewildered by the glare of false glory glittering around public life, forgetful of the fact that true greatness consists in goodness, and true glory may shine forth in the lowliest walks of life and duty. The gift of eloquent public speech may be admirable before the outer world, but the humblest words and deeds in private life are the most admirable before the audience of an angel world.

Some lecturers and writers are continually firing over the heads of the people. Whatever their ideas may be, their language becomes stilted with strides towards the stars, often terminating with a tumble into the muddiest phraseology. The masses of their hearers and readers may start and stare as long as they can keep awake, yet in the end they wonder what it all means, and find nothing pointed or practical adapted to their minds and hearts. This straining after the grandiloquent, the metaphysical, the scientific, the philosophical, is like straining at camels and swallowing gnats; like molehills laboring and bringing forth musquitoes. An unsophisticated old gentleman, hearing a lecturer speak of the "ubiquity of God," wanted to know if "ubiquity" was something good to eat. Exactly so; the people want something to eat; something practical, pointed, plain, comprehensible, digestible, nutritive to the commonest mind and heart. Write and speak to be understood. Now and then we may enjoy a plunge into the profound arcana of subterranean spheres, or a flight into the cerulean heights of the empyrean univercœlum; but we find the multitude are on a matter-of-fact, common-sense plane, and they need language which can be understood without a constant reference to the dictionary. The shortest words and sentences, the fewest adjectives, the simplest phrases, are always the most eloquent and effective. One of the most sublime sentences ever falling from human pen or tongue, contains but two short words, — *Jesus wept!*

The compensation of spiritual laborers has been a subject of much discussion. Lecturers and mediums, as a class, are as unselfish as they can possibly afford to be. Most of them are willing to spend their time, exhaust their energies and work hard, for just what the people are freely disposed and able to render them. But few of them have any other resources or employments outside of the spiritual field. They have been compelled to forsake all else, and yield to the call of the people and the higher intelligence sending them forth on apostolic missions of evangelization. They "go without scrip or purse," and leave behind those who are dependent on their remittance of means to buy bread, fuel, clothing, and other necessities of life. Under these circumstances, it is not strange they should sometimes feel anxious, and become urgent in their demands. The sternest justice and the tenderest humanity demand means. Perhaps, while deeply depressed and embarrassed for the want of means, while suffering anxiety in remembrance of home and creditors who are pressing their claims, while overwhelmed with fears as to the future, and wondering how they are to meet certain inevitable demands, they may seem avaricious or mercenary in asking for money.

Now, while lecturers and mediums have these responsibilities to meet, let them not suffer censure for feeling the need of means. Their reputations often suffer because they lack means to pay their honest debts. And we have known them censured by those very persons who were too mean to pay them anything for their services! Let the public consider these things. It is said, "the laborer is worthy of his hire;" we are to "take no thought for the morrow;" means will be provided; God and the angels will take care of us; we shall have our reward here or in heaven; all of which is very beautiful, and in one sense sublimely true. But we are obliged to keep in view the stern conditions of material life, and remember that this philosophy, in the abstract, will not cash bank notes, or pay landlords, butchers and bakers. Nothing but cash will pass at the counters of the society in which we live. Railroads, markets, printing establishments, take no drafts on the bank of heaven.

Those who are continually prating about this philosophy should give us a few practical lessons; abandon their business, their secular professions and employments, put all their money and real estate out of their hands and beyond their reach, and then go forth laboring for humanity, trusting the Lord to pay all bills. Yet there is a vast difference between true laborers, who seek to devote themselves as unselfishly as possible, and those who seem really mercenary and exacting in their demands. We know of but very few who belong to the latter class. All lecturers and mediums who are truly called and have confidence in their gifts, can trust themselves in the hands of the people, and may fear for no want of means. There are exceptions, but they are exceedingly rare among genuine Spiritualists. A few aggravating cases have come to our knowledge. We knew a trance lecturing and healing medium who was sent after for several miles to lecture an evening and treat the sick daughter of a wealthy farmer, and he received twenty-five cents for his time and service. We remember two similar instances in our own experience; and one place where we lectured and gave a public examination, all entirely satisfactory, and we received fifty-five cents to pay for our service and a stage ride of twenty-five miles. We declined the munificent sum, and deemed it our duty to insist on a specific amount, as the parties were able and wrote us to come. But these are rare exceptions. Where the friends are really poor, the places are in need and are prepared, an appeal is made entirely different from calls coming from places where there are friends blessed with abundance. Yet it matters not how poor or needy certain places may be, we know of no spiritual laborers who can possibly afford to go at their own cost in time, life and money. They have no surplus funds at hand, and while their families, friends and themselves are dependent on their labors for every means of subsistence, and for provisions against future want, they are bound by obligations as sacred as the divinity of their own souls. However deplorable these conditions are, they are inexorable in their demands in the present state of society. And Spiritualists are noble, generous and wise enough to realize these things, and provide for the material recompense of their laborers. They understand that lecturers and mediums can labor only a part of the time; they become overtaxed and exhausted, and are often exposed to changes, trials, bad conditions and disappointments, which render it impossible for them to fulfil a regular course of engagements during the entire year, and from year to year, without any cessation. A lecturer may be away from home for a time and have a number of good engagements paying from five to ten dollars a lecture, and then may visit a number of places without receiving more than expenses, and perchance return home enfeebled, worn out, and unable to labor for months, either in the spiritual or any other field. So with test and healing mediums. Their compensation is not to be measured by the hour or day, for the days and hours of their engagements are comparatively few, and their expenses heavier than in other departments of life, and their labors peculiarly enervating, and disqualifying them for all other avocations. In the "good time coming," we shall need no special classes of laborers like these. All shall become unfolded on higher planes of harmony and communion; and the kingdoms of this world shall become the kingdoms of God, dispensing the bounties of Nature with impartial justice and benevolence.

A right use of the means at the command of all liberalists would result in the more rapid advancement of the cause of truth. If some persons were only as free in the use of their means towards spiritual laborers, as they have been towards the church and popular ministry, and as they are still, our cause would suffer less. Some think they must sustain the church whether their own sentiments are publicly sustained or not. They must take other newspapers, religious and secular, sometimes to the neglect of their own spiritual paper. They must send their children to sectarian Sunday schools, and perhaps are slow to start spiritual schools of their own; though Spiritualists in many places are awaking to the importance of the latter. Liberal schools are now being organized in numerous localities, and a series of books will soon be published adapted to their needs. Some must always have a sectarian minister to perform the marriage ceremony, without knowing that all acceptable spiritual teachers may become legally qualified to officiate on such occasions. So, likewise, in regard to funerals. Should Spiritualists on funeral occasions call in the services of orthodox or other clergymen, who can administer no consolations in accordance with Spiritualism? Mourners are frequently divided in sentiment, and spiritualist friends often yield their choice as to speakers in order that the prejudices of neighbors or relatives may be appeased. Opposing clergymen are invited, and what is the result? On some occasions we remember, where some of the nearest relatives of the deceased were Spiritualists, the minister hurled out wholesale denunciations against Spiritualism, and insisted on his orthodoxy as the only foundation of hope and consolation. And what consolation, we ask, can any orthodox clergyman offer on such an occasion? Unless he proves dishonest and conceals his theology, he must doom the unconverted deceased to a destiny of eternal woe, and can offer no hope to mourners aside from that which is based on a belief in the most terrible dogmas. For our own part, we would sooner consign the remains of deceased friends to the tomb without any form or funeral service, than call on any clergyman whose creed might consign the dead to eternal woe or banish them to eternal silence in some remote realm of the universe, beyond all sympathy and communication, and who might not only insult the living, but harrow their souls with emotions of unutterable agony. The time is fast coming when Spiritualists will no more expose themselves to these mock comforters, but will invariably call on mediums or spiritual speakers to minister to their needs on these occasions of sorrow and bereavement. It is then that Spiritualism is needed most, and its ministry of angels adapts hopes and consolations afforded by no other system of philosophy or religion.

Spiritualists may become cautious in regard to some dishonorable members of the clerical profession. They are found in every part of the land. Some of them deal in wholesale denunciations in their pulpits, yet smile on you most graciously as they meet you in company and on the street. Some of them assume a politic silence in their pulpits, yet sneer at you in private. Some of them profess to be very anxious to investigate, yet give them an opportunity, and they will shrink; or if they have the most positive evidences, they will make no concessions. Some of them will preach sentiments exceedingly liberal, and will talk to your face just as though they were about ready to come out openly, yet all this is only to secure your patronage. There are those who can blow hot and cold, and say good Lord and good devil at the same time. Some clerical functionaries seek to ride the fence; they are on both sides at once. Other characteristics might be delineated, but these are sufficient. The whole clerical profession, however, should not be judged by these miserable specimens, for there are good and noble men in the sectarian ministry, in spite of all the errors of our common humanity.

The ranks of Spiritualism are infested with certain classes of individuals who seek its celestial clothing to cover iniquities of hideous deformity, as there have been impostors in every other great and good cause. Some men, and a few women, driven from the pales of all other society and employment, seek shelter beneath the angel wings of this new dispensation, and claim a charity afforded by no other philosophy or religion. The benevolence Spiritualism extends towards all renders it preeminent over other systems in its power to save the tempted, the fallen, and the outcast, and thousands once abandoned as forever lost have been redeemed by angel love, and sent on their way rejoicing in missions of usefulness. The infidel, the heretic, the slandered, the suspected, the rejected, cut off from all sympathy with old cliques, have found new faith and hope in intercourse with angel friends who see and judge with other than short-sighted mortal eyes; and among Spiritualists they have found large hearts with a charity covering a multitude of sins, long-suffering, kind, forbearing, gentle, easily touched and entreated, hoping all things, believing all things, and never tiring in efforts to seek and save those once regarded lost in evil and error. While we are all conscious of the imperfections to which we are subjected, God forbid we should ever close our hearts against any who are seeking or needing the wiser, purer, better life, no matter how deeply their souls may have been steeped in crime. Let us believe they are not as bad at heart as they may seem in our external, imperfect judgment. Let us learn the nature of their organisms, the education and influences surrounding them, the temptations to which they have been subjected, the struggles through which they have gone, the obstacles they have battled and overcome in spite of all those evils to which they have yielded, the inner springs of their being, the sufferings with which their souls have been wrung in those dark hours when all earth and heaven seemed to abandon them, and the depths of agony in which they sunk when the voice of conscience spoke in thunder tones of self-condemnation and despair. Oh, when we spurn that trembling brother and sister, stricken at our feet, all covered with the curses of alleged guilt, we know not what secret sorrow and woe already overwhelm the crushed soul, and what wailings of desolation and despair may be wrung from the bleeding heart; and where one kind word or warm hand might have saved, a single cold look or frown, or sentence of slight, may drive the sinking spirit down the steeps of everlasting night. One loving sentence from Jesus saved the poor Magdalen; one chiding word or look might have doomed her to remediless infamy.

Yet, alas, there are those who avail themselves of this charitable philosophy of reform only to pervert it and use it as a cloak for the perpetration, concealment, and justification of evils; those who are continually preaching up charity towards others, only that they may have charity exercised towards themselves in regard to evil practices they are constantly perpetrating and excusing, rather than striving to reform. "Neither do I condemn thee, *go and sin no more*," was the charity of the Nazarine. But certain modern charity-mongers, who have stolen the livery of Spiritualism in which to serve the devil of their own selfishness and sensualism, advocate a sort of infernal justification philosophy, which permits them to go on sinning, free from all restraint and condemnation; and if they are cautioned, counselled, or chided in their iniquitous courses, they play the offended penitent, and plead the need of charity and brotherly protection. It is hard to deal with such cases, but they are in our midst and must be met face to face; not with anger or severity, but with kindness, wisdom, and firmness. It is a deplorable fact that there are men and women whose natures are so far perverted and unbalanced, it becomes almost impossible to redeem them while in this rudimental sphere of existence. Hospitals, insane asylums, and prisons are crowded with subjects who are unsafe and irredeemable out in public society as it now is, with all its false and imperfect conditions.

Abandoned men and women have crowded themselves into the ranks of every new popular movement. Primitive Christianity was so infected with impostors, deceivers, and false professors, Christ and the apostles were continually warning the people to beware of "wolves in sheep's clothing." Many of the early believers were charged with heinous crimes. Paul wrote the Corinthian Christians that common report alleged they were licentious. There were those so specious and seductive, the very elect were in danger of being deceived. It is so in the popular churches of to-day, those very churches now charging all sorts of crimes and impositions on Spiritualism. What marvel, then, the Spiritualist ranks should be infested with similar characters, especially since Spiritualism claims no sectarian organization, erects no rigid standards by which to judge all men alike, appoints no popes, bishops, or priests, to rule with pharisaic power, but relies rather, for all tests, on the divine principles of right and rectitude to be unfolded in every human soul, on the spiritual intuitions and perceptions; and, with a charity as broad as human brotherhood, calls on all to "try the spirits" for themselves, "prove all things, and hold fast that which is good." On this broad humanitarian ground, with the heavens bending in benevolence over all, no marvel there are some who rush into the ranks of Spiritualism without the highest motives, since they are continually seeking new fields of operation, and everything good and true under heaven is capable of perversion. Every form of religion has been abused, and it were folly to contend that Spiritualism is an entire exception. The sooner Spiritualists acknowledge this fact, the better will be the issue, and the better shall we be prepared to guard against the evils and errors endangering our future prospects.

The phases of spiritual mediumship, manifestations, and communications, are so numerous, in many cases the phenomena so subtle and startling, the broadest experience and the coolest judgment are requisite to discriminate between the true and false, the lying and reliable, the genuine and deceptive. While the most critical skeptics witness overwhelming manifestations, the credulous and unguarded, earnestly needing, and confidently seeking, sometimes lay themselves open to the basest impositions, and are ready, in their unsophisticated simplicity, to accept as genuine whatever or whoever comes in the name of Spiritualism. Hence the temptation held out to bogus mediums and impostors palming themselves off as the mouthpieces of the angel world. No matter what trash or balderdash emanates from their magic circles or oily tongues, some will regard them as the oracles of heaven. It is time we came to our senses in regard to some of these characters, and begin to learn the business of testing everything and everybody in the light of wisdom as well as charity. If there is another sin under heaven worse than blasphemy, it is that of the impostor who prates of the holy dead and departed, of God and the angel world, while he is only seeking to work upon the sympathies and aspirations of those whom he may victimize. There are those who would coin the tears of mourners in their greed for gold, gloat over the deepest sensibilities of the soul, and with mock messages and manifestations would laugh God and heaven to scorn.

But the most dangerous of all impostors are those of the libertine school. We do not allude to those who are found in the pulpits, or in fashionable society, but to the few who are prowling in the land under the self-assumed sanction of Spiritualism. Some pass as private mediums, some as healing and speaking mediums, and some as inspired normal lecturers. Their modes of operation are various, but there are certain uniform signs of designation. Most of them fancy they have some great mission to perform, and some of them probably possess the intellectual capacity to do a good work. Many of them make large professions of great magnetic powers, and are quite ready to experiment on every attractive subject of the opposite sex. Fastening their eyes on every beautiful form they meet, they begin to calculate as to the opportunities of making some insidious advances. In all such cases they profess to have something peculiar to communicate to the persons in question. If they take them by the hand on first meeting, their grasp is significantly warm and protracted, and they are urgent to call for some very important purpose. In circles they are invariably impressed to be seated next to favorite subjects they have selected, and then all hands must be joined to induce certain conditions. They are sure of being able to exert some extraordinary, mysterious power to aid in the development of mediumship, and in the cure of all sorts of pains, and especially headaches, providing the mediums are of the opposite sex and the pains and aches belong to attractive forms. They believe there is great virtue in the human hand, and are fervent in the apostolic injunction for the laying on of hands and clasping the same. They are kind souls, ever ready to assist the spirits in obtaining influence and control. And the spirits have always something very remarkable to communicate to them and their favorites. Each new person has some brilliant mission to perform, so these prophetic souls say, and they are to become highly essential in unfolding and bringing them out. They can impart influences and counsels of a most momentous character, and if an opportunity offers they begin by harping on affinities, affections, congenialities, mutual attractions, conventionalities, sympathies, and inform the dear suffering feminine hearts how much they are pining, languishing, dying for somebody to love them, and somebody just like themselves.

They are cool, cautious, and calculating at first, and assume an air of sanctity more becoming the saint tnan the serpent. They never lose an opportunity to lay their hands, accidentally, of course, on all agreeable subjects coming within their reach. Neither they nor their spirit friends ever recognize the old and ugly, but are overflowing with impressions and attentions towards those who possess external charms. They are great lovers of humanity, freedom and rights, by all of which they simply mean their right to prowl around the innocent and unsuspecting until ruin is left in their path. If rumors follow them from place to place, they either keep a dignified silence, as though they held all such things in utter insignificance and contempt, and were above suspicion, or they whine about how they and all independent souls are slandered and persecuted for opinion's sake; just as though people knew no difference between suffering for honest opinions and suffering for bad practices.

We might designate other characteristics peculiar to these impostors, but these portraitures are sufficient to enable all intuitive Spiritualists to identify the individuals described, and stand on guard against their wily influences. And what shall be done with such characters? It is not consistent with our philosophy to deal in personal public exposure and denunciation against them, for we may hope something for even the worst men and women; and yet it becomes our duty to defend ourselves, our families, our cause, our sons and daughters, our friends, neighbors and the public, against their baneful influences. They breathe a moral pestilence wherever they go, and attract a class of infernal elements contaminating the very atmosphere of those who are not fortified by the most positive and well-tried virtues. Those whose spiritual intuitions are unfolded are at once set on guard; and these intimations are the surest safeguards where minds are left to act unbiassed by rumor or prejudice. As Spiritualists we claim no infallible right to erect standards by which to judge, exclude, or condemn certain men or women, or forbid them to represent Spiritualism; but as individuals we can unite in erecting a moral sentiment more potent than all external forms and disciplines, in detecting the evil and erroneous, and protecting ourselves against their encroachment. As we invoke the highest influxes of celestial wisdom, truth and love, we become the more intuitive in our perceptions; and the moment we come within the sphere of men and women, we know what they are as well as though their hearts and lives were unfolded on a written scroll.

But, in closing, we may remark that the abuses to which we have adverted are not confined to persons who are travelling as mediums and lecturers. They are found in some public and private circles, among those who profess an interest in Spiritualism only for the purpose of prostituting it to the basest ends. Let Spiritualists, and especially young mediums, beware of these lecherous prowlers; and unless they are sure of bringing them under higher influences, let their presence be shunned, their infernal magnetism be exorcised, and their touch be avoided as loathed and leprous. They are attracted to Spiritualism through the false representations of its opposers, and fancy it may afford them a rich field in which to practise their licentious tendencies. Give them an opportunity, and they are exceedingly free and familiar, profess great anxiety to communicate with spirits, and in the end evince no earnest desire beyond the privilege of gaining access to persons from whose society they would otherwise be excluded. As a preventive of these evils, we would urge a solemn caution against all undue freedoms and confidences with untried strangers, unless they bring unmistakable impressions of pure heart and purpose. And in the formation of circles, caution should be exercised in joining hands with those whose magnetisms may exert a deleterious influence over persons of a negative nature. Mediums and negative individuals who are not positively unfolded in communion with the wisest and best spirits, can seldom sit with joined hands in discordant circles without experiencing some unfavorable influences, whether they are conscious of the fact or otherwise.

But while we are dealing in these hints, let us not be understood as reflecting on mediums in general, nor on circles held by the pure and wise for the legitimate purpose of spiritual unfolding. Nor would we say aught to create anything like unpleasant suspicions against every person not fully known. Let us sometimes be momentarily deceived, rather than always allow ourselves to be haunted with fearful spectres of evil. But with all our charity, we need wisdom; and we may never incautiously expose ourselves or our cause to unnecessary danger. *In our portraitures of libertines and impostors, we may have attributed to them some things which are innocent in themselves, and which pure, noble-minded mediums, lecturers and Spiritualists may practise without having their motives impeached.* We have no sweeping denunciations for any, nor have we any morbid tolerance for those seemingly incorrigible pests, vampires and vultures seeking to prey on the spiritual public and gloat over the tears and blood of innocent souls. We care not whether they assume the name of Spiritualist, Socialist, or Reformer; when the mask is torn off, they stand revealed as they are. God have mercy on them, for they have little or no mercy either for themselves or their victims. There are but comparatively few such in the spiritual ranks, and their career will soon end; for the celestial world beams with a high and holy light, penetrating the darkest chambers of guilt, unmasking iniquity, and enabling Spiritualists to discriminate between true and false. With purer hearts and lives, Heaven help each to become more and more redeemed from seeming evil and error, and more and more consecrated to the redemption of our brothers and sisters.

In alluding to laborers of a questionable and an eccentric character, let us not become indiscriminate or uncharitable. Impostors, imperfect representatives, Judases and Arnolds, have been identified with every good cause on earth. Counterfeits presuppose the existence of something genuine. Christianity has been cursed for ages by innumerable anti-Christs, counterfeiters, pretenders, swindlers, fools, imbeciles, and knaves; and all the churches are so loud in their complaints, they should be cautious in their charges against Spiritualism. It may be, however, that some of those spiritual evangelists whom the public regard as most objectionable and eccentric, after all, have an important mission to fulfil. If they are imperfect, we are reminded that no mortals are perfect, and we are cautioned against setting up any class as our models, our priesthood, our authority. Our cause rests on the reputation of no one class of individuals; it is based on eternal principles; the responsibility rests with individuals; stand on your own dignity, and you will never complain of the injury others are doing the cause. The most unwise and eccentric geniuses may have a mission far beyond our appreciation for the time being. Many of the greatest seers, sages, poets, reformers and philosophers have appeared in violation of popular conventionalities. The ancient Isaiah for three years wandered like a madman through the Holy Land. Homer was a blind itinerant. John the Baptist came howling but half-clothed from the wilderness. A graphic writer, in describing the ancient Hebrew medium, says:—

In his highest form he was a solitary and savage man, residing with lions when he was not waylaying kings, on whose brow the scorching sun of Syria had charactered its fierce and swarthy hue, and whose dark eye swam with fine insanity gathered from solitary communing with the sand, the sea, the mountains and the sky, as well as with the light of a divine afflatus. He had lain in the cockatrice's den; he had put his hand on the hole of the asp; he had spent the night on lion-surrounded trees, and slept amid their hungry roar; he had swam in the Dead Sea, or haunted like a ghost those dreary caves that lowered around it; he had drank of the melted snow on the tops of Lebanon; at Sinai he had traced and trod on the burning footsteps of Jehovah; he had heard messages at midnight which made his hair to arise and his skin to creep; he had been wet with the dews of the night, and girt with the demons of the wilderness; he had been tossed up and down like a leaf, upon the strong and veering storm of his inspiration. He was essentially a lonely man, cut off by gulf upon gulf from tender ties and human associations. He had no home; a wife he might be permitted to marry, but as in the case of Hosea, the permission might only be to him a cause, and to his people an emblem, and when, as in the case of Ezekiel, her death became necessary as a sign, she died, and left him in the same austere seclusion in which he had existed before. The power which came upon him cut, by its fierce coming, all the threads which bound him to his kind, tore him from the plow, or the pastoral solitude, and hurried him to the desert, and thence to the foot of the throne, or to the wheel of the chariot. And how startling his coming to crowned or conquered guilt! Wild from the wilderness, bearded like its lion; the fury of God glaring in his eye; his mantle heaving to his heaving breast; his words stern, swelling, tinged on their edge with terrible poetry; his attitude dignity, his gesture power — how did he burst upon the astonished gaze; how swift and solemn his entrance; how short and spirit-like his stay; how dreamy, yet how distinctly dreadful, the impression made by his words long after they had ceased to tingle on the ear; and how mysterious the solitude into which he seemed to melt away. Poet, nay Prophet, were a feeble name for such a being. He was a momentary incarnation — a meteor kindled at the eye, and blown on by the breath of the Eternal.

CHAPTER IX.

THE CRISES OF THE AGE — PRACTICAL APPEAL TO SPIRITUALISTS — POINTED SUGGESTIONS — PERSONAL AND GENERAL REFORM — INCIDENTS, HOPES, CONSOLATIONS, ENCOURAGEMENTS — NATIONAL CONDITIONS AND SIGNS — CLOSING MESSAGE.

SPIRITUALISTS of the nineteenth century: We are in the midst of a crisis unparalled in human history. After all that has been said and written in regard to the agitations and advancements of the age, but few are prepared to anticipate the momentous issues involved. Only those whose interior vision is opened in communion with celestial intelligences watching from the stand-point of the spirit world can form the most accurate estimate of the responsibilities and results of the impending crises now involving every department of civil, religious and social life. Ancient prophecy pointed to the era in which the "old earth and old heavens," or the preëxisting order of things, should pass away, and a "new earth and new heavens" should take their place, and "all things be made new." The same prediction has been repeated all along through the ages, up to the present time; and during the present spiritual dispensation it has come in thousand-fold forms through thousands of mediums. The whole church, for nearly half a century, had been praying and predicting in accordance with ancient prophets and modern mediums; but when Spiritualism began, and its manifestations and communications indicated the dawn of a celestial era outside of the church, the latter began to retract all it had preached and prayed for, and commenced falling back on old forms, creeds and traditions, and to rely more on conforming to the old order of things than on any new inspirations or unfoldings from the eternal world. Meanwhile, progress has been apparent in every other department of life. Science, art, philosophy, literature, social and civil reform, have advanced so far as to produce radical changes among the masses of the people. These changes have modified all old habits of thought and life, and have been attended by revolutions shaking and unsettling the foundations of old laws, customs and institutions. New mechanical inventions are superseding the old, changing the industrial habits of the people, saving time and labor, affording greater facilities for the cultivation of the intellect, and demonstrating that mind is destined to rule over matter. Literature is effecting a moral and social reform; and as the masses of the people come to a true knowledge of the dignity and divinity of human nature, they demand civil reform, and in rising to assert their rights, civil governments rock and are threatened with revolution.

Spiritualism comes with its manifestations and inspirations from higher worlds, and seeks to inaugurate the kingdom of heaven in every human soul; and as individuals come under its influences in communion with the angels of God, they rely less and less on the authority of transient external laws, customs and institutions, and feel more and more the responsibilities which belong to men and women as brothers and sisters, and as spiritual beings in oneness with God and the myriads peopling the celestial realms. In the light of these facts we need take no alarm at the signs of the times or the revolutions now rocking America. They are harbingers of great changes in the state, the church and society. As Spiritualists, it is not ours to excite alarm or to join with any sect or party engaged in dealing threats or denunciations. Ours is the angelic mission of Wisdom, Truth, Love and Peace. Radical reformers have gone on before us, lifting their loud cries and wielding their battle-axes; ours is a more Christ-like mission, yet none the less earnest and emphatic in urging the need of individual reformation in preparation for the coming kingdom of heaven. Now, in the midst of all these impending revolutions, where are we to look for some substantial foundation of facts and principles on which we can stand and hope not only for individual improvement, but for the peace, harmony and prosperity of our age? No religious body, no political party, no social code now existing, will be found adequate. We may find something good and true in all, and something we may seek to preserve, but we need a new order of things, "new earth and new heavens;" and all the omens of to-day indicate hopeful changes inaugurating the gospel of Spiritualism as absolutely essential to the unbelieving, unsettled, unsaved millions of our people.

There are now over one thousand public lecturers and mediums and two millions of believers in the States, who stand united on this spiritual ground, without any external pledges, or social, sectarian, sectional or political compacts. FRATERNAL SYMPATHY, INDIVIDUAL FREEDOM AND SPIRITUAL INTERCOURSE, — this is the bond of our unity. Most solemnly do we believe the facts, the philosophy, the science, the religion, the practical principles of Spiritualism, are essential to us as individuals and to the redemption of the race. To this end we are laboring and sacrificing; sustaining circles, lecturers, mediums and public meetings; seeking to practise what we profess; circulating tracts, pamphlets, books and spiritual journals, in order that the multitudes may receive the light in which we rejoice with unutterable gratitude. We are now in the midst of agitations well calculated to test our faith and philosophy anew. And how shall we prove ourselves? Shall we join with croakers, cowards, alarmists, and plead that the times are so trying we must abandon our work and let the cause of humanity go back? Now is just the time we need to be tested, and now the time our zeal and self-sacrifice are demanded. A thousand new motives are urging us to renewed interest in our home circles, our public meetings, and in all the auxiliaries of spiritual progress.

While we are urging the importance of Spiritualism, and seeking to unfold its facts and philosophy, it becomes us to keep in view the application of its principles, and its grand practical objects and aims. It is a matter of first moment to demonstrate the immortality and future eternal progress of the whole race. With what joy and rapture have hundreds of thousands welcomed the fresh tidings that the dead live, that man is immortal, that the heavens are opened, that angels come as guardians and guides over the highway of life, that we are all destined to enter celestial spheres of never-ending advancement, that death is but the doorway to eternity, where the departed wait to greet all earth wanderers home. But we have something more to do than sing, and weep, and rejoice over these glorious tidings. Deep principles are involved. The spirits come for other purposes than to excite our joy and wonder, or to appeal to the selfish and sordid. If our interest ends with the external manifestations or with the mere fact of immortal life demonstrated, we have but a very dim view of the great practical aims of Spiritualism. The time has now come when Spiritualists are called on to consider all the bearings and applications of the gospel they profess.

Spiritualism is something more than a belief that spirits exist and communicate; it enjoins stern duties, and practical lessons to be lived out. Some suppose they have nothing to do but receive tests, witness manifestations, hear lectures, attend circles, read of what is going on, and give a sort of theoretical assent. But there is a vast difference between *believing* and *being* a Spiritualist. Why do spirits communicate? For high and holy purposes;

to make men wise, better, purer, kinder; their hearts, lives, and homes more like heaven. It is a joy to know our spirit-friends live, love, and come to us; but if we would be truly benefitted, we must heed the objects for which they come, and make the heart and life such as to attract the high and holy influences they would impart. And we are to remember the many who need the light we claim to have already received, and use all laudable means within our reach to diffuse that light. It were well we inquired as to whether we are doing all we might do in this direction. There are hundreds who are devoting their all to this end, laboring in public and private. How are they sustained, encouraged — lecturers, mediums, and others? The wide field of humanity is opened. "Say not ye, There are four months, and then cometh the harvest. Behold I say unto you, lift up your eyes and look on the fields; for they are white already to harvest. And he that reapeth receiveth the wages, and gathereth fruit unto life eternal; that both he that soweth and he that reapeth may rejoice together. And herein is the saying true, One soweth and another reapeth. I sent you to reap that whereon you bestowed no labor; other men labored, and ye are entered into their labors." To those who have comfortable homes, lucrative employments or professions, and abundant means, it is easy to speculate in regard to the needs of humanity, and the great, glorious duty of somebody going forth with a self-sacrificing heroism. There are spiritual and other reformers who grow exceedingly eloquent on this subject, but are seldom if ever willing to work themselves, or aid others in their labors. Now and then we find rich men in private life who seem fully able to see what a vast harvest stands ready to be reaped, but they fancy the reapers should be sustained, body and soul, families and all, by some superhuman agency. They can *praise* laborers and mediums, but somebody else must pay them, or they may go beggared and in danger of bailiffs. Then we have a class of fancy laborers, who, instead of gleaning the field, are prone to gouging it. They take particular pains to find out what places will pay well, and affix an enormous price to their services. But these classes are exceptions. We have had some experience in public life and labor, and among Spiritualists we have found more magnanimity than among any other class of people. Our faith and philosophy enlarge the soul, and open the heart and hand. We are made to realize the momentousness of our mission as immortal beings, allied to the brotherhood of man on earth and in the heavens; and, while we behold thousands around us wrapped in darkness and despair for the want of that light which has dawned on us from the angel-world, we feel it a cheerful as well as a solemn duty *to give as freely as we have received.* The time is fast coming when those who have means will lavish them more abundantly, and when no worthy laborer shall be oppressed with anxiety in regard to the necessities of material subsistence. If the field of labor has been hard, it has tested those who have entered it, and tried them so far as to enable the public to know who were prepared to endure the heat and burden of the day; who were worthy or otherwise.

As Spiritualists we have a work before us, the importance and magnitude of which but few have fully comprehended. When the manifestations first began, all was joy, wonder, curiosity, and excitement. The idea that the spirit-world was a reality, that it was opened for us to hold perpetual intercourse, that the blessed and beloved came back ever watching and guarding over us, and waiting to welcome us home to realms of beatitude, — all this was so glorious and enrapturing, our exulting souls went nearly wild with rejoicing, and multitudes ran forth to proclaim the tidings. But now the fact of spiritual intercourse has become well-established in the minds and hearts of millions, and the time has come for us to do more than rejoice and exult. It was natural for us to hail the rising sun of Spiritualism with shouts of joy as the clouds of centuries rolled back, and the angels sang, "Glory to God in the highest." But now the sun is up, and we have a practical work to do. Unbroken fields need the plowshare of the pioneer, the seed of truth must be sown where now all is barren, and whitened harvests stand all ready to be reaped. The work needs beginning in our own nature; and well may we each ask what fruit we are yielding as evidence of communion with God and the angel spheres.

While noble sympathy is called out in behalf of those who are suffering for the want of material means, we are reminded of millions who are suffering for the want of the spiritual. Their souls are hungering, thirsting, starving, dying; and they are raising their cry for the bread and water of eternal life. And who responds? Is it the religious world? A large portion of religionists profess to believe countless hosts will be banished to a world of worse than utter destitution and famine — a hell of despair in which they shall wander over burning deserts of eternal death and desolation, without a crumb or a drop of water to relieve their perishing souls. Heaven's board shall be spread with ample provisions for the few favored saints who shall feast on "fat things" and sing songs over the starving hosts howling beneath, while neither God, nor angels, nor saints shall heed their cry or proffer a ray of hope. Good heavens! and this is the awful dogma on which the orthodox world still proposes to feed the souls of humanity. And is it not a libel on God and human nature? Why, if men acted according to this dogma, who would heed the cry of those suffering for bread? What are a few thousands starving for a short time in Kansas or Ireland, compared with countless billions starving, despairing and dying in hell through the measureless ages of eternity!

Yet, let us take even the most liberal gospels of modern churchdom; and what do even these propose to give the people? All the sects opposed to Spiritualism insist that humanity, however spiritually needy and starving to-day, must be fed and sustained alone on what came ages ago and is recorded in the Bible. The Bible is all-sufficient. The bread and the water of life, coming down from heaven centuries ago, is all man needs; he must have no manifestations, no communications, no inspirations, no spiritual or angelic intercourse to-day; all these are unlawful, delusive, diabolical, impossible. Now, this position is just about as rational and humane as it would be to argue that the starving people of Ireland required no fresh provisions; just send them lots of New Testaments; tell them to read and believe about how Jesus fed hungry multitudes in Judea eighteen hundred years ago, and that will answer just as well as though we sent a thousand loads of fresh eatables! This historical feeding would answer a very poor purpose. The hungering multitudes would regard themselves insulted, mocked, and tantalized. Precisely so with the millions who, to-day, are in a destitute spiritual condition, with no faith, no philosophy, no religion adequate to satisfy their wants as beings of immortal progress. We find the masses of the people living with no deep, settled, satisfactory convictions in regard to their own spiritual natures, their relations to each other, to God and the eternal world. How few are living as though they realized their own immortality! how few are devoted to the loftiest aims of existence! how few think of the dead as still living and loving in constant communion! how many are lost on the material plane of life, and abandoned to selfish, sordid, sensual gratifications which fail to satisfy the divinest needs of their souls, and are followed by sadness and satiety!

How many are sitting down, dark and desolate, brooding over sorrows which find no alleviation — over bereavements which enthrone them in lonely despair — over blighted affections and friendships which leave them worse than orphans — over sins which gather like thunder clouds, big with threatening vengeance — over hopes gone out to be re-enkindled no more at the altar-fires of earthly life — over disappointments which leave this world like a vale of tears and a wilderness of woe! And how many, with some faint aspirations after a nobler and better life, are straining their tired vision after the "good time coming" so long foretold by the sages, the prophets and poets of the past!

And what science, what philosophy, what religion shall respond to these wants of the starving, perishing millions? It is Spiritualism. This gospel comes with its angel ministry, the spirits of the great, the good, the beloved; they come on the celestial railway and the celestial telegraph; they come to every heart, every home, every palace, every hamlet; they come to the wandering prodigals in strange lands and to the famishing souls ready to perish along the highway; they come from climes of perennial flowers and from plains waving with harvests of imperishable richness; they come with fresh provisions from our Father's house of many mansions, and bid mortals partake freely.

Some believers, perhaps, are over-anxious to convince others of the truth of Spiritualism. A certain degree of anxiety is enjoined as a duty in behalf of those now under the influence of error, ignorance and prejudice, and in need of the light gladdening along our pathway. It is sad to think of those who are in the darkness of materialism, those who are mournful and apprehensive beneath the awful dogmas of orthodoxy — an angered Deity and doom of eternal dread; and our deepest sympathies are engaged in unfolding the better gospel of an All-loving Father and his ministering spirits. But our sympathies may sometimes mislead our judgments; and our pride, or love of ease and popularity, may run into a species of proselyteism. We have taken our position as Spiritualists, and we seek to convince others in order that we may triumph over them in proving our opinions right and theirs wrong. We are liable to make it a matter of personal competition. We seek to add to our ranks certain individuals who, it is fancied, will add to the strength and respectability of our cause, and take some portion of the burden and reproach from off our own shoulders, enabling us to enjoy more ease and assume less labor and responsibility. Some better motives may mingle with these, but these are sometimes too apparent in efforts made to show off certain mediums and lecturers, in order that opposers may be overwhelmed with manifestations and eloquent productions out-rivaling the world. Sympathy may demand our utmost exertions towards convincing and converting the skeptical, but self-respect and confidence in the cause of eternal truth call on us to check all over-anxiety and over-heated zeal. Men and women will seek Spiritualism for themselves when they begin to feel their need of it; and unless they DO feel their need and are willing to seek somewhat at their own labor and cost, they are not prepared to find or accept it; and it were folly to attempt forcing their convictions. The multitudes are fast coming to realize their spiritual needs. Calmly and confidently pursuing our own course, improving in accordance with the light we are constantly receiving from higher spheres, cultivating our own spiritual natures, harmonizing our own hearts and lives, forming our own circles and unfolding manifestations adapted to conditions, sending out the silent yet mighty influence of noble thoughts and deeds, availing ourselves of all proper means to disseminate the seed of the celestial kingdom, one after another shall fall into our ranks, attracted by the divine magnet of Spiritualism, until the millions of earth shall join the myriads of heaven in anthems of concord.

Never was the demand for spiritual laborers so great as at the present. "The harvest is truly plenteous, but the laborers few." Notwithstanding the many now in the field, still the call is for more, and especially for more of those who are prepared to go forth with the right qualifications and in a self-sacrificing, apostolical spirit. Men and women are needed who are able not only to give the facts, the philosophy and the solid arguments of Spiritualism, but who are inspired with a deep and fervent love for humanity, whose souls are anointed with noble purposes, and whose hearts are warmed and baptized beneath the holy flood tides of angel life. How many thousands, yea millions, are waiting for the fresh bread and water of eternal life! Heaven help the noble band of evangels already in the harvest field, and send forth other laborers into the vineyard!

Well may Spiritualists exclaim, in the language of the pioneer Paul, "Now is the accepted time and now is the day of salvation." Never before were all the signs so encouraging in behalf of those who are laboring and praying for the inauguration of the celestial era. The masses of the people are weary of the heated strife of the age, and are seeking principles involving the spiritual and eternal needs of humanity. Revivalism has died out in the churches, with no hope of a resurrection, and widespread apathy reigns in Zion. Nine-tenths of all the people are waiting for some unfoldings and agitations adapted to man's nature as a social, affectional, religious, spiritual and immortal being. And what save Spiritualism, with all the themes and reforms involved, is so well calculated to arouse the slumbering energies of humanity? The cry of all pioneer souls is, "Repent (or reform) ye, for the kingdom of heaven is at hand."

"O Lord, revive thy work in the midst of the years!" was the prayer of the ancient Habakkuk; and its repetition has long been needed in our generation. As Spiritualists we may pray for it, in words and deeds. We pray for a revival of love to God and the neighbor, not tormenting fear of God nor sectarian, selfish love of the neighbor to get him into our church, our clique, our line of social and secular interests; a revival of true religion, not of forms and creeds, but of deeds of mercy and charity to the needy; a revival of genuine piety, not mere prayers and pretences for filling pockets and purses, but of pure aspirations towards God, and holy sympathies for humanity; a revival of reason and godly affection, not superstition and wrath concerning an angry God and a fabled world of eternal flames, but a spirit of inquiring intelligence to read, investigate, reflect, and a heart earnest in the search of truth and laden with desires for a true life; a revival of rivalry to save souls from sin and error, not to get their names in the church books, but have them down in the book of eternal life in heaven; a revival of gospel preaching, not ranting on old creeds and reproducing the dead letters of history, but preaching from the inspirations of a living God, living Holy Spirit, living Christ, and opened heavens whose angels can give some manifestations of their presence and power.

What are the higher uses of Spiritualism? Compare the condition of those who are in the night of materialism with those whose souls are open to the influxes of the supernal world. The former have no positive evidence of things divine and eternal; no light, no inspiration from Heaven; no consciousness of intercourse with higher spheres of intelligence, and nothing but speculation or history to satisfy their religious needs and aspirations. As Spiritualists, however, we have perpetual demonstration of the existence of an all-present Father Spirit, an angel world peopled by the departed great and good of all ages, and open for descending myriads to visit the planes of humanity with messages and influxes of the most animating import. Those who realize these things cannot feel otherwise than inspired with the holiest, loftiest purposes. What are all the pleasures and pursuits of the passing world, compared with the vereties of immortal life, a spiritual universe revealed by angel hosts in the glory of God and eternity? All these scenes of sensuous existence sink into insignificance, as the expanded soul walks the Mount of Beatitude, communes with the transfigured dead treading the highway of eternal progress, and sweeps its enraptured vision over starry worlds glittering in the celestial empire. We may prize the life that now is, for its manifold beauties, blessings, friendships, loves, and all its ever-moving panorama of scenes and events; but there are ordeals beneath which the soul sometimes sinks, sick and suffering; burdens bending the sternest mortals; disappointments blasting the fairest promises; bereavements rending the stoutest hearts; treacheries lacerating the bosom with unutterable anguish; errors and evils terrible with destruction; unrequited affections ever sighing and sobbing with a desolation akin to despair; and oh, how few of all the hopes once coloring the future with rainbows of delight are ever realized, while clouds darken the heavens, thunders roll and tears fall in showers over the withered flowers of the past!

But in the light of Spiritualism, all the landscape of this life glows in the radiance of the angel world, and angel companions evermore walk by our side, take us by the hand, breathe into our souls influxes born of God, wipe the tears from our eyes, sweep away the clouds once gathering around death, beckon us onward towards the pathway trod by the triumphal hosts of heaven, and wait to welcome us home to everlasting mansions. It is no dream, this glorious gospel of spirit land, for millions are now holding perpetual intercourse with the departed, and receiving the highest incentives to spiritual life and culture. Let us *know* these things, and how elevating the tendency! While the beloved of angel land are ministering fresh messages of divine love, our souls overflow with that same high and holy love for humanity; and all selfishness, lust, pride, hate, must sink before the clear-seeing eyes of heaven. A sainted father, mother, brother, sister, child, friend, beams down like some ever-present sentinel of God. And in view of the eternal destiny opening in the future, who can squander the priceless moments of time, or prostitute to base purposes the God-like energies of our beings? No; this life is too short for its discipline to be lost, and its opportunities too brief and precious to be exchanged for cheating baubles. O God! O ye messengers of the land immortal! lend ye your aids, that each soul, conscious of its eternity, may arise with higher, holier aspirations in accord with the divinity of its unending mission!

It requires no little struggle to attain the true life and our true relations as social and spiritual beings. It is easy enough to float along with the popular current, but it requires true manhood, true womanhood, to strike out from the multitude, and seek the highest ideals of our souls. But few are prepared for this, yet many are continually prating of it. Spiritualists and other reformers are perpetually harping on the need of setting up a standard above the vulgar masses, and the duty of striking out for the path of a true, noble, independent life. Oh, yes; never mind what parties, what churches, what conservative society, what the world or the rabble will say. Be true, be free, be pure, be noble! If your political relations are false, change them for the true. If your church relations are false, remedy them. If your social relations are untrue, correct the evil, and obey the divine laws of harmony and purity. Now, all this is is very fine, heroic talk, but who will dare reduce it to practice? God help us! angels pity us! Many of those very persons who are so loud in heroic talk, perhaps, are among the first to join with the rabble in damning us if we seek to live up to the standard around which they rallied with hypocritical hurrahs. Good Lord deliver us from all would-be reformers who do nothing but prate and pound public platforms, yet never dare practise.

There are penalties, pains, and persecutions attending all radical changes. Sometimes it is like plucking out the right eye, or taking off the right hand. Neighbors may complain, spies may be set on our track, old acquaintances may turn cold, old associations may be broken up, old friends may weep and tremble, and for a time the whole world seem to frown. But the deed must be done. Though the earth yawns beneath our feet, and the human heavens gather black with thunder-clouds, let us be loyal to God, and conscience, and the angel whisperings of the eternal world. Heroic souls, like Jesus, will stand alone with God and angels, rather than barter their ideal of the right, the just, the true, the pure. Transient pains and persecutions are nothing compared with the "eternal weight of glory" crowning the martyr path. Humanity can never be redeemed from its falsities without these startling and radical changes.

Attending the reception and practice of Spiritualism there are some unquestionable trials, and we may rejoice that there are, not only to test its professors, but to intimidate the multitude who might otherwise rush to its embrace with no higher motive than that of satisfying a morbid curiosity or of using it for the basest purposes. It is an easy matter, if you have the means, to take a cushioned pew in a fashionable place of worship, make a modest profession of having experienced religion, sign a creed already manufactured for you, join a church, and then float along with the church-going crowd; but it is quite another thing to break off from the fashionable throng; to battle perhaps with your own prejudices and opinions; in face of frowning priest and people, and perhaps of grieved family and friend, go to a spiritual assemblage or circle; to go again and again, and perhaps get but little at first; to go on, and find yourself at last in the midst of manifestations of the most mysterious and startling character; to find tables, chairs, and other material objects knocked about till all your old ideas are knocked into confusion, and you are left in fearful perplexity; to find manifestations and teachings in one place which seem to contradict what have appeared in another; to find yourself in the actual presence of spiritual intelligences, and there be told you must make your own creed, your own church, be your own priest, and look to God and heaven for help to work out your own salvation with fear and trembling.

And yet, all this, and perhaps much more, will fall to our lot before we have gone far into the field of spiritual phenomena. The subject is beset with so many difficulties, the opposer regards this as an objection to its truthfulness, and informs us the path of truth is so easy he who runs may read, and the wayfaring man though a fool need not err therein. True, he who runs *may* read; but it depends very much on which way he runs. If a man closes his eyes, stops his ears, shakes his head, and then undertakes to run away from these spiritual manifestations, it is probable he will neither read nor understand the truths they reveal. Yet their significance is so simple and plain, the wayfaring man, though a fool, may not err, while the wiseacres of science and theology, in their blindness and bigotry, scoff at the very simplicity of these spirit-demonstrations, and, rejecting them for this very reason, call us fools and lunatics for seeing and believing.

But, however plain and simple the great ideal of Spiritualism may be, we are not to lose sight of the trials and difficulties attending the faithful disciple. We are tried most, perhaps, by the opposition of the church and the priesthood; not the true church, the true priesthood, but the sectarian, those who are wedded to their forms and creeds as though they were infallible, and who denounce Spiritualism because its teachings are not in accordance. God knows we have no malice or unkindness towards either the clerical profession or its churches; and yet we must confess the unwelcome truth, that were it not for their politic hostility to our cause, the masses of the people would at once become enlisted in behalf of this new unfolding. In view of the fact that the clergy and their churches have an opportunity to investigate; that they are continually invited to the work, and the majority *will* not or *dare* not do it; that but very few of those who have investigated and acknowledged themselves convinced, especially among the clergy, have come up to confess it; that most of our pulpits and altars are closed and barricaded against this modern ministry of angels, while they are either thundering alarms and anathemas or growing ominously silent over the rapid progress of spiritual light; — all these, together with many other signs, give us warning that between the church and these angelic powers a conflict is approaching in whose dread ordeal we must all be tried, and a conflict unparalleled in the history of Christianity. We would wage no indiscriminate war against the churches. God forbid. We would give them all praise for what they have *been*, what they have *done*, and what they are now doing to restrain and elevate millions of the race. But let them beware of attempting to shut out God and the manifestations of his holy spirits; beware of attributing these manifestations to Beelzebub, and thereby repeat the blasphemy whose penalty crushed Jerusalem and its proud temple beneath the awful judgment of heaven!

Many of us who were born and bred in Christian churches know what a trial it is to break loose from old ties and associations, and have old friends turn on us with either pity, scorn, reproach, or, perhaps, pour on us the darkest denunciations. But what shall we do? Can we retain our hold on churches which denounce Spiritualism, and at the same time follow the spiritual light we have received? Shall we flatter ourselves that we can effect a compromise between error and truth, hold fellowship with both at once, and, by retaining our place in the temples of old theology, prove successful in bringing over their priesthood and people to the light of this new dispensation? By no means. It would be like putting new wine into old bottles. Why did not Christ and his apostles attempt to compromise with the Jewish church, and to hold their places in the popular synagogues? For the same reasons that we cannot hold popular favor with the churches to-day, and at the same time prove faithful to our convictions of Spiritualism. The moment we make known our convictions, we are called to an account; and the only terms on which we can hold our place is to keep silent or compromise ourselves in a manner to convey the impression that our views and feelings are not materially changed by our faith. And no matter how liberal the church and the priesthood may profess to be towards us, or what compromises they may make in order to retain us, we may rest sure there is something wrong in the compact, something rotten, so long as they refuse to open their eyes and welcome the light now pouring down from heaven with the attendant manifestations of spiritual presence and power.

To realize the glorious fact of immortal life, and intercourse with spirit-intelligences, presses home responsibilities of the most solemn moment. We are to live forever! Death is only a transition to the plains of eternal life, where our work must go on and ever on, augmenting in greatness, grandeur, and glory. Are we devoting ourselves here in preparation for the spheres of celestial companionship? Or are we living as though our stay here were eternal, seeking to carry the world on our backs? If so, death will strip us, and hurl us in transparent nakedness into the presence of God's angel hosts! Some slight cause may topple man's form into the tomb; but all the leagued forces of the material universe cannot confine him there. The feeblest breath of earth may waft away his mortal life; but his spirit will rise over the grave, though swept by the mightiest blasts. Man's dying breath is but the breathing of the first fresh breeze of the morn of an immortal Paradise. His last sigh is the prelude of an unending song of harmony caught by the sons of God gone on in the march of eternal progress. The death-smile that plays on the cold, wan face, is but the gleam of an angel-welcome shining down through the portals of eternity. The good man's death is but his birth into an immortal life made more glorious from the gloom anon gathering over the pathway of a past through which he trod on with triumph towards his God.

Spiritualists and other reformers are constantly accusing religionists of inconsistency in making professions of principles which they fail to practise. These accusations may be founded on fact; yet we may ask whether we have a right to judge or complain, unless we can claim entire consistency and perfection for ourselves. While we are denouncing others, we may listen to angel admonitions whispering within the council-chambers of our own consciences, and saying, "Physician, heal thyself!" Let those who suspect the honesty of others, ask themselves whether they are and always have been entirely free from dishonesty. Let those who censure the alleged weaknesses or failings of others question their own souls, and be sure they are faultless. Do you doubt the purity of others? How is your own heart and imagination? Do you complain of the shortcomings of others, and the insincerity of their professions? How many so-called Spiritualists and reformers might be condemned on the same score! The lofty inculcations of angel wisdom, love, truth, and purity are descending with demonstrations of supernal power, and we make loudest professions of the superiority of our spiritual teachings. But are our thoughts, deeds, and lives of a corresponding character? If not, we stand arraigned at the bar of self-condemnation and judgment, and all our professions recoil on us with sentences of reproach. We cannot shirk the results. Our influence will fail to be felt for good, however specious we may seem in our professions and externals. If our interior nature is untrue, a subtle spiritual influence will go forth for evil in spite of all outward appearances. Practise what you teach and profess. It were better to *live* the truth, and profess nothing, than to profess the truth and live a lying life!

Why do spirits seek to manifest themselves and communicate with mortals? Is it to sanction anything false, selfish, sordid? Anything merely politic, sectarian, time-serving, popular, reputable, fashionable, conventional? No! They come to unfold the divine elements of our being; to shed heaven's light, in which we may read God's laws written in our own souls; to inspire us to be true to ourselves; true to our own most enlightened consciousness; true to the model of heavenly life they are seeking to unfold; true to the purest, deepest affections and aspirations which come in harmony with God and angels. Are we bound to parties, churches, cliques, social influences, or anything else which we know to be false in the sight of Heaven? God and his messengers help us! Dare we be true? How shall we answer? It is easier to praise men and women for their fine sentiments and noble thoughts, than to live in accordance with those thoughts and sentiments. Too much genius and talent are exhausted in the effort to elaborate and publish truth, while too little heroism is manifest in living it out. Any man of tongue or pen can proclaim liberty; but few, however, really dare be free, or face the great battle of menacing myrmidons in the hireling service of social, sectarian, and civil oppression. We bestow the greatest praise on those who have uttered the loftiest sentiments, without asking whether they have proved honest and daring exemplars of what they have uttered, while, perhaps, we treat with contumely and abuse those humbler souls who have really lived out those sentiments. An eminent reformer proves himself a hero in proclaiming the broad principle that "Resistance to tyrants is obedience to God." Yet, when wronged woman rises to throw off the yoke of marital bondage, this same reformer shrinks back and denominates such efforts out of place, and calculated to bring reproach on woman's reform movements. Let silence seal the lips and paralyze the pens of men and women who are not equal to the task of living as they talk. One bold step taken out of the beaten path towards the highway of a true ideal life, shall tell with an eloquence and power mightier than a myriad of voices, — shall prove the signal of hope for millions groaning in bondage.

Many so-called reformers, in common with other people, often manifest great sensitiveness as to what the world will think and say, regardless of what is just, right and true. They are over-anxious about their reputations, and the reputation of "the cause." None, perhaps, may question the motives of some of these sensitive souls, but we *may* question the soundness of their judgment, the breadth of their minds, the independence of their characters. If we are after a good name, or reputation, or what we call popularity, the most direct course for us to pursue would be to abandon

Spiritualism and all progressive ideas, and fall back into popular parties, sects and societies. If we adopt Spiritualism, we fly into the face of an opposing world, and our reputations, for a time, go to the winds. And who cares, while the mind is clear, the soul is free, the conscience is sound, the heart is pure, the life is true, and all heaven bends over us with benedictions of present and eternal recompense? We pity those who undertake to become Spiritualists or reformers, and yet who dare not lift their heads, or open their mouths, or take a single step, without trembling lest somebody think or say something to call in question their character or reputation. Angels blush over such craven souls. Let men and women who profess celestial enlightenment and celestial guidance *be men and women*, though all the world whisper suspicion or deal in diabolical denunciation. But what if people misunderstand us? What if they honestly regard our course as evil, unwise and injurious? Never mind! If your motives are good, if you inflict no evil on others, if you regard the rights of all, if you discharge your every duty according to the convictions of your own conscience, if you are deliberate and wise in all your acts and purposes, if you manifest a kind, loving and forbearing spirit, if you are true to God and humanity as revealed in your inmost soul, if you are guided by the divinest affections of your own being in communion with angel intelligences, then press on your way, firm and unflinching, though all earth and hell howl on your track.

Dare you do this? Then do it, and without whining or wincing. We may remember we owe some obligations to what we call the world, and may not seek to offend honest prejudices and opinions, or rudely assail established laws, customs, conventionalities and institutions. Yet there are times when we are called to speak and act independent of all these, and in seeming violence to the feelings of those once nearest and dearest to our hearts.

And what if we are misunderstood, and for a season made to suffer the deepest sorrow and obloquy? It has been thus with all pure, noble, pioneer souls. We are to find our highest recompense in the consciousness of speaking and acting according to our divinest convictions and affections. If, in so speaking and acting, we come in conflict with the prejudices, the misapprehensions, the evils and errors of the world, we are to remember the greater need of our firmness, freedom, fortitude and heroism. The world can be redeemed from its falsities only so far as we meet those falsities face to face, and rise above them, in spite of all opposing influences. Millions are groaning in social, civil, and religious bondage from which they can never be saved, unless the freed Messiah-souls of this dispensation stand forth as examples of heroism, clothed in the armor of God and the eternal world.

While we are continually extolling the beauties of our spiritual theory, it were commendable to reduce the same to some practical purpose. Angel visitants come on errands of mercy to our common humanity; but how is it with us who profess to give them welcome, and rejoice over the messages and inspirations they bring? As Spiritualists we despise all cant, and would avoid falling into strains of fanatical exhortation; yet it may not come amiss for us, at times, to suffer ourselves to be questioned as to our duties and derelictions. With all our professions of a superior faith and philosophy, how are we living, and how are we dealing with our brothers and sisters about us? Are we seeking to become as true as the angels whose presence we invoke? Are we living conscious of their overshadowing influence, and seeking their smile, the smile of God and the approbation of our inmost souls, rather than the smile of the passing world? Are we endeavoring to become angels of mercy in the daily walks of life, dropping words and deeds worthy of those who profess communion with heaven?

Spiritualists there are who begin to realize their mission. One of our lecturing brethren was walking out in the woodlands near Auburn, when he heard sounds like the groans of a man in deepest agony. He drew near, and found a poor fellow lying on the ground, in intense suffering. Like a good Samaritan, he picked up the sufferer, conveyed him to a healing medium, and the unfortunate man was provided for and treated without money or price. A young man was brutally knocked down in the streets of Auburn, and was supposed to have been killed. A group of men gathered around, but no one for a moment seemed to proffer any relief. A young woman was passing by, and dashing through the crowd of men in defiance of all conventionalities, she took up the head of the young man and rubbed his forehead with the palm of her hand, when he opened his eyes and seemed to speak in gratitude. The young woman was a well-known medium. A poor fugitive woman, with sore and bleeding feet from long travel, knocked at the door of this medium's home, and her feet were washed and her wounds were dressed, and she was sent on her way rejoicing. That poor woman had just been turned coldly and empty from the door of a rich and pious neighbor! A poor outcast woman in Owego, N. Y., was taken into the house of a neighbor, and kept and treated with kindness, until she was at last restored to confidence among her friends. And who was her protector? She was a young widow woman, a medium, and whose house was thrown open for regular circles twice a week.

"Go thou, and do likewise," ye who would prove your faith by your works. Too many, instead of seeking to redeem the unfortunate, are prone to pass hasty sentences of condemnation. "Why judge ye one another?" was the pertinent inquiry of an ancient brother. Do we judge one another in haste or severity? Are we prone to pass sentences of condemnation on our brothers and sisters?

Where is our authority? Before we presume to sit in judgment we need to feel assured that we are qualified for that solemn office. Are we perfect ourselves? None save the All-seeing is prepared to pronounce perfect judgment. Jesus, with his far-seeing soul of love, never judged, never condemned. Read thy brother, thy sister; read them through and through, and understand all the motives and moving main-springs of their being; and perchance thou wilt find more to approve than to condemn. Understand them as thou wouldst be understood, and no whisperings of slander nor curses shall ever pass thy lips. Do not judge of one political party entirely by what other parties may say. If sectional excitements arise, beware of forming one-sided opinions. Do not judge all radical reformers to be fools, fanatics or knaves, because they are denounced in wholesale by conservatives; nor judge all conservatives by the denunciations of certain radicals. Never allow one religious sect to bias you against another; learn the sentiments and positions of all. Do not judge of Spiritualism by what its one-sided opponents may say. If public lecturers or mediums are reported unfavorably, be sure and learn the other side from them or their friends. If social disruptions ensue, be careful how you judge from rumor or scandal. If husbands and wives have difficulties, beware how you interpose. If either party in trouble feels called on to report and to seek sympathy, hear the other party also. And after you have heard all, perhaps it may be impossible for you to pronounce judgment. If disruptions ensue, seek to know all the secret and inmost causes, and keep silence unless you can remedy the evils involved, or offer some palliating consolation. The most terrible evils in society arise from false, hasty, one-sided judgments, prone to pronounce unqualified condemnation. Remember no mortal is totally depraved; there are redeeming traits in all. The most unfortunate are capable of improvement.

When you hear a person pronouncing unqualified censure, you may be sure that person is in the wrong, and lacks not only justice but humanity. In most cases of difficulty between neighbors, families, husbands and wives, there are some causes on both sides, and as we are all liable to err, it becomes us to be exceedingly guarded in our judgment, with our hearts ever open in sympathy and our hands ever ready to aid. Why did Jesus fail to rebuke and pass judgment on the woman of Samaria, who had had several husbands, and was then living with a man to whom she was not legally married? (See John iv.) Because he read her whole life, her whole nature; he saw all the causes and conditions by which she had been influenced. It is thus that angels see us all; and in the same manner God help us to see each other.

We profess to believe there is hope for the reformation of the most unfortunate, yet how few treat each other as though there was any possibility for changes for the better. We are continually judging each other by circumstances, influences and alleged imperfections in the past, forgetful that all the experiences of the past may have brought lessons for improvement in the future. "Go, and sin no more," said Jesus to the unfortunate; but we say, "Go, go, go! hopeless, branded, damned for time and eternity!" Oh, if each woe we pronounced on others were to rebound and fall on our own souls, what curses would crush us, and what wailings of despair would rend the air! What good can I do? is often asked by persons who feel their humility and yet possess a laudable ambition to become great, good and useful. Too often, however, their ambition may be to become great in the esteem of the world. Ah, how worthless is the world's fame compared with that soul-worth, which alone is enduring and divine! What good can I do? It may be little compared with the achievements of the world's great heroes and philanthropists, and yet that little may tell, like the widow's mite, down through ages. It is a little "rap," that tiny sound we hear on the table from some dear returned friend, and yet what great thoughts and emotions are awakened; and that faint vibration seems like an echo ringing through the corridors of eternity. Is there no friend, no neighbor, no fellow-being, to whom you can go and speak one kind word, breathe one hope, and for whom you can perform some good and noble act? Ah, it may be a little thing, but it shall tell through all time. How many hearts are brooding and breaking, how many minds are wrapped in night, how many souls are sinking in silent gloom and despair, how many immortal beings are tending down to destruction and death, while only one word, one look, one smile, one tear, one humble deed, might avert the impending woe! What good can I do? Think for yourself. Make a trial.

Do Spiritualists believe in the duty and possibility of individual reformation? Most assuredly. Yet there are some persons everlastingly prating on reform in general, without making it a personal matter or talking and acting as though they believed it possible for certain individuals ever to change for the better. There are some sham reformers who are the very meanest sneerers, snarlers, fault-finders, backbiters, scandal-mongers, and suspicion-snuffers, whenever certain persons are named whose antecedents may not have squared with their notions of right. Doubtless there *are* unfortunate organisms for whom we can have but little hope of reformation in the present life, yet humanity compels us to hope and labor lovingly for every soul giving sparks of desire and aspiration towards a better life. There are men and women, young and middle-aged, who may have partly wandered for years, yet, while they give any evidences of pure aims and noble purposes, it becomes us as brothers and sisters to drop the tear of sympathy, to seal our lips in silence over the past, extend helping hands, and breathe words of encouragement. Oh, ever thus do God's ministering angels bend over us all; and as we hope for angel ministration in the day of trial and sorrow, we may consider the solemn duty of acting as angels of mercy to others!

Brethren, if a man be overtaken in a fault, ye which are spiritual restore such a one in the spirit of meekness; considering thyself, lest thou also be tempted. — Galatians vi. 1.

Take heed that ye despise not one of these little ones; for I say unto you that in heaven their angels do always behold the face of my Father.—Matt. xviii. 10.

Practical Spiritualism is summed up in one word,— Love; love to God, manifest in love to humanity. While Spiritualists seek no central creed, no fixed platform of intellectual opinion, no rigid system of theology, binding the conscience and trammeling freedom, they are united in the one grand, central element of fraternal love encircling the family of earth and heaven. We can all agree, without controversy, in regard to this central principle, for there is one common chord of benevolence running through the great heart of humanity, which needs only to be touched aright to vibrate in harmony with the angel world. But men may quarrel everlastingly about abstract creeds and systems addressed to the head alone, without coming to any uniform opinion, while their hearts are rent with discord, or left cold, desolate, untouched. The religious world for ages has endeavored to unite in creeds and forms to save humanity; but with what lamentable results! It has not saved even itself, and to-day the churches are found waning and powerless; and while they are contending over the "dry bones" of old faiths and formulas past all resurrection, millions of the ignorant, erring, fallen, and unbelieving are left to pine and perish outside the pale of redemption.

In this emergency Spiritualism makes its advent. It is scouted by sectarians and would-be philosophers, because it begins with no rigid creed or system, but leaves each individual conscience and intellect free to seek and decide for itself, while it first aims to reach the heart and awaken those divine religious affections paramount over every other department of human nature. We thank God and the angel world that Spiritualism comes as a religion of the affections. It embraces all science, philosophy, reason, intellect; but its angel hands reach down through all these and first seek to lay hold of the slumbering chords of the human heart. "He that loveth is born of God, and knoweth God; for God is love." John goes on to say, in substance, that divine love was manifest in Jesus; that men may know whether they have this love by the spiritual witness within them, and that no man can love God without loving his brother man. 1 John iv. Recognizing God as the Father Spirit of all souls, whose essence is love, every spirit or angel commissioned of God to visit humanity must come on errands of love, and is a manifestation of the Christ-principle, the Holy Ghost, or the Holy Host of heaven, whether that spirit or angel be one of the departed saints of sacred history or a little child just gone from the humblest home below. There is no small or great in the spiritual kingdom now being inaugurated on earth, no high or low, no rich or poor, but all are one in the fellowship of love engirting the universe. Could we take some lofty stand-point in the spirit world, and gaze down through all the transient grades and conditions of humanity, seeing as angels see, we should discover one central element of love more or less pervading all souls, and learn that most of the evils, errors, and differences existing among the millions below were less than our false judgment had apprehended, while every being would reveal a germ of divinity destined to mount and burn with glory among the celestial hosts of eternal progress.

Let Spiritualists reduce this gospel to practice, and

what would be the result? We should hesitate to think, speak, or act in violence to the principle of universal love, remembering every thought, word, and deed will tell for good or for evil, affecting we know not how many immortal beings nor how long, and must at last rise in judgment either in time or eternity. Touch but a single chord in the humblest human soul, and the vibration rings through the whole chain of human brotherhood, whether we are conscious of it or otherwise. We forget these men or women are our brothers and sisters, when we treat them as we would not be treated ourselves. We forget they are immortal; that we may meet them in that transparent land where all the past stands revealed in the sight of wisdom; that every impression we make on them, either good or evil, will there meet us in judgment; and that evermore their guardian angels in heaven not only behold the face of our common Father, but watch them as well as ourselves, noting every thought, word or deed we seek to conceal from mortals. We sometimes grow impatient, petulant, indignant, and perhaps vindictive over what we deem the evils and errors of our brothers and sisters, and perchance seek to minister some severe punishment, not to benefit but to injure them. Whenever such feelings arise, we may be sure there is something wrong in ourselves. We assume to be wiser and better than others, and set ourselves up as judges, with authority to condemn. What a mild yet majestic rebuke to all such once came from Him who told the Jews, "He that is without sin among you, let him cast the first stone," and the Magdalen, "Neither do I condemn thee; go and sin no more;" while in the death hour he prayed, "Father, forgive them, for they know not what they do." We need not become blind to the misdirections of our fellows, but see with "larger, holier eyes," in order that we may understand the secret springs and causes, and be prepared to make allowance for whatever falls short of our idea of the right, the just and the pure. In this manner our guardian spirits see us; and as we pray the Father to "forgive us our trespasses as we forgive those who trespass against us," how can we expect lenity in the sight of heaven, while a thought or deed of unkindness, unforgiveness, is manifest towards a child of humanity?

To be consistent Spiritualists, to exemplify the gospel of the spheres in practical, every-day life, an individual as well as a general reform must ensue. We must have done with all laws, creeds, customs, institutions, and opinions which treat man as a fallen, infernal being, naturally prone to evil, and deserving wrath, hatred and punishment, pushing him to destruction and despair. How is it among us now? How even among some called Spiritualists, claiming to hold intercourse with the spheres of angel love? In our thoughts, words, and deeds towards each other, and towards an opposing world, are we always as just, forbearing, kind, loving as our angel friends who come again and again with their messages of mercy, in spite of all our imperfections? They come not to spy out the evil within us, but to call out the good, the pure, the true, the noble. They come not to condemn, but to commiserate, and encourage better purposes and resolutions. If they see faults, it is not to flaunt them before the world, and chide us, but to eradicate with a gentle hand. They seek to know how and why we err, and to pour balm into wounded souls, and take us gently by the hand, while they wipe away the tears. Seeking deep into our hearts, they see there and in surrounding circumstances all the causes that animate us, but they do not tear open our hearts and leave them bleeding and blasted in the bleak winds of the world. Oh, could we always treat each other thus, and the world likewise, how soon would the millennium dawn over the darkness now covering the multitudes crushed beneath the false and the damning judgment of their fellows.

What but the angel ministry can accomplish this glorious work of reform? The church, state, and society of to-day are doing little or nothing towards reaching the better, affectional nature of man, but are mainly engaged in administering the law of fear and force to ferret out and punish the seemingly evil and erroneous. Let the Spiritualists speedily wash their hands from all participation in this bloody, infernal crusade. What if there is a Judas in our very midst,—worse than Judases, impostors, villains, wretches of the deepest dye? let them alone, as Jesus did Judas; for perchance, poor unfortunates, they will soon drive themselves to temporal ruin. Better a millstone were hung about our necks, and cast into the sea, than one human being should ever be hurried to destruction or hindered from reform by a single thought, word, or deed of our own. But shall we not speak out and exonerate the cause of Spiritualism from reproach? Our "cause?" Heaven save us! Humanity, humanity is our cause! And better a thousand professed Spiritualists suffer temporary reproach from the unthinking rabble, than one soul be crushed forever beneath the Juggernaut of an unchristian judgment. It is easy enough to find fault, criticise, scent out, and denounce sinners; but quite another thing to exercise wisdom and charity broad enough to understand all the causes of human imperfection, and apply the means of redemption. It is sometimes hard to keep silent over glaring wrongs, but better we suffer thus than assume the divine prerogative to pass a sentence which may inflict greater wrongs on the offending. "Charity suffereth long and is kind, thinketh no evil," etc., but seeks rather the good and true, and thereby develops the innate elements of goodness and truth found even in the most abandoned.

This gospel of love has been tested by Jesus, John, Fenelon, Howard, Oberlin, and a host of reformers seeking to "overcome evil with good," and now makes fresh appeals from the angel world to Spiritualists. Dear departed ones from the spirit land bend over humanity with messages of love to souls long waiting for some influences to touch them and call forth angel responses. Nothing is so mighty and magical on the human heart as the consciousness of spiritual intercourse, the great fact that heaven is open, its guardianship is constant, and inspirations are direct. Spiritualism has already redeemed thousands, once darkened, buried in materialism, hardened in heart, but now lifting songs heavenward.

An incident occurring many years since illustrates what Spiritualism is doing to-day. A wretched convict for ten years had been suffering solitary confinement in the old Walnut Street Prison, of Philadelphia. He was regarded as hardened beyond all redemption. A genial philanthropist visited the poor man, and spent a long time in conversation. The visitor was about to depart, when the prisoner reached his hand through the iron grating, and beckoning him to return, in a low voice said, "One word more, if you please. You seem to understand these things. *Do the spirits of the departed ever come back to witness the actions and situation of the living?*" "Many people believe it," replied the visitor, "and the Scripture says there is joy in heaven over a sinner that repenteth on earth. It may, therefore, be true." "It may be!" exclaimed the prisoner; and bursting into tears, he added, "My poor, poor mother." The memory of that mother in heaven, and perhaps the thought of her hovering over him in that hour of prison agony, smote the ice long lying around his heart, and melted him into the tenderness of a child once more sobbing on the maternal bosom.

"She died of a starved heart!" writes a brother, alluding to the death of a noble woman whom thousands blessed as an angel of mercy. Some specious, respectable cause was assigned to account for her decease, but in reality she died of broken and starved-heartedness. What plaintive tales might thousands tell of that same disease whose preyings baffle all medical art, and whose pangs are more fearful than ten thousand kings of terror can inflict. Consumption is called a fell destroyer, but the wasting away of one fibre after another till the physical lungs are gone, is a Paradise of death, compared to consumption of soul, and the wasting away of those spiritual heart-fibres of affection which seek to cling around some ideal love and become entwined in divine bonds of conjugal communion. How the world falsifies in its obituaries! Oh, let the dead speak as they are speaking, and angel sympathy shall flow down from the spheres into thousands of hearts now desolate, starving, dying. O man, O woman, whoever thou art thus wasting the divinest affections of thy being, speak! Open thy soul. But, alas, where is the balm, where the physician? Can the church, the state, the society, the schools of medical science, minister to this disease of a starved heart? Nay. They would blister and blast with curses. O God! it is terrible, this tyrant, lashing legions to the wheel, the rack, till one heart-string after another snaps with agony, and the starved spirit shrieks and faints away on the bosom of God. And then the world says he or she died of consumption, and it was a mysterious providence. It is false! and so was the sad life of the departed; and the lying world held its lash over the bleeding heart till it broke and burst its cerements for the land of celestial love and liberty. But, O ye martyrs of starved and bleeding affections, look up! for the dawn of a better dispensation breaks from the bending heavens.

Ah, how many heart-sick toilers and sufferers are waiting for the dawn of that morning whose day shall reveal the long looked-for joys promised in other years! The world seems filled with care and turmoil, and clouds are lowering. Daily duties press with a relentless grasp. The multitudes seem living amid mists and shadows, and chasing phantoms. We each have our worldly pursuits in which we seem absorbed, and yet we care little for these compared with some great purposes and ideals which lie deep within our souls, all unseen by the outer world. Oh that the world might read us, see us, and know us as God and angels see and know! O, beating heart, be still! Celestial watchers are thine, and if thou art true to the divinest intuitions of thine own nature, thou shalt not wait and struggle in vain. Wait a little longer. The loftiest ideals of thy soul shall yet be realized. The discipline of toil, trial, and patience shall prepare thee for a glorious fruition in recompense for all the past.

Skeptics and worldlings, in the sunshine of prosperity, may scoff at the hopes of immortal life, but there are suffering, sorrowing, sinking millions who clutch at the faintest ray gleaming from another and better world. Tears came to the eyes of hundreds as they heard a philanthropist in public convention tell how, in a miserable den in Boston, he found a poor, fallen girl whom he had known in her earlier years of bloom and innocence. Haggard, wretched, bleared, wild with sin and agony, she fell at his feet, bathed in tears, and piteously cried out, "Oh, is there no better world than this? Will there be no better place for me in heaven?" And what could the skeptic have replied? What answer could have been given by the religious pharisee? Answers which have hurled thousands down the steeps of despair. But our philanthropic brother was a Spiritualist, and he told that fallen daughter of a spirit-mother, and of weeping, loving angels, and of an opened heaven bending with a Father's mercy. Let the outcasts of the world realize the truth of Spiritualism, and Spiritualists become ministering angels, and how many despairing souls might rise redeemed and cause heaven to ring with songs of joy.

"Open the door," were the last words of a dying brother, whose funeral the writer attended. The door of the outer tabernacle was opened, the gate of inner life swung back, angel friends waited with a beckoning smile, and the spirit vanished beyond the portals of eternal beatitude. Ah, how many dying souls need the door opened leading into the unknown land! All is dark, dreadful, stifling. Night blackens into palpable horrors, and perchance demons chatter premonitions of eternal despair. Materialism folds its awful pall over the dying, or human dogmas of direst doom thunder mutterings of endless woe. Horrible! "Open the door." Unbar the gates of death. Give back the dead, and let their white hands lead the dying forth amid those "many mansions" whose doors stand open night and day welcoming the sick and weary millions of the Father. "Open the door." How many minds are stifled inside of closed church doors, imprisoned within thick walls of error, prejudice, superstition, ignorance, custom, conventionalism; and how many hearts are smothered amid murky airs gathering around like the vapors of death. "Open the door!" Set the mind free in the air of heaven. Let the heart breathe its native element of love. Let the soul walk forth in the divinity of its nature. Hark! Angel visitors stand knocking at the portals of humanity, bidding us unbar every door that shuts out the light, liberty, love, and truth of God as revealed in nature and the opening spheres.

There are seasons in which the soul seems enshrouded amid clouds of impenetrable gloom, and all hope and joy are hid from our tear-blinded vision. Yet often amid these clouds, shutting out the future and hanging with depression and despair over the human spirit, are heard celestial voices as heard by the wondering disciples on the Mount of Transfiguration: "And there was a cloud that overshadowed them, and a voice came out of the cloud, saying, 'This is my beloved Son.'" Mark ix. 7. In seasons of sunshine and prosperity, we are too often absorbed in the external world to become conscious of the divine voices of heaven or to listen for the still small voice speaking within the temple of our own souls. But when the external world grows dark and ominous clouds lower over our heads, then we are driven into the silent, solemn chambers of our being, and impelled to seek for aids above and beyond. Oh, sad, sobbing soul, be still. Harken to the voices of beatified ones who have passed beyond the cloud and storm, and thou shalt bathe in the light and melody of angel spheres.

The daily experiences of life teach us how transitory are all things of a material nature, and press on us the importance of fixing the affections on foundations spiritual and eternal. The false dreams, the fickle hopes, the flaunting pleasures once so golden with promises of bliss, where are they? A few years, and all are departed, leaving the soul desolate of those divine treasures which are found only in heaven and in foretastes of heavenly beatitude. Life to the multitude seems only a vain seeking, because the diviner needs of the soul are sunk in things transient and sensual. This world is beautiful and blessed, and there are friends here who seem types of celestial being; but all these are unsatisfying unless seen and appreciated in the light of the eternal world. These scenes of beauty, these forms of friendship and love, are passing away; and what sad mutations are made in our brightest hopes, joys and affections! what clouds of doubt and fear overhang our path! what heart-tremblings, agonies and bereavements rend the bosom! But when the heavens are seen opened and angel ones coming in the name of the Father, with a radiance reflecting the glory of hopes and joys, affections infinite and eternal, we can weep unmurmuringly over the dead and departed, and realize there is a clime where the rainbows of promise never fade, where celestial beings shall clasp us in the love of God, and all that was holy, beautiful and true in this life become immortal.

But few can anticipate all the tendencies of Modern Spiritualism. No marvel old conservatives and conformists take alarm at some of its teachings. The present condition of church, state and society is almost universally conceded to be unstable, unsafe, rotten, and fast tending to utter decay. In spite of all desperate efforts at revivalism, the church is rapidly waning among advanced minds. Intelligent doubters and unbelievers are rarely reached, and popular preaching is powerless over the masses, unless it is accompanied by the genius and eloquence of a Beecher, Chapin or King. The young generation grows restive under the restraints of orthodoxy, and the church is rather tolerated than courted as affording anything attractive to the fast spirit of young America. The rising generation is outgrowing the past, and will not suffer the hamperings of old creeds and formulas. "Give us a dash of something new and daring," is the demand of the day. Popular churches are supported more on the score of policy, convenience, conventionalism and self-interest, than on the ground of absolute utility as means of grace and salvation, and but few are looking towards them as refuges from immorality, irreligion and infidelity. In their very bosoms are thousands of secret or open unbelievers, and immoralities of the darkest hue anon crop out. Where are the safeguards of the church, while crimes are repeatedly perpetrated beneath her cloak which almost "turn the cheek of darkness pale"?

Nor is the condition of the state and society more promising. Demagogues are rampant and unblushing with bribes and other iniquities. "The dear people" are mostly made the dupes of designing politicians, seeking to strut in official power, line their pockets, and roll in ease and lust. Even the capital of the nation has been stained with the blood of martyrs, while patriot sires are bending from the heavens with averted eyes over scenes enacted beneath the banner of freedom. All are not corrupt, but "there is something rotten in Denmark." The manner in which governmental affairs have been managed indicates a fearful degeneracy, and the political schools of all the dominant parties have been tending downward. And how is it with what we call "society"? Young men and young women who go out into society there find themselves initiated into arts, conceits, conventionalities, scandals, intrigues, disguises and habits, in nine cases out of ten, corrupting to all that is pure, free, spontaneous, truthful and confiding. Appearances take the place of intrinsic virtues, and the affections are sacrificed to fashions and morbid sentimentalisms which go maudling into miserable marriages of lust or convenience. Go into our modern fashionable society, or into almost any company, whether fashionable or otherwise, where people congregate to while away the time in pleasure, and what are the predominant elements of attraction? Let the experience and observation of each reader answer. Our popular society, in main, is a sham, and a compromise of the individual. Whoever can show off the best, takes the first place, while superficial wit, wealth, brainless loquacity, scandal, gossip, silk, satin and simpering are always at a premium price. The Lord save us from the bore of "society," as it is called! Give us a crust of bread with one true friend, out doors, on a hard rock, rather than a parlor full of sofa-cushioned pimps, primmed up with soulless compliments and conventional hypocrisies. Society as it now is, is a sort of resort for the practice of hypocrisy and the concealment of hearts and souls. Men and women, young and old, go there less to call out and exchange their real thoughts, sentiments and social feelings, than to cater to each other's false tastes, and seek for selfish gratification in ministering to morbid desires, pride, lust and ambition to display. And there amid false glares begin thousands of intrigues and courtships, ending in worse than death, the prostitution of the divinest affections of the sexes.

While these conditions of church, state and society are every day becoming more and more apparent in the light of Spiritualism, many are growing perplexed and alarmed as to final results. A fearful crisis seems impending. It is the inevitable consequence of the revolutionary spirit of the age. Old ideas are fast unsettling. Individualism is taking the place of false, inefficient institutions. It is being demonstrated anew that not only "corporations," but certain laws, customs and creeds, "are soulless," and measurably destroy individual responsibility. Spiritualism, while it recognizes the temporary expediency of certain laws, customs, and institutions, and proposes no direct interference with them, at the same time seeks rather to address the inner consciousness, the divinity of the individual soul, as the highest, most absolute authority. While it proclaims the supremacy of Deity, the influences of the angel world and the fraternity of man, it appeals to the "higher law" written in the heart of humanity and the court within as final authority. Now, while the multitudes have been held so long under false authorities and enslaving restraints, in view of the individual liberty proclaimed by Spiritualism, no marvel many should suffer a rebound to the opposite extreme. In rejecting false authorities, false restraints, there is a tendency to reject all authority, all restraint, and run rampant into a liberty in danger of leading to anarchy and licentiousness. In throwing off the yoke of tyrannical laws, men tend to the opposite extreme, and repudiate all laws and institutions. In breaking loose from the trammels of false creeds and forms, they are in danger of rejecting all beliefs and all religious order. In seeking to escape from false social customs and institutions, they are liable to break loose from all healthful restraints and run into an individual freedom reckless in regard to results. Hence, the numerous outlaws of our day; outlaws to the state, church and society. Among these are found all classes of characters, from the lowest to the highest; the lowest seeking only for the gratification of selfishness and lust; the highest seeking for a reform in which man shall stand forth redeemed, pure and free from all that is false and ignoble. Spiritualists and other reformers, however, are held responsible for all the lawlessness of the age. This is radically wrong and unjust; for what have we to do with the iniquities breaking out in the old state, church and society? Spiritualism enables us to see these evils in a more glaring light, and to point out the cause and cure, but is responsible only in seeking to apply remedies for their eradication. True, Spiritualism opens a broad field of reform, and in seeking to save all it extends the arm of benevolence and charity over the wide domain of humanity. And many who in their wanderings are lost from the folds of state, church and society, are seeking hope and protection beneath this gospel of angel ministration. And what shall be done with them? Many we know are assuming the name of Spiritualism only to abuse its light, and liberty, and love. And what shall we do? Shall we conceal our light, deny our liberty, and turn love into hate, merely because men are liable to abuse these divine gifts? No. Let us rather seek to elevate the principles we profess, and appropriate them to a legitimate reform. What if they are liable to abuse? Light and liberty are the legitimate inheritance of all, and better these were enjoyed, though now and then abused, than that man should be kept in false, ignoble servitude. The young eagle, in the enjoyment of its liberty, may soar too far and become lost in the burning rays of the sun, yet still liberty is the legitimate right. So many in this age of individual freedom are in danger of breaking over the bounds of all social, civil, moral and religious restraint, and perhaps become lost from all the standard safeguards; but there are thousands and millions who need this liberty as their right, and who know how to use it for their own good and the welfare of humanity.

In this impending crisis we have each a heroic work to perform, and one requiring all the moral energies of our nature. While enemies are continually charging on us certain evils and errors growing out of the revolutionary state of our generation, we need the moral courage to face these enemies, and frankly confess that there are evils and errors, and that Spiritualism regards them in a light entirely different from the old schools. As Spiritualists we do not judge the world according to old standards, and have no right to join in the popular cry against every outbreak of what is regarded radical and conventionally wrong. In endeavoring to defend ourselves against popular slander, we are too prone to join the enemy in unqualified denunciations against those who are deemed erroneous and evil. We are too sensitive about our reputation, and not enough so in regard to what is absolutely right, independent of policy. We are anxious to keep our ranks pure, and that is well; but it is more important still that our own hearts, lives and motives should be pure, our aims lofty, unselfish, humanitarian, and let our reputation take care of itself. We need the standard of God and the angel host erected in our midst, let the world do as it will. The time is fast coming when the radical revolutions now upheaving the old order of things will test and try every Spiritualist as by fire. The uprising ranks of humanity are lifting their cry to Heaven for more light and liberty; and the call is rolled from out the angel world, bidding all true, heroic souls to stand up for the RIGHT, come what will, regardless of sect, party, or caste; regardless of name or fame; and heed the voice of God that speaks within, though transient friends forsake, and the outer world howls with denunciation.

The mightiest forces in the natural world are invisible; it is thus in the civil, moral, religious and social. There are unseen spiritual agencies at work in all the revolutions of to-day. The elements are thrown into commotion in preparation for momentous changes, inaugurating a new earth and a new heaven. Similar signs have heralded every great change in the past. There is no cause for alarm; nothing shall pass away or perish except the transient and perishable; the good and true are eternal. Whatever government, church, or state of society, law or custom, can be shaken, ought to be shaken, tested, and if unable to stand, let it fall, and over its ruins will rise that which is enduring. Let parties dissolve, religions disrupt, and false relations be sundered, yet eternal principles will remain, and on these we shall learn to lean, instead of leaning on things external. Just so long as we depend on any false external institutions or opinions, our own individuality is weakened and compromised. We have boasted of free governments, but where have we found free men and free women? We have boasted of religious institutions, but where are religious men and women? We have boasted of social laws and customs, but where are the men and women who are true to their social or affectional natures? We have been leaning so much on externals, we are alarmed at the revolutions upheaving all things external around us. The result will be, we shall be thrown back on our own individuality, and learn to stand up in the divinity of our nature, relying on ourselves and on Heaven alone. Many are being scattered, lost, wrecked, and filled with consternation and gloom, because they have no cultured character, no unfolded individuality, and no communion with the eternal world to afford the strength and inspiration they need. Why are so many to-day stripped of all external relations and dependencies, and thrown out into the great world amid all the belligerent elements? Because this discipline is essential to prepare them for their work, and for a higher, truer life. This terrible discipline is essential to all, and we are all to pass through it; there is no escape. National calamities are ominous of the fearful ordeal by which every man and woman in this generation must be tried. We may mock at the calamity of others, or pity or condemn them for things which seem evil, or we may shirk certain responsibilities, and seek to hide ourselves beneath compromises, in order that we may avert the storm; but the storm will come, and the flood and the fire, and we must all be tried. We may fancy ourselves secure and safe from the impending crisis, but the crisis will surely come, and the sooner we are prepared for it the better. Confessions and exposures of terrible experiences in the past are prophetic of more startling revelations soon to be made. The hitherto hidden things of darkness are coming to light beneath the opened heavens; we must all stand up and open our souls, and the past and present of our lives must be seen and known; compromises and efforts at concealment will avail nothing; the veil must be stripped from us, and all shams, lies and hypocrisies be dispelled. America is now in a civil crisis, testing all traitors and calling out all true loyalists; this is typical of the moral, religious and social crisis now coming. Conservative communities and thousands of sensitive Spiritualists have already been shocked and alarmed at disruptions and revelations; but these past revelations are nothing, compared with what shall yet come. We are over a volcano whose fires will soon belch forth with lurid hues; we shall be astounded at the revelations of the past and present lives of thousands whom we scarcely suspected, and thousands once exceedingly sensitive as to their reputations and the opinions of their friends and the world. It is the great day of tribulation, of judgment, the Christ advent of the nineteenth century; the heavens are opened and the angel armies are descending. Thrown back on ourselves, we must learn to stand alone, and then we are enabled to call into activity every power of our being. At times we need to stand out alone, away even from the influence, the sympathies of nearest and dearest friends. It was thus the Man of Sorrows stood; at one time forty days in the wilderness, and there buffeting alone, he triumphed, and then angels came and ministered to him. It is not until we have learned to stand alone, and have fought the battles of our own souls, that we are entitled to enjoy peace and the communion of ministering angels.

How may we live a true, harmonic spiritual life? is the anxious inquiry of many aspiring souls. A few random hints may sum up the whole.

1. To live a true life, remember the need of taking care of the body, as well as the soul. 2. Study all the laws of your being, and heed them, remembering the penalty of violating them is inevitable. 3. Cleanliness is next to godliness. 4. Bathe yourself at least once a week, if not oftener, and expose the whole body, while rubbing it, once every day. 5. Call the mind into activity; exercise the will, and let your whole system be animated with a vivid consciousness of the supreme control of your spiritual powers over all physical conditions. 6. Never confine yourself too long at once in the house, but go out into God's great laboratory and inhale the invigorating elements of nature. 7. Walk erect, with your brow lifted hopefully towards the heavens, seeking to realize the all-pervading atmosphere of the spirit world. 8. Study the demands of your nature, and eat and drink only that which you know is best adapted to your organism. 9.

Be temperate in all things. 10. Keep your passions, appetites, propensities, and all your faculties in harmonic activity, without any excesses or undue penances. 11. Neither eat, drink, dress, or do anything else merely to be fashionable or to please others, where no principles are involved. 12. Let all your relations, dealings, intercourses, and pursuits be regulated by your own sense of right, and not by the dictation of others, and give others the same right. 13. If you are not adapted to one pursuit, seek another, and let no failures dishearten you. 14. Sleep regularly, all you need; be sure your apartment is well aired; change your garments on retiring and rising, and air them thoroughly. 15. In sickness partake of nothing to feed disease; fasting is better than feasting or physicking; invoke the healing powers of the natural and spiritual worlds. 16. Give yourself rest and recreation as absolutely essential. 17. Count existence to be a blessing, and realize what it is to *be;* thank God; stand up; take courage; be hopeful and cheerful under all circumstances, remembering God reigns aright, and will overrule all things for good. 18. Remember the young, the aged, the infirm, the whole world, and realize you exert a constant influence for either good or evil. 19. Do unto others as you would have others do unto you in similar circumstances. 20. Be free in all things as far as you can without infringing on the freedom of others. 21. If you do what you please, do it at your own cost, and be sure you involve nobody else against their choice. 22. Mind your own business, and allow your neighbors to mind theirs. 23. Judge not, lest ye be judged. 24. As you would have others palliate your alleged faults, seek to palliate theirs. 25. Thou shalt love thy neighbor, not only as thyself, but better than thyself, when his misfortunes call for thee. 26. "Be not overcome of evil, but overcome evil with good." 27. Ask no forgiveness in thine own behalf, till thou hast, by forgiving all others, put thyself in a condition to receive and appreciate forgiveness. 28. "To thine own self be true, and thou canst not be false to any other man." 29. Treat the religious prejudices and all other predilections of your fellow-beings as tenderly as you would have your own treated. 30. There is no more just cause to quarrel about differences in opinion and practice than there is about differences in looks, features, or organizations. 31. Seek to be contented in whatever lot of life you cannot improve. 32. Let your standard be according to your highest ideal of a true life; yet do not murmur or grow impatient because you are not able to attain perfection at once. 33. Remember, though life is eternal, every moment is too precious for even one to be lost. 34. Let your deeds speak louder than your professions. 35. Have more regard for the approbation of your own conscience and the angel world than for the applause of superficial mortals. 36. The humblest path of duty may be higher in the sight of Heaven than the loftiest summit of popular ambition, or the field of human glory. 37. Treat your fellow-beings as though you realized them immortal, guarded by angel friends, and destined to meet them in the light of eternity. 38. Let no sorrows, trials, obstacles, defeats, persecutions, or sufferings rob you of the heroic hopes and purposes of ultimate triumph and ultimate recompense. 39. Be like angels towards your friends and fellow-beings around you, if you would attract angelic aids and influences, and become conscious at the presence of angel guardians. 40. If you would realize heaven begun on earth, and be prepared for a cordial welcome into the celestial spheres, seek to make your whole life heavenly, and worthy of the companionship of celestial guests.

The rapidity with which manifestations have spread, and the avidity with which they are believed, together with the fact that all past ages have demonstrated something similar, suggest to us, that man has a spiritual nature which cannot be satisfied without a belief in Spiritualism. This belief expands his soul with all the great hopes and aspirations which leap beyond the skies, and is the citadel on which he stands when all other foundations are swept away on the winds and waves of time. Without a consciousness of something within him which shall survive the mutations of time, something allied to God and another realm of higher intelligences, what were this life to the suffering millions? And it is to this consciousness we must appeal, if we would have Spiritualism reach the hearts of the people.

Outward manifestations alone will not regenerate the masses; they can only arrest their attention during a season of curiosity and excitement, which will soon pass away, and leave them worse than at first, unless the moral principles involved are recognized and enforced, and the evidence goes down into their hearts to awaken the internal witness. You go to your skeptical brother, and tell him of the wonderful manifestations you have seen and which he may see; but perhaps he treats your story with levity. But you then appeal to his own interior nature; you ask if he has not some hopes, some desires, some affections which reach beyond the grave; if some dear one has not gone before him, with whom he would like to commune, and if he would not feel happier and better to know all this. And he will cease his levity, and perchance, while his bosom heaves, a tear will steal into his eyes; and he will turn away, resolved to seek for light, and to search his own soul.

Oh, could we but touch the right chord in the hearts of our brothers and sisters, we should no longer suffer their raillery, but feel their hands grasped in warm fellowship and see their faces wet with streams of joy and love! We may pass by none without remembering all are of one family with us and with the same yearnings after something higher and better than we now seem to enjoy, and that something is unfolded by the spiritual gospel. It appeals to the common wants of humanity, and when rightly presented and appreciated finds an answer in every soul. It points us to the material universe as the glorious temple of God; from the earth beneath to the highest arch of heaven vocal with everlasting harmony, and radiant with love. It reveals the eternal relations of man to man, man with his God, man with other worlds and other intelligences peopling the realms of immensity, and opens holy and loving communion between every domain of an immeasurable universe. It expands our being with great thoughts that mount beyond this globe, and wing their way, with electric speed, from star to star, ranging along the distant firmament. The dull multitudes plodding along life as though there were nought to do but eat, drink and die, are startled with new views of the mission of man, and begin to feel there is a divinity within allied to God, and destined to walk eternity in the companionship of angels. The poor, the lowly, the lost are lifted up in communion with worlds and beings of kingly glory and grandeur, and no longer feel they are the reprobates of God and the offcasts of creation. This gospel equalizes all grades and conditions in one bond of fraternity, and makes the rich and poor sit down together as common guests at the board around which angels minister celestial messages. No lines are drawn in the kingdom of spiritual love and truth. The opening heavens shine down as brightly through lowly hamlets and dingy dungeons, as on gilded palaces and proud spires piercing the clouds; and with noiseless flight the spirit-bands wing their way down over the wide planes of humanity, whispering the music of the spheres to attune our souls in harmony with the sons of God shouting their anthems amid the melody of the morning stars of primeval creation. And they come with light to shine along the darkest path of life, and with beacons to point our way over the billows which shall soon waft our spirits whither the generations of the past have gone before us.

And shall we despise a gospel like this? Shall we turn deaf ears and closed eyes to the evidences that come to our very doors, and into the circles of our homes? We cannot. When once the evidence sinks deep into our souls, we cling to it as the very stronghold of our being, and are prepared to meet whatever of scorn, of derision, of wrath, of persecution or of suffering, the world may pour on us. Scoffing throngs may follow our track, and denounce us dupes and knaves; poverty may pinch and beggar the poor pioneers who stand forth breasting the public storm, without purse or scrip, pelted by the pitiless elements; yet we can afford to suffer on and wait in patient serenity for the time when all shall behold the unfolding glories now dawning on us from the spheres. The time will come when those who now stand on cold or opposing ground shall yield their hold, and file in with the gathering ranks of spiritual progress. The time hastens when, as on Pentecost, thousands shall be born in a day, and this generation shall see the light long foretold by seers and sages of olden eras. It may be that many shall pause in the midst of private griefs and disasters; in the midst of sickness, sorrow and death, which nothing but the consolations of this gospel can assuage. Or it may be in the midst of revolutions rocking thrones and empires, or dread calamities sweeping continents with consternation and alarm; but the time hastens when God and the celestial hosts shall gather in majesty to awake the slumbering world to a solemn consciousness of the reality of things spiritual and eternal.

Sons and daughters of earth, lift ye up your bowed brows, and bathe in the auroral light gleaming from celestial spheres! Through ages of darkness the gathered armies of God have watched from the Mounts of Beatitude over the mourning, bleeding millions of humanity waiting for the dawn of that millennial morn in which new-born hopes and loves shall blend in rainbow promises, spanning thunder-clouds charged with dread and alarm. Centuries have passed, empires and kingdoms have crumbled, hierarchies have been rolled away amid the melting elements, new states and institutions have risen from the ruins of the past, and behold the heavens unrolled, and their gates thrown back for the inauguration of the last dispensation destined to crown the race with glory and grandeur. No Sinai shall quake, no Olympus shall thunder, no Jerusalem shall be clothed in the tragic drapery of Calvary, no war-gods shall rattle their fiery chariots over continents deluged in blood, no dogmas of human terror, like volcanic flames, shall heave forth edicts of damnation on trembling millions; but the mountain-tops of the century shall gleam with the sunlight of angel faces, and echo the harmonic songs of the empyrean. Tidings already break from the myriad lips of the beloved and beatified bending with benedictions over the hearts and homes of humanity. Fear not! Hells may clang with alarms, and millions turn pale amid revolutions threatening thrones and republics, but the guardians of the Eternal sit calm in the council-chambers of heaven, and over the turbulent sea of human discord breathe the air and pour the oil of celestial harmony. Sit calm in the temple of thine own soul amid the din and jar of the outer world, and thou shalt hear cadences echoing down from the grand anthem evermore sounding through the corridors of the upper world. Scenes shall soon unfold to human vision transcending what olden seers and sages longed to behold. Millions of mortals shall bathe in the coming Pentecost of ages. Arise, priests, rulers, and people, arise! Shake off the dust of olden time, and stand forth in the light and life of the new-born year of Jubilee. Gird on thy sandals anew, and catch the mantles of the ascended as they come back in chariots of lightning with the flames of a living inspiration. Dash each tear from thine eye, stifle each fear, fling thy sighs to the winds, walk forth with the tread of a god in thy footstep, fighting life's battles side by side with that celestial army "whose white tents are already struck for the morning march of eternity."

Hear, O earth, while the heavens bend, and messengers of the Divine proclaim anew the tidings of the descending kingdom. The holy prophecies of all ages point with sublime significance to revolutions now rocking the entire globe. Old foundations are crumbling, the old earth is trembling, the elements of the past are melting with fervent heat, the heavens are being rolled together as a scroll, civil governments are rent like the veil of the olden temple, mythological religions are fading like shadows before the noonday glory, social institutions are sinking amid the cry of millions for more light and liberty, and the nations are running to and fro in dismay.

O America, America! first-born child of the father and mother of olden republics gone down in the night of ages! Why stand ye aghast, sons and daughters of the Western world? Behold the isles and continents of the Orient, with their millions long gazing with steadfast hopes on the millennial star rising and culminating its radiance over the land of the setting sun. Why start ye with alarm at the war-cry and tremble as though demons had broken the bounds of hell, hurling brands of destruction destined to dethrone the Almighty, and roll back the tide of eternal progress? The Lord God Omnipotent reigneth! The council-chambers of the eternal world stand open, and the congresses of celestial empires are seeking to guide the destiny of nations. The ascended saints, sages, and patriots of America, the heroes and victors of battle-fields once red with blood and glorious with the trophies of freedom, and all the armies bearing palms on the plains of immortal life, now bend with wisdom over the conflict rending your continent, bidding you still remember the brotherhood of the race; and above the clamor of belligerent hosts, the clash of arms and the thunder of artillery, listen once more to angel anthems of peace and good-will. And behold, not far distant, beyond the smoke of passing battles, a new-born earth shall bloom, and the opening heavens shall beam with millennial beatitudes on millions now standing in the awe of suspense, wild with dismay, and wrapped in the pall of mourning.

INDEX.

BIBLE PASSAGES REFERRED TO, OR QUOTED, IN HARMONY WITH SPIRITUALISM.

An Eye-Opener; or CATHOLICISM UNMASKED. By a Catholic Priest. 40 cts, postage free.

Answers to Charges of Belief in Modern Revelation, &c. By Mr. and Mrs. A. E. Newton. 10 cents, postage 2c.

Arcana of Nature; or the History and Laws of Creation. By Hudson Tuttle. 1st vol. $1.25, postage 16c.

Arcana of Nature; or the Philosophy of Spiritual Existence and of the Spirit World. By Hudson Tuttle. 2d vol. $1.00, postage 16c.

Blossoms of our Spring. A poetic work. By Hudson and Emma Tuttle. Price $1.00, postage 20c.

Familiar Spirits, AND SPIRITUAL MANIFESTATIONS: being a series of articles by Dr. Enoch Pond, Professor in the Bangor Theological Seminary, with a reply, by A. Bingham, Esq., of Boston. 15 cents, postage 4c.

Further Communications from the World of Spirits, on subjects highly important to the human family. By Joshua, Solomon and others. 50 cents, postage 8c.; cloth 75c., postage 12c.

Incidents in my Life. By D. D. Home, with an introduction by Judge Edmunds. $1.25, postage, free.

Legalized Prostitution; or Marriage as it Is, and Marriage as it should be, philosophically considered. By Chas. S. Woodruff, M. D. 75 cents, postage 16c.

Messages FROM THE SUPERIOR STATE. Communicated by John Murray, through J. M. Spear. 50 cents, postage 12c.

New Testament Miracles, and Modern Miracles. The comparative amount of evidence for each; the nature of both; testimony of a hundred witnesses. An Essay read before the Divinity School, Cambridge. By J. H. Fowler, 30 cents, postage 4c.

Plain Guide to Spiritualism. A Spiritual Hand-Book. By Uriah Clark. Cloth, $1.00, postage 16c.; paper, 75 cents, postage 8c.

Poems from the Inner Life. By Miss Lizzie Doten. Price, full gilt, $1.75, postage free; plain, $1.00, postage 16c.

Reply to the Rev. Dr. W. P. Lunt's Discourse against the Spiritual Philosophy. By Miss Elizabeth R. Torrey. 15 cents, postage 2c.

Spirit Manifestations: being an Exposition of Views respecting the Principal Facts, Causes and Peculiarities involved, together with interesting Phenomenal Statements and Communications. By Adin Ballou. Paper 50 cents, postage 6c.; cloth 75 cents, postage 12c.

The Bible; Is it of Divine Origin, Authority and Influence? By S. J. Finney. Cloth 40 cents, postage 8c.

The Fugitive Wife. By Warren Chase. 25 cents, postage free; cloth 40 cts. postage free.

The Gospel of Harmony. By Mrs. E. Goodrich Willard. Price 30 cents, postage 4c.

The History of Dungeon Rock. 25 cents, postage 2c.

The Kingdom of Heaven; OR THE GOLDEN AGE. By E. W. Loveland. 75 cents, postage 12c.

The "Ministry of Angels" Realized. A letter to the Edwards Congregational Church, Boston. By A. E. Newton. 15 cents, postage 2c.

The Philosophy of Creation; unfolding the Laws of the Progressive Development of Nature, and embracing the Philosophy of Man, Spirit, and the Spirit World. By Thomas Paine, through the hand of Horace Wood, medium. Cloth, 40 cents, postage 8c.

The Psalms of Life: a compilation of Psalms, Hymns, Chants, and Anthems, &c., embodying the Spiritual, Reformatory and Progressive sentiment of the present age. By John S. Adams. $1.00, postage 16c.

The Religion of Manhood; OR, THE AGE OF THOUGHT. By Dr. J. H. Robinson. Bound in muslin, 75 cents, postage 12c.

The Soul of Things; or PSYCHOMETRIC RESEARCHES AND DISCOVERIES. By William and Elizabeth M. F. Denton. Price, $1.25, postage 20c.

The Spirit Minstrel. A collection of Hymns and Music for the use of Spiritualists in their Circles and Public Meetings. Sixth edition, enlarged. By J. B. Packard and J. S. Loveland Paper, 25c., postage free; cloth 38 cents, postage free.

The Spiritual Reasoner. 50 cents, postage 12c.

Twelve Messages from the spirit of John Quincy Adams, through Joseph B. Stiles, medium, to Josiah Brigham. $1.50, postage 32c.

Who is God? A Few Thoughts on Nature and Nature's God, and Man's Relation thereto. By A. P. M'Combs. 10 cents, postage 2c.

Woodman's Three Lectures on Spiritualism, in reply to Wm. T. Dwight, D. D. 20 cents, postage 4c.

ENGLISH WORKS ON SPIRITUALISM.

Night Side of Nature: OR, GHOSTS AND GHOSTS-SEERS. By Catherine Crowe. Price, $1.00, postage 20c.

Light in the Valley. MY EXPERIENCE IN SPIRITUALISM. By Mrs. Newton Crosland. Illustrated with about twenty plain and colored engravings. $1.00, postage 16c.

MISCELLANEOUS AND REFORM WORKS.

A False and True Revival of Religion. By Theodore Parker. 8 cents.

An Essay ON THE TRIAL BY JURY. By Lysander Spooner. Leather, $1.50, postage 20c.; cloth $1.00, postage 16c.; paper 75 cents, postage 8c.

A Sermon ON FALSE AND TRUE THEOLOGY. By Theodore Parker. 8 cents.

A Voice from the Prison, OR TRUTHS FOR THE MULTITUDE. By James A. Clay. 75 cents, postage 12c.

A Wreath for St. Crispin: being Sketches of Eminent Shoemakers. By J. Prince. 40 cents, postage 12c.

Battle Record OF THE AMERICAN REBELLION. By Horace E. Dresser, A. M. Price 25 cents, postage 2c.

Christ and the Pharisees upon the Sabbath. By a Student of Divinity. 20 cents, postage 4c.

Consumption. How to Prevent it, and How to cure it. By James C. Jackson, M. D. $2.00, postage 24c.

Eight Historical and Critical Lectures on the Bible. By John Prince. $1.00, postage 16c.

Eliza Woodson; OR, THE EARLY DAYS OF ONE OF THE WORLD'S WORKERS. A Story of American Life. Price, $1.25, postage free.

Eugene Becklard's Physiological Mysteries and Revelations. 25 cents, postage 4c.

Facts and Important Information for Young Men, on the subject of Masturbation. 12 cents, postage free.

Facts and Important Information for Young Women on the same subject. 12 cents, postage free.

Hesper, the Home Spirit. A Story of Household Labor and Love. By Miss Lizzie Doten. Price 80 cents, postage 12c.

Love and Mock Love. By Geo. Stearns. 25 cents, postage 4c.

Marriage and Parentage; or the Reproductive Element in Man, as a means to his Elevation and Happiness. By Henry C Wright. $1.00, postage 20c.

Optimism, THE LESSON OF AGES. By Benjamin Blood. 60 cents, postage 12c.

Pathology of the Reproductive Organs. By Drs. Trall and Jackson. Price $4.00, postage 36c.

Peculiar. A Tale of the Great Transition. By Epes Sargent. Price $1.50, postage free.

Personal Memoir OF DANIEL DRAYTON. 25 cents. Cloth 40c.

Reedeemer and Redeemed. By Rev. Charles Beecher. Price, $1.50, postage free.

Report OF AN EXTRAORDINARY CHURCH TRIAL: Conservatives *versus* Progressives. By Philo Hermes. 15 cents, postage 2c.

Six Years in a Georgia Prison. Narrative of Lewis W. Paine, who was the sufferer. Paper 25 cents, postage 4c.; cloth 40 cents, postage 12c.

The American Crisis; OR THE TRIAL AND TRIUMPH OF DEMOCRACY. By Warren Chase. 20 cents, postage free.

The Apocryphal New Testament. 75 cents, postage 16c.

The Book of Notions, compiled by John Hayward, author of several Gazetteers and other works. Paper 50 cents, postage 8c.; cloth 75 cents, postage 16c.

The Curability of Consumption DEMONSTRATED ON NATURAL PRINCIPLES. By Andrew Stone, M. D. Price, $1.50, postage free.

The Effect of on Slavery on the American People. By Theodore Parker. 8 cents.

The Empire of the Mother over the Character and Destiny of the Race. By Henry C. Wright. In paper covers 35 cents, postage 4c.; in cloth 50 cents, postage 8c.

The Errors of the Bible, Demonstrated by the Truths of Nature; or Man's only Infallible Rule of Faith and Practice. By Henry C. Wright. Paper 25 cents, postage 4 cents; cloth 40 cents, postage 8c.

The Habits of Good Society. A Hand-Book of Etiquette for Ladies and Gentlemen. Large 12mo., elegant cloth binding. Price, $1.50, postage free.

The Hierophant; OR GLEANINGS FROM THE PAST. Being an Exposition of Biblical Astronomy. Price, 75 cents, postage free.

The Koran. Translated into English immediately from the original Arabic. Price, $1.25, postage free.

The Life of Jesus. By Ernest Renan. Translated from the original French, by Charles Edwin Wilbour. Price $1.50, postage free.

The Mistake of Christendom; or, Jesus and his Gospel, before Paul and Christianity. By George Stearns. $1.00, postage 16c.

The Revival of Religion which we Need. By Theodore Parker. 8 cents.

The Relation of Slavery to a Republican Form of Government. By Theodore Parker. 8 cents.

The Self-Abnegationist, or Earth's true King and Queen. By Henry C. Wright. In paper covers 40 cents, postage 4c.; in cloth 55 cents, postage 8c.

The Science of Man APPLIED TO EPIDEMICS; their Cause, Cure, and Prevention. By Lewis S. Hough. (Man's Life in his Universe.) Cloth 75 cents, postage 12c.

The Unwelcome Child; or, The Crime of an Undesigned and Undesired Maternity. By Henry C. Wright. Paper 25 cents, postage 4c.; cloth 40 cents, postage 8c.

Thirty-Two Wonders; or the Skill displayed in the Miracles of Jesus. By Prof. M. Durais. Paper 25 cents, postage 2c.; cloth 40 cents, postage 8c.

Unconstitutionality of Slavery. By Lysander Spooner. Paper 75 cents, postage 8c.; cloth $1.00, postage 16c.

BOOKS FOR THE YOUNG.

Any book on this list will be sent by mail, and postage paid, on receipt of price. Special pains will be taken to select suitable Books for Libraries. A liberal discount to the Trade and to Libraries.

Spiritual Sunday School Manual, for forming and conducting Sunday Schools on a new and simple plan, and for home use. Readings, Responses, Invocations, Questions, Lessons, Gems of Wisdom, Little Spiritual Stories, Infant Questions and Lessons, Songs and Hymns. By Uriah Clark. 144 pages. 30 cents.

A Kiss for a Blow. H. C. Wright. 38 and 50 cents.

A New Flower for Children. L. Maria Child. (Illustrated.) $1.00

Adventures of James Capen Adams, Mountaineer and Grizzly Bear Hunter of California. T. H. Kittell. (Engravings.) $1.50

A Picture Alphabet of Animals and Birds. Stories and Hymns. (Illustrated.) 63 cents.

All for the Best. T. S. Arthur. 63 cents.

Anything for Sport. Mrs. Tuthill. 50 cents.

Arabian Nights' Entertainment. $1.25

Arbell's School Days. Jane W. Hooper. (Illustrated.) $1.00

A Strike for Freedom. Mrs. Tuthill. 50 cents.
Audubon, the Naturalist: ADVENTURES AND DISCOVERIES. Mrs. H. St. John. (Illustrated.) $1.00
A Will and a Way. From the German. (Illustrated.) $1.00
Belle and Lilly; OR THE GOLDEN RULE, for girls. (Illustrated,) $1.00
Bears of Augustusburg. (Illustrated.) $1.00
Boy of Spirit. Mrs. Tuthill. 50 cents.
Boy of Mt. Rhigi. Miss C. M. Sedgwick. 75 cents.
Bear Hunters of the Rocky Mountains. Anne Bowman. (Illustrated.) $1.00
Boarding-School Girl. Mrs. Tuthill. (With Illustrations.) 60 cents.
Christmas Eve, AND OTHER STORIES. From the German. (Illustrated.) 63c.
Canadian Crusoes. Catherine Parr Thraill. (Illustrated.) $1.00
Children's Friend. M. Berquin. (Illustrated.) $1.00
Cousin's Hatty's Stories and Hymns. (Illustrated.) 50 cents.
Childhood of Mary Leeson. Mary Howitt. 50 cents.
Children's Trials. Rope-Dancers, and Other Tales. (Illustrated.) $1.00
Children's Year. Mary Howitt. (Illustrated.) $1.00
Dog Crusoe. R. M. Ballantyne. $1.00
Dick Rodney. Adventures of an Eton Boy. (With Illustrations.) $1.00
Eskdale Herd Boy. A Scottish Tale. Mrs. Blackford. (Illustrated.) 75 cents.
Ellen Stanley, AND OTHER STORIES. 50 cents.
Florence Erwin's Three Homes. A Tale of North and South. $1.00
Flowers for Children. L. Maria Child. $1.00
Fanny Gray. (Illustrated, in a box.) $1.00
Frank Wildman's Adventures. Frederick Gerstaecker. (Illustrated.) $1.00
Georgie and his Dog, AND OTHER STORIES. (Engravings.) 63 cents.
Gorilla-Hunters; A TALE OF AFRICA. R. M. Ballantyne. (Illustrated.) $1.00
Grimm's Tales and Stories. (Numerous Illustrations.) $1.75
Harry and Aggie; OR THE RIDE. (Illustrated.) $1.00
Hurrah for the Holidays. (Illustrated.) $1.00
Hymns, Songs, and Fables. Mrs. Follen. 50 cents.
Happy Days. (Illustrated.) 60 cents.
Holly and Mistletoe. From the German. (Engravings.) $1.25
Hurrah for New England. (Illustrated.) 50 cents.
I Will be a Soldier. Mrs. Tuthill. (Illustrated.) 75 cents.
I Will be a Gentleman. Mrs. Tuthill. (Illustrated.) 50 cents.
I Will be a Lady. Mrs. Tuthill. 50 cents.
John Chinaman. W. Dalton. (Illustrated.) $1.00
Jack in the Forecastle; SEA-LIFE ILLUSTRATED. $1.50
Johnny and Maggie, AND OTHER STORIES. (With illustrations.) 40 cents.
Just in Time, AND OTHER STORIES. (Illustrated.) 40 cents.
Keeper's Travels in Search of his Master. (Illustrated.) 60 cents.
Kangaroo Hunters, Anne Bowman. (Illustrated.) $1.00
Leila. Ann Fraser Tytler. (Engravings.) $1.00
Leila in England; continuation of "Leila." (Illustrated.) $1.00
Leila at Home; continuation of "Leila in England." (Illustrated.) $1.00
Little Frankie and his Mother. Mrs. Madeline Leslie. (Illustrated.) 38 cts.
Little Frankie and his Father. Mrs. Madeline Leslie. 38 cents.
Little Frankie at his Plays. 38 cents.
Little by Little; OR THE CRUISE OF A FLYAWAY. O. Optic. (Illustrated.) 84c.
Little Frankie and his Cousin. 38 cents.
Little Frankie on a Journey. 38 cents.
Little Frankie at School. 38 cents.
Life of Lafayette. E. Cecil. (Engravings.) $1.00
Land of the Sun; KATE AND WILLIE IN CUBA. Cornelia H. Jenks. (Illustrated.) 75 cents.
Life of Washington. E. Cecil. (Engravings.) $1.00
Mary and Florence. Ann Frazer Tytler. (Illustrated.) $1.00
Mary and Florence at Sixteen. Ann Frazer Tytler. $1.00
Molly and Kitty; WITH OTHER TALES. (Engravings.) $1.00
Many a Little makes a Mickle. From the German. (Illustrated.) $1.00
Miss Edgeworth's Early Lessons. "Frank," "Sequel to Frank," "Rosamond," "Harry and Lucy." 5 vols. $5.00

www.ingramcontent.com/pod-product-compliance
Lightning Source LLC
LaVergne TN
LVHW021252110826
845151LV00004BA/1045

* 9 7 8 1 4 2 5 5 2 8 6 0 7 *